THE D DAY LANDINGS

THE D DAY LANDINGS

Philip Warner

𝕿𝖍𝖊 𝕯𝖆𝖎𝖑𝖞 𝕿𝖊𝖑𝖊𝖌𝖗𝖆𝖕𝖍

Pen & Sword
MILITARY

First published in Great Britain in 2004 by
Pen & Sword Military
an imprint of
Pen & Sword Books Ltd
47 Church Street
Barnsley
South Yorkshire
S70 2AS

ISBN 1 84415 109 3

A CIP catalogue record for this book is
available from the British Library

Printed and bound in England by
CPI UK

For a complete list of Pen & Sword titles please contact
PEN & SWORD BOOKS LIMITED
47 Church Street, Barnsley, South Yorkshire, S70 2AS, England
E-mail: enquiries@pen-and-sword.co.uk
Website: www.pen-and-sword.co.uk

Contents

Foreword

By W. F. Deedes

That early June dawn some saw breaking over the greatest sea-borne invasion ever launched is now sixty years behind us. Memories of our feat of arms are fading. This year's anniversary will be the last in which survivors are likely to take part in considerable numbers, for most of them are now over 80 years of age. Yet it was an event that ought not soon to be forgotten. For it was not simply a vast international military operation that succeeded against the odds; and one which called for human endeavour on a heroic scale. As Philip Warner observes in his Introduction of quarter of a century ago, it was made possible by the ordinary man. It was the sum of his courage that led to our success. And the cemeteries scattered through this region of France remind us of the extent of his sacrifice.

Many accounts of this extraordinary day have already been written, but just how it felt to storm those fortified beaches and what it took to keep going through that long day is best conveyed through these snatches of personal recollection. This is a story from which all of us, and particularly the descendants of those who took part, can draw pride.

For consider the circumstances. In 1940 we were driven from France and were lucky to retrieve most of our Army. Thereafter we knew that to win the war we would have one day to storm our way back into Europe against a coastline heavily fortified by Germany. Russia wanted us to go in 1943 to relieve the pressure on their Armies. 'Second Front Now!' was the cry of their sympathisers. Churchill, Roosevelt and their generals resisted enormous pressure until we were thoroughly ready. Even then the bad weather which led to the postponement of D Day by 24 hours made it a close-run thing. And the storm of 19 June destroyed some of our rapidly assembled harbours and severely hindered reinforcements.

This gathering together of recollections is a tribute to those who led the way. Those of us who came a little later found it rough going, but we encountered nothing comparable to what these men faced on those Normandy beaches early in the morning of 6 June. Like all great battles it was won primarily by valour, as Warner puts it, the valour of 'unassuming men'. He is right in saying that many of them performed deeds of which they never believed themselves capable.

Much ingenuity too went into the success of that day. The tale told here by Stuart Hills of the Sherwood Rangers is worth a second glance, for it tells of the Duplex Drive tanks which were on the beaches some while before the Germans expected to see tanks. Hills had the misfortune to sink, but there were enough of them on shore to level heavy and accurate fire at Germany's fortified machine gun posts and so save many lives.

In reading through these accounts with pride and thankfulness, we may well say 'never again'. Yet it would be wrong to say, 'we would never be able to do it again.' In our Services today are men and women fully qualified to follow in the footsteps of those who contribute to these pages. Let's just say it was no end of a lesson, which Europe appears to have taken to heart. Therefore the sacrifices made on that day were not altogether in vain.

TO FREDA
Without whom this book would
not have been possible

Acknowledgements

First I must thank *The Daily Telegraph* which printed a letter from me which asked for survivors of D Day to get in touch with me. They did, in their hundreds.

Secondly I wish to thank Mademoiselle de Berenger, Director of the Museum at Arromanches, who very kindly arranged interviews, and supplied valuable information and photographs.

Thirdly I wish to thank all those who wrote to me, telephoned me and talked to me. When so many went to so much trouble, and entrusted me with valuable and cherished maps and photographs, it would not be fair to mention individual names without mentioning all. So much relevant and interesting material was supplied that in order to achieve a fair balance much had to be omitted. However, where contributions have been severely shortened, or even omitted, it should be remembered that the full texts will have been deposited in the archives of the Imperial War Museum for the benefit of future scholars and students.

P.W.
1980

Introduction

This is a book about men of action, men who were there. Much of it is written by them. Although those who fought in the battle are proud to have been a part of it, they would be extremely embarrassed at the idea that they were heroic figures. For many it was their first time in action and, with others of more experience, they hoped they would prove equal to the occasion, would give leadership where it was needed, and not show fear or doubt. The greatest dread of many was to be incapacitated by sea-sickness and to be unable to perform their task when the time came. Whatever the future had in store for them they hoped to meet it bravely, perhaps with a smile. Some survived the landings but were killed later. Many of those who wrote to me assured me that the part they played was of little importance. Nevertheless unless they had been there and doing all and more than could be expected of them all the great plans would have come to nothing.

On 6th June 1944 there took place the greatest seaborne invasion in the history of mankind. The Allies, who had been planning and preparing for that day for over four years, launched a massive assault on the northern shore of France. It was on a scale which is never likely to be repeated, for the development of weapons of mass destruction has made it unlikely that such a large, vulnerable concentration of force would ever be assembled again. In a war which saw one massive military action after another – the blitzkrieg, the German invasion of Russia, Stalingrad, the Italian campaign – D Day stands supreme. It has been celebrated as a triumph of planning, of international co-operation, of combined operations, of political foresight. In this maelstrom of analysis, self-congratulation, and euphoria one fact seems to have been glossed over. It was made possible by the ordinary man.

Most of this book consists of the recollections of unassuming men. They found themselves on that day and the succeeding days in extraordinary situations, performing deeds of which they did not even know they were capable, and which in retrospect seem so fantastic as to be scarcely believable. For the facts of D Day are that it was such an enormous and unique occasion that even though a man had been a soldier, sailor or airman most of his adult life and had exercised his skills in similar though lesser events, the assault was on such a scale that it made everyone a novice, whether general or private, whether pilot flying high over the battlefield or private crawling over it and digging in.

As often happens in modern battles the most dangerous and unpleasant place to be was not necessarily in front at the point of attack but some distance behind it. If you are the assaulting infantry you do not see many dead and wounded, either your own or those of the enemy, unless there has been very effective preliminary bombardment. Your own and enemy dead are left behind as you press forward. The people who see the really gruesome side of war are the medical men who try to repair the casualties and the chaplains who have to bury many of them. But there was one thought which was common to all who took part. It could have been much worse. Fortunately for the Allies, the Germans were deceived over both the date and place of the landings. Had they not been, and therefore not been taken by surprise, D Day could have been even bloodier than it was. And there were several occasions when the outcome of the battle could have been very different from what it eventually became.

The term D Day landings does not, of course, mean merely those landings which took place on 6th June 1944. The D Day phase continued until 18th June, when the bridgehead was considered to have been adequately consolidated. Up until the latter date there was a reasonable chance that the Germans could put in a counter-offensive and sweep all the invasion forces back into the sea – a Dunkirk on an even more horrific scale with little chance of rescue.

But over to the events themselves.

It may come as a surprise to many that immediately after Britain had been ignominiously swept out of France in June 1940 planning to return should have begun. Thus, even when this country was under close and immediate threat of invasion, plans were being made to return to the Continent. In 1943 the commanders for the great occasion were appointed. General Eisenhower (USA) was to be the supreme commander but Air Chief Marshal Sir Arthur Tedder (Britain) was to be deputy-commander, and Lieutenant-General Bedell-Smith (USA) was to be chief of staff. The overall name for the landing was 'Overlord', and two armies would be used : the American 1st Army under Lieutenant-General Omar Bradley and the British 2nd Army under Lieutenant-General Miles Dempsey. The cross-Channel part of the invasion was known as 'Neptune' and for this the joint armies, which were called 21st Army Group, were commanded by General Bernard Montgomery, the victor of Alamein.

Once the troops were ashore, Eisenhower was to take supreme command and Montgomery and Bradley would command their respective armies under him. Eisenhower's genius lay not in military skill but in the ability to create harmony among the diverse and individualistic personalities who worked in SHAEF (Supreme Headquarters Allied Expeditionary Force). An additional problem for Eisenhower was to make sure Europe obtained its fair share of American resources, particularly of landing craft, of which a considerable – some say disproportionate – number were being allocated to the Pacific area.

The central problem of the landings was to put ashore sufficient troops to defeat the Germans confronting them, but not in such concentration that they would strangle themselves in the bottleneck and thus simplify the task of the opposition. The limit to the number of divisions was the quantity of shipping needed to transport them.

For Neptune all the commanders were British : General Sir Bernard Montgomery was 21st Army Group (as mentioned), Admiral Sir Bertram Ramsay and Air Chief Marshal Sir Trafford Leigh-Mallory. The Allied plan was to make an assault with 37 divisions. Each division usually consisted of 15,000 men. It was divided into three brigades with supporting artillery. Each brigade consisted of three battalions; the approximate strength of a battalion varied between 500 and 850. A regiment may have one or more battalions in it; in wartime most regiments were expanded to have many battalions. A man landing at D Day could therefore have belonged to a battalion which only existed in wartime : in certain cases he may have belonged to a battalion in a regiment which has subsequently been merged with another regiment. Thus a man serving in a battalion of the Manchester Regiment would today find his regimental home in the King's Regiment, a combination of the King's Liverpool and the Manchester Regiment. In an armoured division one of the brigades consisted of three tank battalions, and another brigade consisted of lorry-borne infantry who would be needed in the event of a breakthrough. This is where the basic simplicity ends, for once we enter into detail we find that every division incorporated a host of other units such as engineers, machine-gunners, signals, medical services, mortar companies, reconnaissance units, pioneers, anti-tank units, chaplains, camouflage, anti-aircraft, and so on. Inevitably an army includes a large number of people who are in units which are described as 'supporting arms or services'. In fact everything except the infantry and armoured corps is breezily dismissed by Army organisations as not being 'fighting' arms. Thus engineers who led the infantry through the minefield at Alamein, gunners who often hold isolated posts, and signals who may well find themselves behind the enemy lines, are 'supporting' arms. 'Services' are referred to in an almost mediaeval manner. Nevertheless without these the army would quickly cease to function. They carry out such essential tasks as transporting anything from food to ammunition, the preparation and distribution of food and, by no means least, operate the recovery sections which ensure that damaged equipment – from tanks to guns – is quickly repaired and brought back into the battle. If the tide turns and the army is pushed back, every one of these 'supporters and services' can take his place in the line, with the exception of chaplains and doctors who are barred by convention from doing so.

Such is the complexity of modern war that in every army there are numbers of what soldiers tend to refer to as 'funnies'. They are specialised units consisting of men trained for unorthodox tasks. The task might range from detecting and dismantling booby-traps to capturing senior enemy officers by means of a swift raid behind the lines. Thus the initial plan to land in France, in the first two days, a total of 176,475 men, 3,000 guns, 1,500 tanks, and 15,000 other assorted vehicles, was not as simple as it looks on paper, even if it looks simple there.

Against the assault force of 37 divisions the Germans had 60 (11 armoured) divisions, but these were extended over a wide front; Field Marshal von Rundstedt had the task of deploying them in the defence of France, Belgium and Holland. Von Rundstedt formed the opinion that his forces were over-extended and would have preferred to withdraw to a shorter line along the German frontier. However, Hitler would have none of this and sent Field Marshal Rommel to command the troops in France while leaving von Rundstedt in overall command. Rommel would have preferred to launch the full German effort against the troops as they came on to the beaches but von Rundstedt was of the opinion that it would be better to reserve the main German strength for a massive counter-attack when the Allies had a good portion of their troops ashore but before they had consolidated. This led to a compromise in which the German infantry was positioned well forward while the armour was held back for the decisive counter-blow. The German dispositions caused some surprise to the RAF reconnaissance and bomber aircraft but less to the SHAEF planners who, by virtue of the Enigma machine, knew what was in the minds of the German General Staff.

The Germans expected that the main Allied landing would be in the Pas de Calais (the area around Calais). They had been encouraged to believe this by various complicated deception operations. The deception had been created by false reports from 'turned' spies, by dummy concentration of troops in south-east England and East Anglia, and by heading off German reconnaissance from areas, such as the south-west, where our forces were really concentrated. So convinced were the Germans that the Pas de Calais was where the main Allied thrust would fall that even when the Allies had successfully landed at the other end of Normandy and were driving inland the German High Command still believed that it was only a feint move which had been unexpectedly successful and was being reinforced for that reason; even at that stage they believed that a second, greater, blow would come to the Calais district.

The deception over the landing illustrated one of the classic situations of sea-borne assaults versus land defence. The invader from sea (or air) can choose his assault point at will and progress to it far faster than the defender can move his troops over land. However, landing from the sea or air has many hazards and unless the position can be consolidated very quickly the invaders will soon be overwhelmed by superior numbers. Preventing that happening became a vital part of Allied strategy.

The first essential was to deceive the enemy over the actual landing area which, we saw, was done. The second was to hamper the movement of German divisions which would otherwise be rushed to annihilate the troops which had landed. The latter was accomplished in various ways. Extensive bombing of roads, railways, and bridges made progress slow, and the damage by bombs was greatly increased by sabotage from Resistance forces. Finally the assault area was sealed off by air landings along the flanks, a process which was made immensely more difficult by having to be begun in the dark.

At every moment in this vast enterprise someone, somewhere, was doing something extremely difficult and dangerous. Skill on an unprecedented scale was shown by men who did not realise they possessed it. A simple example is that of the minesweepers clearing a path for the convoys. As the minesweepers could not move at less than $7\frac{1}{2}$ knots and the convoys could not move faster than 5 knots this meant the former regularly reversing course and regaining station in variable tides. Impossible – but it was done.

The invasion plan, in very simple form, was to train and then assemble adequate numbers of suitable units at points where they could be transported to France, then transport them, then reinforce and relieve them. Training them for the tasks they would tackle on arrival would take months, if not years, and require complete familiarisation with the essential equipment. While this was going on, especially in the latter stages, complete secrecy must be preserved. (As we see later, there were one or two occasions when secrecy was accidentally breached but without ill-effects.)

Then came the process of delivery. For this, they and their equipment must be loaded on sea or air transports and, while being transported, be protected from enemy interference by air or sea. On arrival they must be disembarked quickly and provided with adequate supplies.

Clearly the most delicate phase of this long-drawn operation would be the actual landing. The lesson which had been learnt in the early stages of the war was that infantry on its own could not defeat armoured divisions. It was therefore essential that tanks should land with the infantry of the assault force. Later, when a port had been captured, unloading tanks would be a less hazardous process than running them off ships on to the beaches. For the disembarkation of tanks and soldiers huge numbers of suitable craft would be required. This led to the development of a whole family of landing craft of which the first had been the Landing Craft (Tank) in 1940. LCTs and their sisters are usually thought of as an American invention owing to the American skill at producing them in vast numbers. In fact they derived from an idea of Churchill's in 1917, an idea which was revived in 1940 so that Combined Operations Headquarters had a prototype on the water at the end of that year. LCTs were flat-bottomed (thus unsuitable for rough seas) and had a hinged ramp door in the bow. As the LCT reached the beach the ramp was lowered and the tanks ran down it and up on to the beach. However the possibilities of this operation going wrong in rough water, bad-weather, and overcrowded beaches need little imagination. A larger and better version of this vessel was the Landing Ship Tank which could even carry LCTs on its upper deck and travel at 10 knots over open water. However this supplemented rather than superseded LCTs. There were also LSHs (Landing Ship Headquarters) which were joint military/naval headquarters. They could carry over 400 people and were equipped with the normal aids of a joint command post.

LS(I)s were Landing Ships Infantry and were for the most part adapted passenger or cargo ships. They carried a variety of assault landing craft; these were mainly flat-bottomed boats with the capacity to make almost anyone seasick in rough water. Among the other members of this family were Landing Ship Dock, Landing Ship Gantry, Landing Ship Sternchute, Landing Craft Assault (an armoured craft of ten tons with a low silhouette and silent engines) and Rhino ferries. Rhino ferries were 400-ton steel rafts which were used for unloading LSTs in deep water. All these vehicles were severely functional, which is one way of saying that some were more hideously uncomfortable than others.

However, valuable and ingenious though all these craft were, they were not a substitute for a proper harbour, and Churchill therefore proposed that the Allies should take a proper harbour with them. Two were built, each about the size of Dover Harbour. They were code-named Mulberries. They consisted of an inner breakwater of concrete caissons which would be sunk on the bottom, another floating breakwater of the hulks of old ships, and four floating piers which ran outwards and rose and fell with the tide, enabling small freighters to discharge cargo on to them at any time. But as soon as possible a major port, possibly Cherbourg, would have to be captured.

The chosen landing area was 50 miles wide and extended from Orne on the left to the Vire estuary on the right. There were five main assault beaches. The Americans had two of these: Utah and Omaha, and the British three: Gold, Juno and Sword. The right flank of the American assault was to be shielded by the 82nd and 101st American Airborne Divisions, which it was planned to drop near Carentan. The left flank of the British assault was to be protected by the 6th Airborne Division which was to parachute in to the east of Caen. The initial assault would be carried out by the British 3rd Division on Sword, by the 3rd Canadian Division on Juno, by the 50th Division on Gold, 1st US Division on Omaha, and 4th US Division on Utah.

Nobody expected the landings to go exactly to plan for most of the commanders were aware of the phenomenon known as the 'fog of war'. The 'fog of war' is that great cloud of uncertainty and potential chaos which descends on any force as it moves up to engage the enemy. Unexpected delays occur, errors are made, incorrect deci-

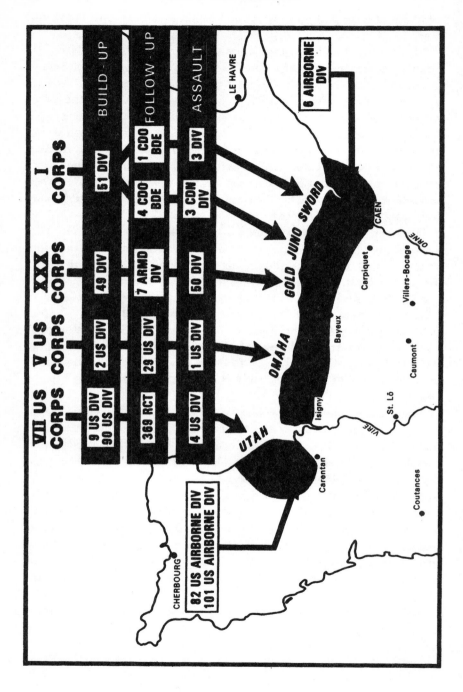

sions are transmitted as orders and before the enemy (who has his own fog, of course) is engaged, considerable disruption is experienced. When the armies engage, the fog thickens rapidly, and units encounter friends where they expected enemy and enemy where they expected friends.

In spite of heroic efforts to keep them clear, most routes are hopelessly congested by vehicles trying to move forward while others, having discharged their loads, and perhaps filled up with casualties or prisoners, are trying to move back. Enemy shelling or bombing of crossroads increases the dislocation.

Apart from the administration problems involved in the large-scale movement of troops there were numerous other factors to interfere with the landings. Inevitably, there was a resolute German defence behind a host of lethal deterrents which included underwater obstacles, mined posts, anti-tank ditches and broad minefields. Underwater obstacles damaged numerous LCTs, an unexpectedly high tide narrowed the beach area and caused unbelievable congestion, but a bonus was that the Allied air forces gave the invasion complete protection from air attack.

Hours before the seaborne landings began, parachutists and gliders were moving to their appointed tasks. One of the most effective and vital of these was that performed by a force of 200 men travelling in six gliders. They were drawn from the Oxford and Bucks Light Infantry (now 1st Greenjackets) and Royal Engineers. Their task was to prevent the Germans demolishing two bridges near Benouville as these were vital to the second phase of General Montgomery's plan. Like all vital bridges the two were already wired for demolition as part of the defensive plan and it was essential to seize them before the charges could be blown. As they were heavily defended and were a small target, and there was a strong cross wind, it was an astonishing feat to crashland the gliders near them, capture the bridges and defend them against counter-attack. Parachutists and gliders were soon coming down all over the surrounding countryside but inevitably there were some disasters owing to the strong winds and navigation errors in the dark. Some gliders broke their tows in the squalls over the Channel and foundered. In spite of tremendous difficulties and considerable losses, 6th Airborne Division had reached and dealt with its most important objectives.

On the opposite (right) flank, the Americans had organised a much larger drop, a total of 12,000 parachutists. Unfortunately for them the dropping zone was badly flooded and as much of the water was covered by green weed, to a descending parachutist it looked like green fields. Landing in the dark, when weighed down with heavy equipment meant that many were drowned. Others came down in wooded areas where it was impossible to find landmarks. High winds and heavy anti-aircraft fire put many of the pilots off course and many drops occurred in areas miles away from their proper destination. The gliders fared even worse but with amazing American luck and a strong dash of initiative there were enough troops on the ground to interfere seriously with German efforts to contain the move. One of the unexpected bonuses from this disastrous scattering of the parachutists was that German Intelligence was utterly baffled by the manoeuvre; it was impossible to make any tactical sense out of such a diversity of scattered landings and as a result the Germans did not respond to it in the way they should have done.

The landing on Utah beach was another example of Americans being luckier than they might have been. To guide them in, they had two patrol boats and a radar boat. Unfortunately one patrol boat was sunk and the radar boat fouled its propeller. This coincided with an unexpectedly strong tide which swept the entire convoy – now with the loss of the radar boat unable to fix its position – and the landing was made a mile to the south of its proper destination. However, on the wrong beach they landed thousands of men and their equipment for a loss of only 12 killed and 100 wounded. An inspired decision by Brigadier-General Theodore Roosevelt took them straight inland, instead of their trying to find their originally allotted landing point.

Less happy were the Americans at Omaha. At best it was a difficult, well-defended landing point. Here they had no luck at all and lost 3,000 in getting ashore. But subsequently it appeared that many of their troubles were of their own making. They loaded up their assault craft twelve miles out. This was so that the loading would be outside the range of enemy fire, but it also meant that the assault craft were swamped by heavy seas. Their efforts by sea and air bombardment to reduce the German opposition to the landing were much less successful than they had been expected to be. An interesting point which emerges from the recollections later was that a contingent of rocket-bearing ships which might perhaps have been destined to assist the Omaha landings was far off course at the beginning of the day and did not appear to be heading in the right direction until late evening. Eventually, at a cost which caused the beach to be christened 'Bloody Omaha', the Americans established themselves. This they

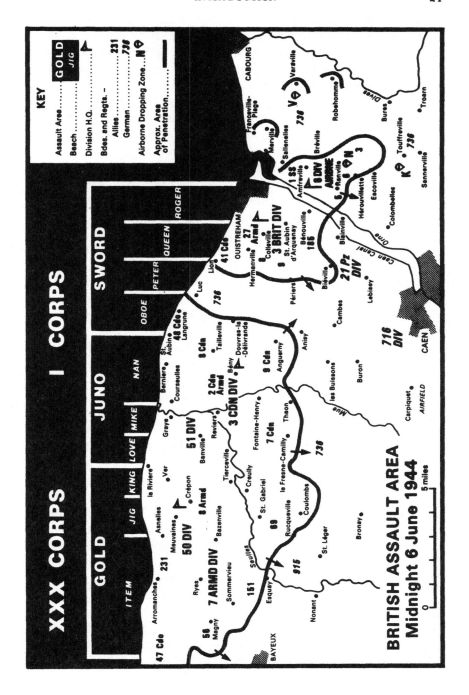

BRITISH ASSAULT AREA
Midnight 6 June 1944

owed to their courage and determination rather than their foresight
and skill. They were also assisted by the fact that the Germans had
been over-optimistic in believing the landing had been repulsed and
had withdrawn some troops to deploy against the British 50th Division
which was now approaching Bayeux.

Next to Omaha and in the very centre of the landing area was
Gold, which had been allotted to the 50th (Northumbrian) Division.
This was by no means an easy area. It had the same weather conditions as Omaha, but the unloading took place much closer in and
the division were well served by a long and accurate bombardment
of enemy strongholds by the Royal Navy. But Gold saw its losses too.
These were minimised by experience which had been learnt on other
difficult occasions. The bad luck included a high tide which covered
many of the underwater obstacles and meant that frogmen had to
deal with these in extremely difficult conditions. The DD (Amphibian)
tanks could not be landed in such rough water and had to go in
later straight on to the beach. This meant that the infantry lacked
their support at a critical moment. But 'the funnies' (the special
equipment like 'flail' tanks and 'Crocodile' Flame-throwers and
AVRE – heavy tanks used for breaking through obstacles) were
remarkably successful. 50th Division was accompanied by the famous
'Desert Rats' – the 7th Armoured Division who were no newcomers
to battlefields. Tremendous impetus built up in this area and if von
Rundstedt had been able to launch his cherished counter-attack it
would not have been likely to have had much success. This too was
an area where the work of the French Resistance and other behind-
the-line saboteurs completely dislocated German plans for reinforce-
ment.

Juno was allotted to 3rd Canadian Division who were considered
to have the dash and stamina to drive inland towards Caen – a most
important objective. Accordingly, 3rd Canadian Division, supported
by 2nd Canadian Armoured Brigade, was given the furthest objective
of the day – the capture of Carpiquet aerodrome eleven miles from the
beach. The Canadians did not quite reach it, but they covered seven
miles and, considering the weather and the beach obstacles, that was
a staggering success. Bringing in the landing craft was a particularly
delicate task. The tide had to be sufficiently high for the boats to ride
over the reefs off the coast but the very fact that it was high enough
for that meant that the underwater obstacles (which would have been
observable at low tide) were now hidden. Although frogmen, working
in very rough water, blew up many of the underwater obstacles, they

could not possibly deal with all in the time available; thus many LCTs were sunk coming in.

The landing beach was heavily mined and also well covered by defensive fire. Outstanding courage in the face of heavy losses enabled the leading units to dash across the beach; and conditions for the second wave were slightly easier in consequence, but well-positioned defences are not easily eliminated, nor are mines cleared immediately. As the beach was narrow, the congestion was appalling, and units which were badly needed further up the line could not get through. When eventually they did do so further congestion occurred at points where the Germans were putting up dogged resistance. The Juno assault was an outstanding success, more so than anyone could really have expected. Nevertheless it fell just short of its last objective, the Carpiquet airport, and it took a month before that site, so vital to the capture of Caen, was finally overrun. Juno beach saw determined fighting by 41 and 48 Royal Marine Commandos but both units ran into defences of such solidity and strength that it was impossible to break through without tanks, which were not available at the time.

While the Canadians were thus busily avenging the bloody repulse they had encountered at Dieppe two years earlier, the British on Sword beach had Dunkirk equally firmly in mind. On Sword everyone was fully determined that mistakes would be reduced to the minimum by foresight, preparation and care. A sample of this thinking was shown by the preliminary placing of two midget submarines. These lay on the bottom for two days and nights waiting to surface, at the due moment, and mark the outside edges of the assault lane with winking lights. In the event nearly all the assault craft landed at the right time in the right places.

But Sword had its problems. The tide was faster and stronger here. Many of the booby traps and stakes were already submerged by the time H hour (0725) approached. The water was too rough for amphibious (DD) tanks and these could not therefore be landed with the first waves. The tanks would have been very useful but the setback was minimised by the successful work of the 'funnies' who preceded the infantry and cleared many of the beach obstacles. The 'funnies' here were heavy demolition tanks (the AVREs), 'flail tanks', which used chains to beat a path through minefields, and mine detectors. By evening the assault battalions had fought their way six miles inland and had linked up with the Canadians.

While these assaults were pressing ahead everything which could be done to assist them was being done with vigour and precision. The

Navy pounded German gun emplacements and defences ahead of the advancing Allied infantry and the Air Forces prevented the Germans from being reinforced with necessary ammunition and stores. The Germans fought with great tenacity but eventually the combination of a shortage of ammunition and a vigorous and sustained frontal assault on their positions wore them down. But this did not mean that some German strongpoints did not prove fanatically determined in their resistance. The one at Merville which, with its four heavy guns, dominated the Sword and Juno beaches, is at this moment (1980) being restored by a fund raised by the Airborne Assault Normandy Trust, which is formed mainly by Senior and Retired Officers of the Parachute Regiment.

Many individuals and many units fought with distinction and bravery and it may not seem fair to single out some for mention when others, equally deserving, are not named. But the dash for Caen which was made by the KSLI (King's Shropshire Light Infantry) was perhaps one of the most inspired actions of the war. Lacking tank support, the KSLI requested permission to go it alone on foot. But they were supported by a squadron of tanks of the Staffordshire Yeomanry and even though they ran into a group of forty German tanks managed to thrust their way forward to within two miles of the vital city of Caen. There, alas without reserves or support, they had to halt within sight of their objective. Few could have equalled their effort; no one could have done more.

It would be a month before Caen was taken and the first main stage of the invasion completed, but the achievement so far was profoundly satisfying. The German counter-attack had still to come and the assault on Caen itself would be exhausting and costly; there could still be disasters. The German plan was to assemble a sufficiently large force to make a counter-attack crushing, but the Allies, aided by inspired air support, maintained such a pressure that the Germans were constantly having to reinforce the damaged parts of their own line. The Allies had their disasters but they were due to weather rather than German opposition. The Channel weather was continuously and exceptionally bad, culminating in a storm on 19th June which damaged the American Mulberry beyond the possibility of repair. The British Mulberry, also damaged, now had to handle greater than expected quantities of stores. But by that date much vital territory had already been won. The Americans were fast approaching Cherbourg, which they captured on 26th June. On the 26th General Dempsey began a thrust which soon had a four-mile deep wedge in the German defences; this could well be a decisive breakthrough.

From then on events moved rapidly – for a time. The Americans broke out and thrust deep through the German lines, the German 7th Army was destroyed at Falaise, Paris was liberated. The war could have been finished within six months if the Supreme Commander had let either Montgomery or Patton exploit the breakthrough they had established. Unfortunately there was insufficient petrol for two thrusts, only enough for one. The only wrong decision that could be made was to share the petrol equally, and that was the decision which was taken. In consequence surprise, initiative and advantage were all lost, and the Germans were given time to stabilise. The war in the west could not easily be lost now, in spite of the reverse in the Ardennes, but the tapering off of the great effort which had put the Allies ashore and cut deep into the German defences was a disaster which had not merely military, but political and economic consequences.

CHAPTER ONE

Invasion from the Air:
the RAF, the Gliders, and the Parachutists

The order in which accounts by individuals appear here is, whenever possible, the order in which they entered the battle. Some of the first people to be concerned in the D Day fighting set off the night before by air and arrived early on the scene; others embarked and began a slower journey by sea. The task of the air forces was to saturate the German defences with bombs, to report every activity, and to tow gliders and drop parachutists. The task of the airborne troops was to destroy enemy positions but also to keep intact certain bridges which would be needed by the Allies later. Thus it was vital to destroy the gun emplacement at Merville but equally important to ensure that the bridges over the Orne remained intact.

For those immediately concerned this meant a difficult air journey on a stormy night, a jump or glider landing in the dark, and the problems of finding comrades and equipment in a scattered landing in enemy-held territory.

The Royal Engineers, who would lead the assault on the beaches, were also represented by thirty officers and men in the glider party which captured Ranville and Bénouville bridges in one of the most critical operations of the assault. Needless to say, the brilliant parachute and glider operations were not without high cost. The official figures were that fourteen thousand sorties were flown by the Allied Air Forces on 5th/6th June and 127 aircraft had been lost. By the end of 6th June six hundred airborne troops had been killed, six hundred more were missing, and one hundred glider pilots were killed or missing. British and Canadian casualties in air and seaborne landings totalled 3,000 (one third of which were Canadians). The Americans lost six thousand in their airborne and seaborne assaults, and approximately half of these were on Omaha beach.

*

From Flight Lieutenant P. M. Bristow, a member of C Flight
575 Squadron, based at Broadwell in the Cotswolds
Once we had been given our first briefing and knew the DZ [dropping zone] and the glider targets, a tight security clamp was imposed. No one was allowed off the camp, no letters were collected though we received incoming mail, and no telephone calls were permitted. Even an Ensa concert party arriving by coach was turned away. On the other hand all our flight commanders went over to Netheravon for a special briefing. This was the operational centre for our part of the show and one of them told me later that he came out of the briefing room and put through a call to his girl friend in London.

During these days we studied photographs, large-scale maps and then we got a sand table of the coastline with the river Orne running up to Caen. We were even shown a film of the run-in from the coast line to the DZ. I think much of the success of the final operation was due to these visual aids we were given in the last few days.

On the morning of 5th June we had a pep-talk from the colonel in charge of the paratroops. By 1800 hours all our aircraft were marshalled on the perimeter track and taxi tracks so they could file out in the correct order for take-off. I forget now how many aircraft went from Broadwell that evening but I think it was two or three squadrons. I do remember that not only was mine the last squadron to go, but as I was in 'C' flight I was amongst the last of our squadron. It was a long wait and not without anxiety, for one had no sort of idea what reception we might meet. I do remember a strong sense of occasion and however small the part one felt one was taking part in an historic event.

The first to get airborne in the last of the daylight were all towing gliders. Never shall I forget the first one of all, for he had just about used up all the runway and was still on the ground. Around the periphery of the airfield stretched a low dry-stone Cotswold wall and a load of shingle had been tipped against this wall at either end of all the runways. It may have been imagination, and remember the light was failing, it may have been a despairing heave back on the control column or it may have been a bit of both; but it always seemed to all of us who were watching that the Dakota ran its wheels up the shingle bank and was literally catapulted into the air. At zero feet it staggered along too low to make a turn but with a line of electricity grid pylons not far in front. Next day in the mess the pilot said the trip had been uneventful apart from the take-off. To the best of my memory take-off proceeded without a single hitch.

Aircraft carrying paratroops started their take-off about an hour later and not until it was quite dark. There should have been a full moon that night but there was 10/10ths cloud cover so the night was dark. We had normal runway lighting for take-off but no navigation lights were used and we had to observe strict radio silence. Our signal to go was a green light from the control caravan at the end of the runway and we went off at pretty long intervals of say one minute and thirty seconds. There was certainly no sign of the aircraft ahead of you by the time it was your turn to go. The whole flight was scheduled : So long after take-off and turn on to such and such a course, after another interval turn to a different heading, with times to leave our coast at Littlehampton, to make landfall at Normandy and a time to drop. Streams of aircraft were going off from several other airfields, many destined for the same DZ so they all had to be interlocked. So far as I could judge the staff work must have been good.

We were supposed to be flying in Vees of three and I was third in my Vee so I kept my throttles well open to catch up the others in front. Formation flying is not a normal part of a transport pilot's expertise, but we had done a little in the preceding months but not at night, yet here we were on a particularly dark night. I eventually caught up with the fellows in front and found there were four of them. I decided I should be much more relaxed if I dropped back and flew on my own.

Bill Dyson was giving me regular fixes from his Gee box and confirmed we were on course and running to time. We had taken off at 2330 and were due to drop at 0100. Our stick went down within 30 seconds of the exact scheduled time.

We were carrying twenty paratroopers and an Alsatian dog that had been trained to jump from the back of a lorry. On a temporary rack fitted below the belly of the aircraft we carried a number of small anti-personnel bombs. We had been briefed to drop these as we crossed the Normandy beaches so that if there were any defenders they would be encouraged to keep their heads down. There were also a couple of folding motor-cycles in cylindrical canisters.

Shortly before we made landfall something exploded on the land right ahead. A vast sheet of yellow flame lit up the sky for a second or two and in that I saw a line of aeroplanes all going the same way, all at the same height, and I was part of this mad game of follow-my-leader. I made myself think I was all alone on a night exercise on Salisbury Plain, but kept very keyed up to take smart evasive action if I got close enough to anyone else to see them. I felt the slip-stream from other aeroplanes in front from time to time but once that rather shattering fire had died down never actually saw another.

Bill Dyson and the Gee box brought us in for a perfect landfall and Robbie Burns and I found we could see enough to make our way visually to the DZ. Robbie was an RAF navigator and was just ex-Ulster University. He was a bright boy. There were not always enough pilots for every crew to have a second pilot, so I was given Robbie as a map reader and that was a lucky day.

We had been told we should be crossing heavy gun emplacements and that our bombers would be dealing with them before we arrived to prevent them bombarding the Navy. Whatever had happened to them had burnt them up to such effect that we passed over a number of glowing plates of ferro-concrete. The heat must have been generated inside but here was the topside of a concrete roof glowing like a red-hot plate of steel. I have always wanted to know more about those glowing gun-pits.

Rebecca-Eureka was working by now to help lead us in. This was a short-range homing device actuated from a portable ground station. Now the illuminated direction Tee could also be seen and we were almost there. The paratroops had been standing lined up with the red light on – well back from the door opening – and at this point they got the amber and would go on the green. Doug Strake, my Canadian W/Op, was acting jump-master and was able to speak to me down the intercom and he told me all was ready and well. I had started the drop at the right height, the right speed and all was as right as we could make it until I lost contact with Doug. I should wait for him to tell me it was O.K. to open up, but he was silent and we were steadily losing height and advancing on the Germans who were clearly belligerent as witness the flames in the sky not long before. I was sure it was one of our lot that had bought it, though I was later told it was a Stirling. A moment later and Doug came through again to say everything had gone and I opened throttles, made a climbing turn to port and disappeared into cloud where we all felt nice and snug.

When he rejoined us in the cockpit Doug told us that the dog, who with his handler was the last to go, had followed the others all the way to the door and as it came to his turn to follow his handler out he decided this was not the same thing at all as jumping from the back of a lorry, had backed away from the door and retired to the front of the fuselage. Doug had had to unplug himself from the intercom, catch the dog and literally throw him out. Several weeks later he met one of our stick in Oxford who had been sent home wounded and he said they had eventually found the dog.

We came below cloud some ten miles short of Littlehampton and I remember laughing out loud at what we saw. Marking our landfall were three pairs of searchlights, each pair meeting at the cloud base. There they were, three inverted Vees to say, 'This way home boys!' It was the final crowning note of complete air supremacy. We had come a long way since June 1940.

*

From Mr F. J. Parslow, Warrant Officer Navigator
I was a WO Nav/B in an Albemarle towing a Horsa glider on 6th June 1944 to Caen. Prior to dropping our glider, I saw a Hamilton about one mile in front of us carrying, as I recollect, troops on the upper deck and a tank on the lower. Suddenly the tank broke through the front of the glider plummeting to the sea, followed by the glider, which had been cast off from the towing aircraft.

After dropping our glider we were immediately hit by anti-aircraft fire and the starboard engine and the rest of the wing outward fell off. We crash-landed at Greenham Common. The only casualty amongst the crew was the rear-gunner who was hit by shrapnel in the backside. He also had the wire connecting his parachute handle to his parachute shot through, and was most upset until I gave him my parachute. I was, you must understand, no hero, as we flew all the way back to England at about 100 feet and in as straight a line as possible, so a parachute was superfluous.

I was in 296 Squadron, stationed at Brize Norton.

*

From Wing Commander J. H. Dyer, MA, AMBIM, RAF (Retd)
On checking my log book I find the following entry:
  a. Date: 6 Jun 44
  b. Hour: 0250 (i.e. take off)
  c. Aircraft Type and No: Lancaster Y NE 165/G
  d. Pilot: Wing Commander J. B. Tait, DSO (x4) DFC (x2)
  e. Duty: Navigator
  f. Remarks: Ops Military Installations at St Pierre du Mont

(in the area of St Pierre-Eglise and Barfleur) in the
Cherbourg peninsular – Controller

  g. Flying Times (Night) 4.00 hrs.

At that time Wing Commander 'Willie' Tait, later better known as
CO of No 617 (Dambusters) Squadron and leader of the operations
which finally sank the *Tirpitz*, was undertaking a tour as a 'Master
Bomber' or Controller at RAF, Coningsby, Lincs, and I was one of
two navigators in his Lancaster, which carried some additions to the
standard equipment of those days. The other navigator was Squadron
Leader Ciano ('The Count'), reputed to be a member of the family
of the then Italian Foreign Minister! He happened to be just about
the top operator in Bomber Command of equipment known as H2S,
and my first impression, when crossing over the English Channel,
came from the picture he produced on the radar screen of what
appeared to be almost solid masses of formated blips heading towards
the Normandy beaches, which in turn produced the remark from a
crew member: 'Some Commando raid!' From this you will understand such was security that none of us in the crew, except probably
the pilot, had any idea that this was D Day. In fact a week earlier,
on 28th May 1944, when we had been detailed to bomb a gun
emplacement in the same area we were most surprised when this
operation did not turn out to be part of the invasion of the European
mainland.

Our task on D Day was to control and direct the bombing of a
battery of six coastal guns by a force of about 120 Lancasters of
No 5 Group. I gathered subsequently that five of the six guns were
completely knocked out and what impressed me most about the
operation at the time was the total lack of opposition either from
the ground or from the air. For those of us brought up on bombing
Berlin and the Ruhr etc, this was almost a novel experience, which
was not lost incidentally on our lords and masters. At that time there
was some delay in the output from training of bomber crews and to
help solve the problem operations against targets in the occupied
countries were temporarily reduced in value in respect of completing
a tour of operations (normally thirty for the first tour, and twenty
for second and subsequent tours) to one-third of an operation. Indeed
on this occasion so quiet was it when the bombing was completed that
the Master Bomber ordered the attacking force to return to base
whilst he gave us for about 45 minutes a unique 'grandstand' view
of the landing craft, etc, approaching the beaches. The early morning
skies were grey and overcast and the approach was unopposed, allow-

ing our wireless operator to flash messages of encouragement on the Aldis lamp to the invading forces below.

My final memory of this day relates to our return to RAF Coningsby. After the usual debriefing we returned to the officers' mess for the traditional post flight breakfast of bacon and eggs. On this occasion hardly had we sat down when a message came through requiring us to return to the Operations Block for a fresh briefing and thus to this day I still feel cheated of half a fried egg and a rasher of bacon!

Such are my memories and impressions as an airman of the D Day landings – the easiest operational sortie of my tour, which later counted as a full and not a third of a sortie.

*

From Flight-Lieutenant J. H. T. Russell, RAF

I took part in the D Day landings, but as an RAF pilot; I did not land in Normandy. Having done a stint as a night bomber pilot on Wellingtons in 99 Squadron Bomber Command in the summer and autumn of 1941, I was posted with 99 Squadron to the Far East and when we had re-formed as a squadron in India in 1942 we were engaged in night bombing operations over Japanese occupied Burma and daylight sweeps over the Bay of Bengal. At the end of 1943 I was posted back to the UK and I expected to do a short conversion course on to Lancasters or Halifaxes and then back into the fray in Bomber Command.

But the dear old Air Ministry thought otherwise. I was instructed to report to No 42 Operational Training Unit at Ashbourne, Derbyshire, which was equipped with Whitleys, Albemarles and troop-carrying gliders. I had never been inside a Whitley, never seen troop-carrying gliders and never even heard of an Albemarle, and I recall being a little surprised when I was informed that I was to instruct pilots straight from flying school in the art of flying Whitleys and of towing gliders with them. Our task was to train the pilots and crews who would tow the glider-borne troops when the circumstances arose.

Late in May 1944 word came through from above that the instructors of No 42 OTU were to provide crews for twelve Albemarles to take part in the D Day landing.

I did a quick conversion course on to Albemarles on 29th and 30th May and on 2nd June off I went with my crew to Hampstead Norris, the satellite airfield to Harwell in Oxfordshire. In my log book there is a reference to 'No 42 Special Mission Flight' – I cannot recall whether we gave ourselves this title or whether it had official blessing. But it sounded impressive and we convinced ourselves that if the Hun heard of our existence he would shudder in his jackboots. It sounded even more impressive and mysterious when abbreviated to 'No 42 SMF' – was this the secret weapon to win the war?

On D Day take-off must have been about midnight because I recall that we had to be over the French coast at 01.20. Our task was to drop 'window'* as the 6th Airborne Division were towed in gliders across the Channel and put down in Normandy. We were to fly at spot-on 1,200 feet and we were required to keep a very accurate time schedule to be at certain points at very definite times.

I kept my head in the 'office' with my eyes glued on the airspeed indicator and altimeter, but I can well remember being surrounded by other aircraft. I could see the shipping in the Channel and gunfire on the enemy coast. We were not molested by night fighters or flak but I seem to remember that, of the twelve aircraft of No 42 SMF which took part, only eight returned.

On landing back at Hampstead Norris, instead of going to bed, we listened to the radio and I think it was at 9 a.m. that the world was informed that we were back in Europe.

Duty done, it was back to Ashbourne to train more crews for what lay ahead – in the event Arnhem.

*

From the Reverend Lieutenant-Colonel A. R. Clark, MC
The longest day was, for me, actually a night and a day, the night being the day before, if you know what I mean.

At the end of May 1944, I was in command of a company of the 13th Parachute Battalion (Lancs). We were one day whisked away to a place unknown but quickly termed by all ranks as the Concentration Camp. This concentration did not concern, to my mind, the numbers of troops in one spot so much as the amount of briefing, checking and counter-checking down to the last detail, almost down to each man's individual role in the forthcoming invasion. We learned here that the objective of the 6th Airborne Division was Normandy – in a part so very much resembling the country round Oxon – Gloucester – Wiltshire borders where so much of our training over

*Material to upset enemy radar.

the past months had been carried out.

We had come to know how imminent was the invasion since we were kept constantly up to date with the meteorological situation. We learned that since the immediate weather conditions were not too propitious and that the long range weather forecast was anything but good for an airborne invasion, what had to be done would just have to be done almost at a moment's notice.

June 4th arrived offering little hope. 5th June was forecast as 'clearing temporarily after a doubtful start'. 6th June offered a ray of hope, not that any necessity for concern was in evidence from our side of the Channel, where we were impatiently waiting at Broadwell Airfield, since the weather there was not at all bad. Broadwell, how-ever, was quite a distance from the planned DZ at Ranville in the Calvados district of Normandy, where such matters as visibility and wind velocity were of vital importance.

One thing I do remember about this time. I remember thinking that it would surely have pleased my old Granny, whose concern I could never forget for our personal cleanliness, and also that of our linen – 'in case you should ever get knocked down in the street and have to be admitted to hospital, and then what would people think?', and this despite the fact that getting knocked down in the street in her era, when the fastest traffic – a runaway horse going at 12 mph, was most unlikely. However, to return to our projected invasion of Hitler's Europe by the 6th Airborne Division. The point was that before the final dénouement we managed to get a bath. This, I felt, would fit in well with General Boy Browning's precept, as well as my Granny's, that no man of the Airborne Forces under his command should go into battle unprepared to meet his Maker. Neither was this precept forgotten, in the sense in which *he* had intended it.

In the gathering dusk of the evening of 5th June 1944, off the perimeter track of Broadwell Airfield could just be distinguished parties of what might have been men, had it not been for the shape-lessness of their appearance. Perhaps a better description would have been that of many caravans of heavily laden camels silhouetted against the darkening horizon, all making, with that peculiar gait known only to an over-loaded camel, for one assembly point. At that rendezvous, the ceremony which was to take place there seemed at that moment to be the most natural in the world. It was the expression of the loyal offering of self to the interest of what seemed right and proper, to-gether with the confession of a newly found trust that had never before had the opportunity of rising to the surface to declare itself.

The many shapeless caravans converged, and, like camels, sank to their knees. What matter that prayer was made by a Methodist, or a Muslim, Catholic or Congregationalist, Sadhu or Salvationist : the intention was the same. So all six hundred of our battalion, led by Padre Boy Foy, acknowledged our need and our dependence, our fear and yet our trust, our inadequacy and yet our resolve. How inspired, I thought, had been the powers that be when they designated that mighty and yet puny effort to shake off the shackles of oppression from a continent fettered as it had been for four years, as 'Operation Overlord'. That may have been the name on the operation order, but it was more. It was a prayer. There was another prayer being offered by six hundred men of one Parachute Battalion, the 13th (Lancashire) Battalion. It was written on their battalion flag; a black one, bearing, under the parachute badge the red rose of Lancashire and the motto 'Win or Die'.

It is strange what inconsequential matters occupy our thoughts, and indeed remain in them, during moments of stress. The two points that stood out most persistently in my mind on emplaning were, first, that in the dimmed interior lighting of the Dakota, and due to a previous application to our faces of brown greasepaint, I could not recognise a single one of the men with me. All were rendered additionally shapeless by the acquisition of a parachute on the back and a very large kit-bag strapped to the right leg of each. How very disconcerting this was. To me it seemed like being given a tune to play without the provision of the necessary music, or a note that I could recognise..

Secondly, as the RAF dispatcher came aft, carefully checking the equipment of each man, I saw that, praise be to God, he was a 'blue job', and no brash American. I was to learn that only a couple of weeks before he had been flown back from Burma where he had been supply-dropping to the Chindits. I was comforted by the thought that here, at any rate, was no novice.

He indicated to me the large insulated tea container fixed to the floor of the fuselage, opposite me and slightly to the right. It was conveniently placed for operation by Albert, my batman, the only man I recognised really, and then only by reason of the fact that he had lost some of the camouflage paint from the region of his left eye. The name 'Chirgwin' came quite unbidden to my mind.

There was one more thing that I knew, and that was the location of Private Bamber. He was No 20 in the stick, that is to say right forward of me, the farthest man away from me on the starboard side of the plane; diagonally opposite, so to speak. My concern for his whereabouts was twofold. First, that as he was normally airsick even before the plane was airborne, I had to ensure his fitness to jump at the appropriate moment, and, secondly, since he was the Company HQ 38 set operator on the wireless, I could pass to him as soon as might be after landing a number of 38 set batteries which I had somewhat overgenerously offered to stow in my own kitbag for him. At the time of packing last minute items, the way he had looked at me, for all the world like a little dog put 'on trust' by his handler, had roused in me a sense of pity which was really most unsoldierly, at the apparent mountain of kit he was endeavouring to stow away in his kitbag.

I was not aware of all he was trying to take, but I do know some of the contents of my own kitbag, which rendered the weight of it rather more than I could lift. When I look back I shudder at the recollection of that load. In the kitbag were stowed the following:

Small pack containing – washing and shaving kit; change of underclothes and socks; gym shoes; knife, fork and spoon; gas cape and groundsheet; water bottle (full); drinking mug; gas mask; mess tin, containing a 48 hour ration pack. Then there was Sten gun and spare magazines (filled with 9 mm ammn); 2 lbs spare Plastic HE (always handy); 2 full belts of 303 Vickers ammn. (weight?); 2 filled Bren mags; 1 shovel GS; 1 pair wire cutters; 3 spare wireless batteries (for Bamber).

Since all these items would obviously not be immediately to hand on landing, the 'important' items were carried on my person. They consisted of:

Basic Equipment, i.e. belt and straps; 2 ammunition pouches (each containing 2 x 36 grenades (primed)), holster containing 45 automatic (loaded). In the bosom of my battle dress blouse two pounds of Plastic HE; one Webley revolver (spare and loaded), and one hunting horn. In the large patch pocket of my trousers – maps and message pads. In the field dressing pocket on the other leg – customary first aid kit plus a tube of morphine. In a hidden pocket down the outside seam of my right trouser-leg – a particularly hard and unaccommodating Commando fighting knife.

The list was not yet complete, for in the inside breast pocket of my battle dress blouse was my escape wallet, containing compass, pep pills, escape maps and foreign currency.

In the tail pocket or pouch of my camouflage smock reposed an

Army pullover, stocking hat and red beret. Oh, and I almost forgot, over all – the toggle rope.

When I shudder now at my recollection of the weight of the equipment listed, I suppose I should have shuddered still more at the possible result of detonation. Strangely, however, that thought never entered my mind at the time. As long as I could hobble from my position in the plane to the exit door I felt reassured that I should be able to cope, since the kitbag, once lowered to the end of its rope while I was descending through the air, would reach the ground one second before I did, and provide an anchorage. This was perhaps going to be necessary as we were given to understand that the wind speed was likely to be above normal, in fact probably over the limit of what was considered safe for a training jump.

Before emplaning I had seen RAF engineers loading bombs, apparently one to each plane, which we were to let go on passing over Cabourg, thereby, hopefully perhaps, misleading the Germans into the supposition that we were just another bombing raid. The thought did just cross my mind that it would be just too bad if someone up at the pilot's end inadvertently pressed the wrong button as we were starting up, but the matter was quickly banished from my thoughts as the next door plane's engine burst into a roar, to be followed immediately by ours -which, having revved up to some shuddering speed as though flexing its muscles for the job, calmed down again a little.

We rolled forward, took a short run, and I felt that lack of bumping which indicated our being airborne, saw obliquely through the open door the ground which should have been below swing upward to my right, and felt the 'clunk' of the wheels as they were retracted into their flying position. We were off. We were coming Over Lord.

It was natural I suppose that as far as the men were concerned silence reigned in the plane for some time, though on what each of us was centring his thoughts one could only guess. Our RAF despatcher appeared beside me, rather in the manner of a ghost. The look on his face, the only white face in the plane, asked if everything was all right. I asked him how Bamber was. He departed to find out and returned after a couple of minutes to report 'OK'. To my incredulous and inane enquiry as to why he had not been sick he could give no answer.

This passage of words had the effect of starting the general conversation among us. First between immediate neighbours, then soon with buddies on the opposite side of the fuselage. Voices were raised against the noise of the engines. Laughter broke out at the crude inanities that normally pass between soldiers. The tension was eased. We were back to normal, or as nearly back to normal as a score of men about to make a parachute jump could be. Someone started to sing. The tune was taken up by the whole stick, with such volume that the noise of the engines was scarcely heard above it, and served only to maintain the rhythm of that very rhythmical hymn, 'Onward Christian Soldiers'. Strange that *that* song should come spontaneously to the throats of *us*, whose usual marching songs, though 'soldierly', were usually anything but Christian! The occasion, however, seemed to call forth the appropriate incidental music. It went on verse after verse, though each was mostly a repetition of the first and only well known one.

It was the appearance of the despatcher again that caused the singing to die away. He said that there was flak coming up ahead. We were getting near the French coast. I couldn't see *ahead* from where I was sitting but I did look down through the door and could see in the brilliant moonlight between the patchy clouds the little points of darkness made visible by their tiny white wakes – the invasion craft below in the Channel. Then came the long white line of surf, and suddenly as we banked slightly to starboard the flak was visible. The despatcher shouted 'Cabourg'. Shortly afterwards we were into the flak. It came up at us rather like fireworks. Our aircraft instead of rising and increasing speed seemed to slow down. It dropped lower, altering course slightly a couple of times. I did think that on this occasion the pilot might just have complied with his orders to drop the bomb not worrying particularly when or where. However he was presumably at last satisfied with his effort, for we started to rise and the engines took on a, for me, much healthier note. The despatcher appeared with what I could feel was a puckish smile on his face as he shouted 'Bombs away', with all the aplomb of a bomb aimer who had just released a stick of one thousand pounders into Hitler's front garden.

Something hit us. The sound was rather like that of a dustbin being emptied, but there was no apparent damage at the moment. It wasn't until a minute or so later when Albert's next-door neighbour jokingly accused him of having made a pool on the floor that we discovered that the tea container had sustained a direct hit from the flak. This was held to be a heinous crime on the part of Jerry, for which we resolved he should pay dearly in due course.

I could tell that it would not be long now before we were

required to do more than sit and sing 'Onward Christian Soldiers', though we did manage a final roaring first verse. The despatcher was beginning to get edgy, making frequent trips to the pilot's cabin and ceasing individual attention to us. At last he came back from the cockpit saying something to each man as he came, first on his left and then on his right. I could not hear until he was four men away from me what the message was, although I guessed, and correctly too. 'Five minutes to go.' Those nervous motions, so well known and yet unnoticed by those making them, began again; the fidgeting with and preliminary tap on quick-release boxes, the tightening of the chin straps, the glance at the hooks on the static lines, verifying that the safety pin was safely home; that the kitbag was safely fastened to the leg – all those little things we so often cursed ourselves for doing, well knowing that they were just signs of nervousness.

So intent were we on these last fidgetings that the next order came as a shock. 'Stand to the door.' God, that kitbag was heavy. But I made the doorway, to be almost pitched out as the plane rolled. It took all the strength of my left hand on the door lintel to prevent a very premature exit. I heard a soft voice with a Bootle accent behind me enquire 'All right, Sir?' and all I could do was nod. It was not easy to screw my head into the right position to see that little red light up by my left ear, when it came on. But the old butterflies in the midriff had gone. I even remember thinking amusedly that there would be no yellow light between the red and the green like you get at the crossroads, and, there, flick, the red was on. The green followed quickly and I was away.

I noticed no opening of the parachute. All my attention was given up to that pernicious and unmanageable kitbag. I strove frantically to slow down its speed of descent, but the sudden transition from falling to its being supported by the chute canopy had started the rope slipping through my fingers. I thanked God for the provision of double thickness silk gloves. Without them I should have had little flesh left on my hands. I waited it seemed like minutes, though it could obviously have been just one second for the final sickening and awful tug of some two hundred or so pounds' dead weight snatching at my middle at 32 feet per second per second. It never happened! The rope, held now in my nerveless fingers still remained there, but there was no weight of any bag. No indication of what had happened to it. It had gone. I could only suppose that the stitching had been rotten and had allowed rope and bag to part company. In my usual facetious way I hoped that if it had not descended on the head of some unsuspecting Kraut it had at least given him pneumonia from the draught of its passing.

With this contretemps behind me I had soon to look to my landing. It was not easy to judge the wind. There was no comforting red smoke candle. I was coming down into what seemed to me to be a large wood containing many clearings. Suddenly I was down. The trees of which the wood was composed were sufficient to subdue the wind so that the canopy of my chute subsided gently on the ground – much more gently than I had done. Planes were droning overhead. Away to the north I could hear gunfire of some sort. I remained lying down while I released the parachute harness and divested myself of the awkward enveloping jumping jacket.

It was perhaps as well that I did so. I felt a sudden obligation to cease struggling like a rabbit in a snare so that I could listen and observe. I had landed in a small clearing surrounded by, as far as I could see in the intermittent moonlight, orchards, which indeed they were. I was roughly in the centre of a field some fifty yards square. The cause of my sudden concern was that I thought I heard voices. A few seconds of absolute stillness on my part confirmed the fact. I *could* hear voices from just inside the orchard on the south side. Now came the crucial question, 'English or German?'. I had not long to wait for the answer. Three figures emerged through the hedge on the south side of my clearing. They were muttering together, but strain as I might I could not make out one syllable of their conversation. Then in that strangely capricious way that a breeze has of changing direction, it brought me their scent. I couldn't describe it, except perhaps to say that the nearest description which comes to mind was that of a cross between the plasticine we used to use at school and a new cheap brand of scented soap. My mind went back to, of all places, Cheshunt College, Cambridge. Not that I had ever contemplated studying for holy orders in the non-conformist Church, but I had indeed attended a course of instruction there in 1943. The nature of this course had been the study of German Army Identification and Intelligence. During this course uniforms and equipment had been produced for inspection. These had most probably been laundered before we examined them, nevertheless a distinct odour had remained clinging to them. It hung on the air now. I think that they saw nothing although their suspicions were aroused.

They may possibly have seen the flash of my arm as it described an arc in their general direction to release from my hand the 36-grenade which I dare not hold any longer since the fuse had been struck for at least a second already. In fact I believe it never reached the ground before it exploded. Although I say it myself, it was a good throw. I didn't wait to see the result, but on the explosion I was up on my feet and running like a hare in the direction I judged north-west to be. After about a minute I pulled up, partly through want of breath but also, having managed to subdue my feeling of panic, to say to myself aloud, I believe 'You – – – brave paratrooper'.

I set off in the general direction in which I believed the rendezvous to be, at a somewhat steadier pace than I had started, and now, as far as I could see, entirely alone in a large and uninhabited area of the Calvados region of Normandy. All the aircraft seemed to have departed, and comparative silence reigned; silence enough for me, after a space of some ten minutes during which I must have traversed the best part of a mile, to catch a most peculiar sound. It was like that which a rabbit makes when caught in a snare, though it must have been a rabbit as big as a sheep from the noise. The wire was occasionally being pulled so taut that it positively twanged like a violin G string. As I again debated with myself 'One of ours or one of theirs?' my doubts were resolved by hearing a voice which this time I could distinguish, by the hoarsely whispered intensity and urgency of its English appeal, the burden of which was, when separated from a perhaps understandable flow of invective, 'Cunning-ton! Cunnington! Come and help me out of this (qualified) mess.' It was Bill Harris, the Battalion 2 i/c.

I saw what had happened to him when I approached and identi-fied myself as a friend, though not his batman Cunnington. In crossing a post and wire fence which had not been as taut as it might have been, a lower strand had become crossed over the upper, thereby trapping his foot most effectively, and suspending it four feet above ground where it was impossible for him to reach it unaided so that he could free himself. I was able to put him to rights in a few seconds. Since he was bound for a different rendezvous from mine we de-parted our separate ways in the gradually increasing darkness as the clouds covered the moon.

As I plodded on, suddenly from way ahead in the direction I was going came a sound as welcome as I had ever heard – a hunting horn. It was fainter and farther away than I had expected it to be. The sound it uttered was quite distinguishable even if not made by a practised trumpeter. 'Dit-dah-dit-dit,' the morse letter 'L'; L for Lancashire and L for Luard. I judged it to be about a mile farther on and increased my pace confidently.

I arrived eventually. Albert, who had arrived at the RV some full
ten minutes before me and now figuratively wagging his tail like a
pleased puppy re-united with a long absent master, greeted me, heard
my tale of woe concerning the lost kitbag and, after a minute or so's
absence returned with a sten gun and haversack, remarking, 'There's
bags of these lying about around here,' by which I gathered that two
or three of them were spare since their owners had become casualties
either on landing or very shortly after.

There wasn't much time for conjecture or further debate as suddenly the tell-tale sound of mortar fire from the north-east assailed
our ears, to be followed within the expected few seconds by the crunch
of the bombs – too close to be pleasant. I would have loved to go
forward into the beckoning and comparative safety of the edge of
Ranville village, but orders said otherwise. 'C' Company HQ and
No 9 Platoon were to remain at the RV as reserve, until the village
was captured and then move in to protect the left flank of Battalion
HQ. The only thing that had not gone more or less to plan was that
No 9 Platoon was conspicuous by its absence.

Progress seemed slow. Apart from the very regular and frequent
arrival of a bunch of mortar bombs nothing much appeared to be
happening. Then we began to advance slowly, haltingly, into the
south-west edge of the village. As we did so the man about whom I
had forgotten in the preoccupation of the preceding hours, or months,
or aeons, appeared. So uncertain was I of the period of time that
had elapsed since we left Broadwell airfield that I felt obliged to look
at my watch, for the first time. It said 0205 hours. Only three hours
earlier we had been in England.

The soldier who approached me was Private Bamber. The usual
rueful smile was on his face under the paint.

'Message from HQ, sir. Ranville captured,' he reported in his doeful
voice, as though apologising for some oversight, but then that was
always his way. I felt constrained to ask him how he had enjoyed
the flight.

'First time in all me life I've never been sick, sir,' he said, again
almost apologetically as a smile of triumph transformed his face. It
was the first and only time I can ever recall that he was able so to
report.

As we drew further into the village the gliders landed. We could
see them in the dawn light being towed overhead and then released
to circle clumsily, and sometimes finally crash through the trees before
coming to rest on the landing zone. I remember thinking, somewhat

ungrammatically, 'Rather them than us', to have arrived in such an uncomfortable fashion, having little power to influence direction, destination or disembarkation once they were committed to such flimsy, three-ply aerial trailers.

The light seemed to materialise quite suddenly as we emerged from the village's southern end with its cover of tall trees, into the north-western outskirts with its church on the crossroads, conveniently close to the château and the presbytery, in the garden of which Battalion HQ was set up, with our Company HQ a trifle close, I thought. Our company was, though, somewhat naked by reason of the non-arrival of 9 Platoon.

Across the north end of the little orchard in which we had stopped, and separated from it by a 'Gloucestershire' type stone wall, ran the narrow country road. On the other side of this road there stood a rather long, three-storeyed house. From the windows of this waved hands and pieces of cloth as though tentatively offering either friendship or surrender, dependent upon which might best be received by us, the new eruption into the lives of the occupants. A section of No 8 Platoon, having taken up position astride the road, tried their hands at making friends, but the little group of occupants were very scary. I didn't blame them after what the village had very recently been through.

The area now appeared quiet. But not for long. Soon a terrific barrage started from way up in the north as the guns of the Royal Navy opened up. It seemed to me perhaps as well that I had traversed that two and a half miles from the spot where I had landed, since the burst of heavy shells seemed to come from just that very spot. 'H' hour had arrived – 0700 hours. I pictured the scene on the beaches as the assault craft grounded, let down their ramps and vomited forth tiny little men into the uncertain and unfriendly surf, to struggle manfully on to the beaches against an enemy as tough and determined as any they were ever likely to encounter. In spite of certain difficulties I myself had encountered on arrival I preferred my method of getting to the scene of action.

Through the day the occasional mortar bomb still burst uncomfortably close. Now was not the time to forget Brigadier Nigel Poett's maxim, 'Dig or Die.' How thankful I was to be for the possession of two pounds of plastic HE. The noise of our beating into the hard unyielding Gloucester type stony ground of a four-foot length of piping was soon heard, interspersed with warning shouts of 'Take cover', just in case, as the charges dropped into the bottom of the deep hole made, were detonated. One would blow a nice spherical hole below ground which could fairly quickly be converted into a trench large enough to accommodate a soldier yearning for the instant and necessary cover such as it could provide.

There was no denying that the enemy was persistent, and also that he was far from inaccurate in his fire on us. It was, of course, inevitable that the reason should at last be borne in on us : the church tower, that rather strange edifice built separately from the church proper although an integral part of it. We investigated it. The cause of the previously persistent though unexplained arrival of mortar fire coincided with the movement or gatherings on our part was made clear, but not before a sudden well-directed concentration of bombs on the crossroads had coincided with the moment chosen by various rather indispensable members of the company, to assemble there to exchange news and views on the tactical situation. That moment cost the company the platoon commanders of Nos 7 and 8 Platoons, the company sergeant major, the colour sergeant and a couple of men, all at one fell swoop.

It was too late that the offending 'spy' was located in his signalling post at the top of the church steeple. The previously unexplained ringing of the church bell at odd moments ceased forthwith.

Since George Lee, our No 9 Platoon commander, together with the bulk of his platoon had not been seen or heard of since the drop, in fact since we took off for France, I found myself the sole remaining officer in the company. I remained so for a considerable period.

But I am still alive, as you can perhaps see.

(The Rev) Lieutenant-Colonel Clark, MC, aged 75, is now a Military Knight at Windsor Castle. He had originally joined the Army as a trooper in the Life Guards, and after leaving the Army as a lieutenant-colonel, took Holy Orders and became a missionary to Pakistan for 25 years.

*

From Mr John Weathers
A brief rundown as to my 'status' as at 6th June 1944 : Private Soldier in Signals Platoon, HQ Company, 12th (Yorks) Parachute Battalion, 5th Brigade, 6th Airborne Division. I was 19½ years of age at that time.

Thirty-five years ago on 4th June, as I recall, my personal feelings were of great apprehension, wondering what I had 'let myself in for' by volunteering for the Parachute Regiment. 'Chutes were drawn about mid-day on that day, only to be returned shortly afterwards – D Day had been postponed, just when one was 'up tight' thinking this is it. At the same time there was a sense of false security in that the unknown was to be delayed. On 5th June, 'chutes were drawn again. No postponement this time – faces now 'blacked up', all equipment, especially the parachute, checked over many times. By the time emplaning took place (time of no return), about 2300 hours, I recall everyone looking like Christmas trees without the fairy lights – 'chutes on backs, steel helmets with all the camouflage decorations on, personal weapons, and in my case I was to drop with a carrier pigeon in a cylindrical container hung about my neck. I was also carrying a supply of corn with which to sustain the pigeon and I remember wondering if perhaps I would, within the next day or so, be needing it for my own survival. I think at this time there was much 'brave' chit-chat etc, so that any fears one might have had were at least for the moment forgotten.

It was an uneventful crossing until the French coast was reached, when the aircraft was suddenly struck on the underside by flak, obviously from a German shore battery. I remember the dull thuds which seemed to reverberate right through the floor of the plane and right up my body. The pilot must have decided on evasive action, and we were all thrown about to a greater or lesser degree which not unnaturally brought forth a choice sample of opinions vocally. 'Red Light' came on very abruptly, this being the signal to make oneself ready for the 'Long Drop'. I remember a feeling of nervous tension, the plane's engines were throttled back and all seemed relatively quiet; one had so often had this experience in training, but this was for real. The 'Green Light' followed very quickly; there was no time now for much thought, it was a case of follow the man in front, when he disappeared you knew you were on your way. A rush of air, the 'chute exploded open and all was quiet; tension seemed to have gone. I was out of that plane, floating down, thinking how good it was to be away from the dark belly of that Stirling bomber from which I had 'escaped' – then my thoughts came to wondering as to what sort of greeting I was to expect on landing, or indeed as to where I should land. But land I did, of course, all alone, about three minutes past 0100 hours – very dark, very quiet, very wet – disposed of 'chute, knelt on ground, heart thumping, waiting, wondering as to next move. Only two hours or so before I had been back in England, safe, near home, and now here – thinking back like this now makes one's heart beat a little faster, as the complexity of it comes back to one. On my feet now and sensing I was not where I ought to be, nothing familiar to tie up with the briefing session we went through, I was suddenly aware of someone's presence only five to ten yards away. 'Friend or foe' was my immediate thought, but before I made a move I was challenged for the password, and fortunately in a voice that I recognised as belonging to my signals officer. However, through stupidity, or the suddenness of everything, I just could not remember the password. I felt sure that to hesitate too long could be fatal for my wellbeing, so I remember saying 'It's me, sir. Private Weathers.' This fortunately sufficed.

Our plane load was dropped just inland from the coastal town of Cabourg on the River Dives, an area which the Germans had pre-flooded as a welcome gesture for us. This was some twelve miles or so from the battalion dropping zone, and what was left of darkness that morning was spent trying not to be spotted by the enemy and looking for somewhere safe to hide up. Dawn came – before we welcomed it. By now there were some four or five of us who had met up and formed a little party. We waded across the river – in daylight now – and were engulfed in thick oozing mud, for it was low tide, up to our armpits. This was not a very nice experience, nor one from which I expected to emerge. I vividly recall the utter exhaustion when we dragged ourselves out and had a small bank (no more than three feet) to negotiate – it was like trying to climb Snowdon. We reached the shelter of a barn and hid in the upper storey which was full of straw bales. I attempted to clean the filth from myself and my sten gun – it was far from being in working condition. The following morning a Frenchman approached in a canoe through the swamp and he took us one at a time in the canoe to a safer farm – here again we were in hiding in a loft, and the whole area was surrounded by Germans. I have recently discovered that the Frenchman was subsequently shot by the Germans.

About 13th/14th June I was wounded on the outskirts of Sallen-elles and picked up by a Commando unit and back in England about 21st or 22nd June.

To sum up briefly what my personal emotions were during those first hours in France on 6th June. I think I was more apprehensive than frightened, although there were frightening moments. Certainly I was bewildered and very frustrated indeed at being virtually of no use because we were dropped in the wrong place. I never recovered my radio set and could not play the role for which I had been trained.

The pigeon, by the way, I released because of lack of food and I was afraid it might drown. It did return to England, alas, with no message on its leg.

*

From Mr G. T. Radmore

On D Day I was a captain in Royal Signals, Signals Officer of the 5th Parachute Brigade in command of the 5th Parachute Brigade Signals Section comprising myself, a subaltern Gordon Royle, and ninety other ranks. When I had done my course in parachuting at Ringway, on my first parade of the 5th Parachute Brigade Signals which I formed, the sergeant marched up to report and to my amazement it was the same old regular Sergeant Moore who had been with me at Dunkirk. As he saluted he whispered: 'Christ, not you again, sir!'

On 5th June we moved to Fairford. I stopped at a pub on the way for a drink and the publican said, 'I wonder when the invasion is going to start?' I said, 'I've no idea.' What would he have thought if he'd known.

I was responsible for providing wireless communication from Brigade HQ to all battalions, with a link to the UK. I flew in a Stirling with a bicycle and I remember the floor hatch being opened and seeing the surf of the coast of France. From the exit from the Stirling to the ground seemed only a short time as I think we were dropped from 500 feet. It was exhilarating once down, although I remember in the air seeing some flak and thinking I would not shoot pheasants again as I knew what they must feel like!

The DZ* seemed teeming with people. I had no idea where I was and was convinced I'd been dropped in the wrong place. A private soldier was very indignant with me for being in the wrong DZ – as he thought, incorrectly.

I gathered some men and heard a vehicle. Just as we were about to open fire, we realised they were English. They turned out to be two Naval signallers who'd dropped with us to work wireless to *Warspite* and *Roberts* (a monitor†) who were to give us artillery support. When I asked them what the devil they thought they were doing they said that in the Navy they had not been taught how to march and so they'd

*Dropping zone.

†A ship used for bombardment.

knocked off the Germans in the Volkswagen and were driving to the DZ.

Shortly after I met our intelligence officer, Maurice Dolden, and we agreed we were lost. We then came upon a signpost and I said to him that as there were no umpires on this exercise we should cheat. He got on my shoulders and very gingerly ran a torch along it. At that moment we heard a hunting horn which was our rallying signal and made our way to the quarry which was our RV. The first to arrive had been Leonard Mosley, war correspondent of the *Daily Sketch*, who was already busy with his story.

We stayed there and heard the first gliders coming in quite near us with their wings being ripped off on the poles which the Germans had erected. Just after dawn we moved to our first Brigade HQ by the bridge on the east of the Orne. In the meantime one of my corporals and two men had disconnected the main German telephone line which I'd spotted from an air photo.

One of our tasks was to get a telephone line across the bridge to 7 Parachute Battalion on the west of the Bénouville bridge. My line party were all wounded by fire from a maternity home, but one of my corporals, Waters, a regular and a Yorkshireman, got covering fire from one of the men and took the line across and kept the line going under heavy fire. For this he got an immediate MM.* A few days later our lines were being cut, so he lay in the ditch and shot the German who was doing it, arriving back to report to me with a tin hat and a pair of jackboots. Sadly, after behaving continuously in Normandy with great gallantry, he was blown up in a grenade accident at Bulford on our return.

I recall the following incidents in the early hours of D Day.

General Gale arrived in his jodhpurs in great form and gave me a terrific rocket because my cook, Lance Corporal Moreno, had opened up on some snipers. I had not included Moreno (an underchef from one of the big London hotels) in my original jump, but he had been so upset that I gave him some spare equipment and let him come. He was longing to kill Germans and could not resist opening fire at the first provocation. So I claim the first rocket in the invasion as well as the first telephone line!

We had set up part of a farm as the officers' mess – I think it was the cowshed – and I remember having breakfast there. It was an assault ration out of a mess tin, but Nigel Poett insisted quite rightly

*Military Medal.

that we behave normally and have it in the mess. I also remember listening to the BBC news announcing the landings, and working a wireless set to the Commando brigade commanded by Lord Lovat and hearing his pipes in the distance.

That evening we moved into the lodge of the Château de Ranville. The Countess Rohan Chabot was the local mayor and superb as she drove round in her donkey cart. She was embarrassed that her donkey objected to mortaring and was worried that the citizens of Ranville might think her frightened. She told me in later years when I visited her that the first she knew of the invasion was when two of our men came to the door in the early hours of the morning. She rushed up to her husband and said : 'The Tommies are here.'

He said : 'Don't be a damn fool, it's Germans dressed up. You will probably be taken out and shot.'

'In that case,' she said, 'I'll go and do my hair because it would look very bad for a Frenchwoman in my position to be shot with her hair looking untidy.'

I recall visiting the 13 Parachute Battalion and seeing Major Ford, a keen falconer, with a German falcon he'd found in one of their positions.

After the drop, I collected almost all my men except Gordon Royle who had been killed trying to take on a German machine-gun. I also had one glider missing, which must have come down in the sea. I remember burying my dead in the cemetery at Ranville, where they still are.

Later we moved to Lemesnil, which we took over from the 3rd Parachute Brigade. There was a porcelain factory next door, only a few hundred yards from the front line, run by Monsieur du Pont, a large Norman who refused to be evacuated and kept on producing ornaments (one of which I have) right through the battle.

My friend, Hugh Ward, a captain in the Worcestershire Yeomanry, our gunners, was killed in the attack on Bréville. I knew him well because he hunted the regimental beagles at Bulford and I took them out for him once or twice. He was the forward observation officer in the attack by 12 Parachute Battalion on Bréville. The first salvo killed him. His batman, who had been a hunt servant, asked me what to do with Hugh Ward's hunting horn, and I suggested it be buried with him. He lies with his horn in the churchyard at Bréville and not in the Airborne cemetery.

I recall the elation after landing at getting there after months of training and remembered those famous words of Shakespeare : 'And

gentlemen in England now abed Shall think themselves accurs'd they
were not here.'

One final story. My friend John Wilkes was signal officer of the
3rd Parachute Brigade. We had agreed a private frequency on which
we were to call each other at set times and say 'Tally Ho' which
meant 'I'm all right!' I called him and got no answer and found out
later he'd been dropped east of the Dive by mistake and taken
prisoner. The worst of his experiences was that when he was captured
the Germans took his hunting horn and trampled it under their jackboots. When he complained to the German captain of bad treatment,
the German said : 'But Hauptmann Wilkes, we did not invite you
here.'

I asked a Frenchwoman two days after the landing why she was
still putting up poles on the DZ. She said, 'The Germans told us to
do it and no one told us to stop.'

*

From Mr L. M. Cloutt
We were promised moonlight for our airborne operation on D Day.
In fact, as co-pilot with the responsibility for map-reading on the final
dropping run, I had to strain to follow the terrain and, to help,
opened the side window in the Dakota. Alas, most of my large-scale
map was sucked out and I was left grasping a mere fragment, which
I still have as a souvenir. Fortunately we had been well briefed on
several visits to Netheravon, where there was an excellent model of the
dropping area and where film was shown under various simulated
light conditions and we felt as confident as possible in the circumstances that our paratroops did drop in the right area.

I was flying with 271 Squadron from Down Ampney. Later in the
campaign we crashed near Caen, but that's another story.

*

From Mr G. H. Heaton, ex-Staff Sergeant, Glider Pilot Regiment
I was with C Squadron of the Glider Pilot Regiment, flying Hamilcar
gliders from Tarrant Rushton, Dorset, and took part in the landing
on the evening of D Day, 6th June, at about 9 p.m.

As far as I can remember, thirty Hamilcars took off, most of them
carrying Tetrarch tanks, with their crews, of the Light Reconnaissance
Squadron. Four Hamilcars, however, of which mine was one, carried
petrol and ammunition for supplying the tanks. The pilots of these

four gliders were issued with parachutes, unlike all the other glider pilots who did not enjoy this privilege, as they usually carried troops; the theory of this was presumably that as the troops did not have parachutes it would have been bad for morale if the pilots were seen to have them! I must say that we did wonder at the time what earthly use the parachutes would have been if we had been hit, in view of the nature of the loads we were carrying.

My memory is of an uneventful trip, and I was greatly impressed by the swarms of Mustang fighters escorting us across the Channel and by the sight of the Royal Navy firing broadsides into the German defences on the coast of Normandy.

Our landing was, however, more tricky; there was a certain amount of small arms fire, including tracers, coming up at us, and the field in which we landed near Ranville had got telegraph poles erected in it to hinder the landings. We came in rather fast with our wings hitting the odd telegraph pole, which proved to be no obstruction, but just as I thought we were going too fast and would end up in an orchard at the end of the field, a Tetrarch which had just driven out of the Hamilcar landing before we did, proceeded at right angles across our landing path. The tank commander, who was standing in his little turret, took one look, mouthed imprecations and leaped from the tank a second or two before we hit it at a speed of 90 to 100 mph. My first pilot, Charles Channell, and I jumped from our cockpit, forgetting in the heat of the moment:

(a) that my flying helmet with its intercom was still plugged into its socket, thus wrenching my neck; and

(b) that the Hamilcar cockpit was situated on the top of the glider, some 15 to 20 feet above the ground.

After looking around we found the tank upside down underneath our load, with grenades and cannon shells dropping like ripe plums from their containers into the field, and a strong smell of petrol. It was somewhat discouraging to see one or two gliders nearby burning fiercely as they had been mortared by the Germans. Staff Sergeant Channel and I managed to get the unfortunate tank driver and gunner out of the tank; I am glad to say they were still alive, but not very pleased and somewhat shaken. We then adjourned to the nearby orchard, which otherwise we would have landed in the middle of, and proceeded to dig a hole where we spent a rather disturbed night with a number of other glider pilots who had landed more uneventfully.

The following morning while we were brewing up some disgusting small blocks of porridge and beef cubes, and watching the Germans near Caen, who were sporadically mortaring us, I was somewhat surprised to see the burly and battleworn figures with blackened faces of the Royal Marine Commandos coming up to join us and immediately digging far deeper holes than we had scraped out. One Commando then sat on the edge and cut another notch in his fighting knife; they had fought their way up from the beaches.

After breakfast we proceeded to walk, in our red berets and with our rifles slung over our shoulders, through a cornfield with poppies and other wild flowers growing in it, a few of which I picked as a souvenir. We crossed the famous bridge over the Orne canal and river, seeing where our comrade Horsa gliders had landed in the small hours of 6th June and captured what is now known as Pegasus Bridge. The bodies of dead German soldiers were lying about and on the bridge was a German staff car with the occupants dead in it, and the back seat full of silks, perfume and drink; they had obviously been on the way back from an enjoyable short leave when they were unfortunately caught up in the invasion. We walked back to the beaches, some three or four miles away, meeting as we did so British troops, either on foot or on bicycles, who looked somewhat askance at us, as we appeared to be going the wrong way. We then boarded a landing craft to take us back to England to prepare for the next operation.

By this time we were somewhat tired, as the benzedrine which had been issued and taken before setting out the previous evening had worn off, but I recall that we were dive bombed by an odd German aircraft which had escaped the clutches of the RAF; we were however too tired to care. The following morning two or three of us were brewing up our little camp stoves for another dose of the emergency rations, when a member of the Royal Navy crew of the landing craft pointed out that our lighted stoves were on the lid of their flare box, so we enjoyed an interrupted meal.

We reached Newhaven and were greeted by the good ladies of the WVS, who gave us free copies of the *Daily Mirror*, which turned out to be that of the previous day and had on the front page the usual map with 'Dad's Army' arrows showing where the invasion was taking place. I was somewhat upset that we could not have had an up-to-date newspaper given to us.

Anyway, having hit a British tank when landing, going at 90 mph, with several tons of petrol and ammunition aboard, and surviving without a scratch, I have felt ever since that each day I have lived is a bonus. Incidentally, we did hear later that the tank had been recovered and was back in action within 24 hours, with the crew safe and well. If they survived that, they deserved to survive the further fighting they undoubtedly took part in.

*

From Mr H. Howard, ex-Staff Sergeant, Glider Pilot Regiment
I was a first pilot in 15 Flight, 'F' Squadron of the Glider Pilot Regiment and my second pilot was Sergeant Holman with whom I had only flown for twenty minutes prior to Operation Mallard, which was a landing on the evening of D Day to reinforce the earlier airborne operations which took place in the very early hours of 6th June.

Sixth Airborne Division were untried in battle but, like everyone else who had trained and trained again for the invasion, we were raring to go.

I recall the briefing, the maps and photographs of the approach along the River Orne and Caen Canal to the landing zone near Ranville, and the gaiety of the twenty-six RUR* who filed aboard my Horsa glider. Soon came take-off; I had gained sufficient speed on tow behind my Dakota tug to lift the glider off the runway to a position just above the tug's slipstream; we were over half-way down the airfield when to my horror because the tug was still on the deck its undercarriage started to rise and the aircraft bellied on to the runway with sparks flying everywhere. I realised immediately that it could not become airborne and my speed was carrying me over and past the tug. There was still some runway ahead of me, so I released the tow rope, applied full flaps and touched down beyond the tug which I saw as I passed over it had fortunately slewed to starboard on to the grass verge. This meant the runway was still clear for further combinations to take off, provided of course that I did not block it with my aircraft.

Although the Horsa was equipped with a skid which was designed for landing in a shorter distance than would be possible with the undercarriage, we had long learned to keep the wheels intact and not to jettison them. They were fitted with hydraulic brakes which meant that upon touching down the glider could be steered left or right for a distance if there was an obstruction straight ahead. The skid method gave no such choice and the braking system was almost as effective in terms of distance travelled before stopping. I dared not apply brakes and rudder too quickly in case we ground looped and came

*Royal Ulster Rifles.

to grief. The perimeter fence was looming up very quickly but fortunately I successfully turned left off the runway and came to rest
near the perimeter track. You can imagine the Irish comment which
came back to me from the strapped-in platoon in the main fuselage.

I think we all felt relief and disappointment. But no sooner had my
co-pilot and I taken full stock of the situation than we heard the
roar of one of the station tractors and before we could fully realise it,
we were hitched up, taken back to the start line and coupled to one
of the reserve tugs. Meantime the full stream from Broadwell had
taken off, but by cutting the corners whilst the whole airborne armada
was forming up over southern England, I found myself back in
correct formation for the Channel crossing and landing in Normandy.

My impressions of the immense amount of shipping; the 'spot-on'
approach to the LZ (Landing Zone) by my tug crew; their message
of good luck over the tow-rope intercom before I cast off for the
landing; the concentration involved in watching airspeed, avoiding
other gliders on the final circuit and choosing the most open landing
space amongst the haphazard array of gliders already on the zone
from the earlier lift; and the hope that the German ack-ack fire
together with their mortar barrage on the ground would miss us –
these impressions were certainly noted, but somehow were of little
consequence compared with the excitement – for me at least – of the
original take-off.

We pilots, unlike our gliders, were not expendable, and after
digging-in for the night in a wood bordering the LZ and standing-to
at dawn on D + 1 for the counter-attack which never came in my
sector, we were relieved by Lord Lovat's Commando and apart from
being sniped at by a lone German in a church tower we eventually
found our way back to the coast at Ouistreham where we were taken
aboard a landing craft, and returned safely to England for debriefing.

I am very proud to have been in the vanguard on D Day, and
perhaps I was lucky that because of the superb training and organisation for that fateful day, matters went so well for me that my 24
hours of action could well have been one of the several practice
operations which preceded D Day, and which, when one remembers
the chaos of some of those, were probably as dangerous.

*

*From Mr W. W. Brown, ex-Trooper, 6th Airborne Armoured Recce
   Regiment*

We got all ready to be off on the 5th, then were told that there would
be a postponement because of the weather, but that on the next day
we would leave, whatever the weather. The crossing was quite uneventful; I remember and have repeatedly been teased about it, that
I finished reading *The Times* on the way over and also that for a short
moment I felt sick and so did many others, whether from air-sickness
or from excitement I don't know. We could not see out of any
window and did not know when we crossed the coast of England nor
when we reached France, but we could feel when our glider became
detached from the towing plane and began to descend. As we landed
with a bump we heard two or three shots fired but never found out
where they came from nor whether they were fired at us or by our
people already on the ground.

We stormed out of the gliders and I well remember my amazement
that the spot at which we landed looked exactly as we were told to
expect. We had been given descriptions and been shown photos;
there were biggish trees and we had to assemble near one of these,
and there it really was. At that moment I admired the efficiency of
all the arrangements, but from then onwards it all became very much
a shambles. It was late afternoon by then; we occupied an orchard
close by and when not on guard-duty slept quite peacefully. Next
morning and during the next few days any impression of efficiency
quickly disappeared. We didn't know what was going on and it
seemed to me (I cannot be certain about this, of course) that higher
up, in the regiment or in the division, they too did not know much
more. We got into our Jeeps, drove a few hundred yards or half a
mile to the left or to the right and back again. Once we saw a few
German soldiers a few hundred yards away and we were immediately
ordered by our lieutenant to move off in the opposite direction. Some
of our troop were disgusted, they wanted to have a go at Jerry; I
tried to reason with them that after all we were supposed to be a
reconnaissance unit and were not meant to shoot at whomsoever we
encountered, but they continued to despise the lieutenant.

On another occasion two German soldiers were shot quite near us.
I, speaking German, was called to examine their papers: they were
Poles or Lithuanians, members of a work-force attached to the
German Army; they might possibly have been trying to surrender
to us.

At first I imagined that we were a side-show, a diversion, and I awaited the news that the real invasion, near Dover across the narrowest stretch of the Channel, had begun, but after a few days I could in my mind unravel the situation. We heard the news, of course, on our wireless sets and I quickly got the impression (a correct one as I soon found out, but at the time I found it very difficult to convince my fellow-soldiers, who were beginning to be fed up) that although things had not gone according to plan and that Caen, which should have been taken in the first few days, was still holding out, a situation had been produced where our pinning down practically all the German soldiers in the area meant that the Americans could advance on the right flank against very little opposition.

I have omitted to say that the orchards where we spent the first few nights were near Ranville, just east of the Pegasus bridge which we crossed several times to the west, for supplies etc; we got to the landing beaches on some of our trips west, once even as far as Bayeux.

May I add two stories: the first one is hearsay, but from all that was said at the time I am pretty certain that it is true and you may even hear it from someone who was there. When the 51st Highland Division, with all their fame and glory of the Desert battles crossed the Pegasus bridge on the way east, D plus three or four, and saw the various signs and emblems the proud Parachute Regiment had put up they tore them down and replaced them with their own signs; not for long, however.

The other story is about Montgomery; in the spring, a few weeks before D Day, he came to inspect us and gave a pep-talk. He seemed very tired and his speech, short as it was, was quite nonsensical. He said we are going to win and repeated two or three times that we had our successes before; we had pushed the Germans into the sea in North Africa and we are going to push them into the sea again. Applause and cheers from everybody; it seemed to me that I was the only one who realised that this time the idea was to push the Germans not into the sea but away from it.

*

From Mr B. A. Tomblin, ex-Glider Pilot Regiment
June 6th was nine minutes old when six combinations of Halifax bombers towing Horsa gliders crossed the Normandy coast in patchy cloud. The gliders were released as the coast was crossed, and with complete success they landed within 47 yards of an important swing

bridge over the Caen Canal. The bridge was captured with the help of the Parachute Regiment, and thus the first breach of the so-called West Wall of the German fortress had been made. (The bridge was later re-named Pegasus bridge.)

At dawn British Commando forces landed on the beaches at Ouistreham, and American forces landed to the west of these positions along the Normandy coast.

At RAF Down Ampney, Wiltshire, where I was stationed with 'E' Squadron of the Glider Pilot Regiment, the scene was like many of our recent operational exercises – down the centre of the long runway cutting through this lovely rural countryside stood two long rows of Horsa gliders, with their tow-ropes snaking away neatly into the tails of Dakota tug aircraft, likewise lined up outside the gliders. We had been confined to the camp during the last week, and had attended numerous briefings and studied aerial photographs of the area we were to land our gliders in. Any outgoing letters were strictly censored, and, despite the excitement of this undertaking upon which we were to embark, thoughts of my pregnant wife remained uppermost. Would I survive another three months to see my first son, or would he say 'I never knew my father'?

Two days before our glider had been carefully loaded with a Jeep, the responsibility of which rested entirely upon the pilot. A careless loading plan could mean an unbalanced aircraft in free flight, and the inevitable loss of control followed by a crash landing.

It was our privilege to carry airborne troops of the Oxfordshire and Buckinghamshire Light Infantry, who had become part of the newly-formed 6th Airborne Division.

With the gliders lined up on the runway we walked along to read the various inscriptions written on them, some intelligent, some rude, some humorous. Had Dr Goebbels been able to read these inscriptions he would have used them as a prime example of the degenerate English mentality. Nevertheless, it was an impressive sight and a comforting thought that this same gathering was taking place on many airfields in England to form the mightiest invasion force ever to take place in history. One small sneaking comfort to me was the fact that some weeks previously I had given to my wife a grid map of Europe and by a secret code had been able to indicate to her where I was headed, and when the invasion was announced to the nation she knew I was there.

We were aware that a small spearhead had landed just after midnight, and were anxious to get there and give them support.

Our take-off was timed for 6 p.m. and our task was to land east of
the Caen Canal and ahead of the ground troops which had assaulted
the beaches during the day. Our squadron was honoured to be the
first to land on our pre-selected zone, and my aircraft was lying third
on the runway. During the afternoon we gathered near our gliders,
supervised the loading of the troops and arms, and said our goodbyes
to our brother pilots.

Whilst we were busying ourselves strapping into the cockpits and
checking the controls, the pilots of the Dakotas were running up
their engines and doing their final checks. Naturally, we were apprehensive, but being busy absorbed most of our thoughts. My co-pilot,
Lieutenant Alec Johnstone, was a grand chap, full of dry wit. We were
very friendly with the RAF tug crews, having trained and lived with
them for months, and were privileged to have a wing commander
flying our tug. (The day after D Day this wing commander gave a
broadcast on the BBC of the event, and on VJ night he was killed by
a firework whilst celebrating a victorious war.)

At last the appointed hour arrived, and it seemed that the whole
of the RAF personnel on the station had turned out to wish us well.
The sound of engines grew, the controlling ground crews waved their
batons, and the first glider parked in front of us slowly began to move
along the runway – our part of the invasion had begun. The second
glider rumbled away, and then came our turn. The Dakota gently
moved forward, took up the slack on the rope, and then at the signal
from the ground erks she opened her throttles. Brakes off, we rolled
forward slowly, then accelerating until our controls seemed to come
alive. Soon our speed reached 70 mph and on easing the stick back
slowly the Horsa sluggishly came off the ground. The control of a
heavy glider requires much more physical effort than a powered plane.
We held her as close to the ground as possible so that the Dakota
could keep her tail down and get airborne as soon as possible.

Gradually the tug became airborne, and together we began to
climb into the evening June sky, just missing, as always, the spire of
Cricklade village church and flying over the local pub where the
Airborne had devoured many a pint. Would we ever return to this
small part of rural England, or was this the beginning of the end –
if it was we would take many a German with us.

We performed a slow climbing turn, following the previous gliders
– it was a slow climb – we weighed approximately 8,000 lbs. On our
turn we could look back at our airfield and saw the remaining
gliders leaving one by one, as quickly as safety intervals would allow.

The success of a mass Airborne landing depends on putting down as large a number of men, as quickly as possible, in a small area, and to this end our stream of aircraft now headed to pre-arranged meetings with other squadrons becoming airborne from airfields all over the south and east of England.

From RAF Down Ampney our squadron flew northwards to Pershore in Worcestershire, and then turned southwards towards the English Channel, collecting squadron after squadron behind us. We flew over the South Downs, and then came the moment of truth : the coast at Littlehampton appeared and the sea towards France stretched out before us. This was it – no turning back now – what turmoil would we land ourselves in? Thoughts raced through our minds, and it was with a feeling of sadness that we watched the English countryside disappear behind us.

We were only flying about 500 feet high, and Alec and I constantly relieved one another flying the machine. Our tug then descended down to the sea, almost to the wave tops and we raced across the Channel at about 130 mph trying to keep below the German radar search. The black paint on our faces had now become streaked with sweat. Glider pilots become fighting soldiers on landing, and flying a glider wearing full Army uniform plus revolvers, rifles, pockets stuffed with hand grenades, can become a very warm business on a June evening.

The troops in the fuselage seemed quite happy, although the yawing of the glider had brought on a certain amount of air sickness. We were visited in the cockpit frequently by an Army padre watching points, and who, we hoped, was saying more than the normal amount of prayers for us.

Reaching the halfway mark across the Channel our tug aircraft started to climb, and then to our great delight we were joined by our escort of RAF fighters – we were told that 25 squadrons of Spitfires and Mustangs would escort us – the sight of so many business-like fighters really boosted us. They flew close alongside giving us cheery waves from their cockpits, and one could immediately discount the thought of being helplessly shot down.

Our next surprise before land came into view was the sight of a fleet of ships. Some were towing rafts carrying 50 lorries on each raft, and it seemed uncanny seeing large numbers of lorries apparently parked on the Channel waiting to go to the beaches.

Reverberations then reached our ears, and we found ourselves flying fast towards the Normandy beaches. Underneath us the Royal

Navy was firing shells fast and furious to targets inland, and the old
HMS *Warspite* was using her 16-inch guns to launch her huge shells
at the German defences. The blast from her guns could be felt in
the glider.

Pretty lights floated up to us, and it was not until something hit
our starboard that we realised it was anti-aircraft fire. Black puffs
of smoke formed around us, but did not give us any impression of
being dangerous. The tug pilot's voice came over the inter-com. 'Tug
to Glider: we are on our run in. Pull off in your own time.' Glider
to Tug: 'OK, we can see our field. Cheerio. Thank you.' Tug to
Glider: 'Cheerio. All the best. See you in the mess.'

From the photographs shown to us on our briefing our landing
zone could be clearly identified. It was a large field on the east side
of the Caen and Orne Canal, alongside a triangular-shaped wood.
Being third in line, our task was to land at the far end of the field
forming the first of a third column. We were to land regardless of
wind direction – a difficult feat with a heavily loaded glider. It was
difficult to realise that at this moment the Allies were using 5,000
ships, 11,000 aircraft and 2,000,000 men on this invasion.

The tow release lever was pulled, and the twin grapples fell downwards and away from the wing roots – the Dakota slipped away back
towards the RAF mess. Stick back to gain height and our best
gliding speed of about 8 mph. At this stage our thoughts were
interrupted by the Army padre standing in the cockpit doorway
praying loudly, no doubt because of our suspected ability to put this
aircraft down safely.

A slow-descending half-turn brought us into line with our intended
landing position, and we glided gently towards it. This was the great
moment. What was waiting for us? Was it the right field? Half-flap
was applied, and the aircraft's nose dipped slightly. Nearer and
nearer we raced towards the field, and then to our horror we saw
that the landing zone had been sown with poles about 15 feet in
height, inviting us to crash amongst them. There was nothing in the
briefing about this possibility, neither was there anything we could
do about it – a glider can't go up again! Full flap was applied, and
as the huge flaps came down into position we glided down towards
the poles trying to steer a course between them. We held off just
above the poles as long as possible, and as we lost speed we pushed
the nose between the poles as best we could.

'Hold tight,' I shouted, and as we touched the ground the tip of
the starboard wing struck a pole. We slewed round in a half-circle

and came to a full stop. Relief must have shown on all our faces, but was short-lived – there was a crash somewhere behind, a sound of rending wood, and on looking back we saw that another glider had collided with our tail, wrenching it almost off – just where we would have to take it off to get the Jeep out. This saved us a good ten minutes.

The airborne troops pushed their door open, and leapt out in the cornfield – they collected together and having oriented themselves set off to their rendezvous. Alec and I unbuckled ourselves, collected our personal arms together and prepared ourselves to change our role from airmen to soldiers. We stepped down into the field of golden corn, only to be greeted by bullets whining past us. We ducked down into the corn, and for a moment stared at the incoming black cloud of gliders and tug-aircraft. If we were scared, what must a German soldier think to see that mass of angry red-bereted men flying towards them. We later learned that when we reached the French coast, the last of the glider armada was leaving England.

We crept and crawled to our nearby rendezvous at the edge of the wood, keeping a keen eye out for gliders landing all around us. The poles were certainly preventing the neat mass landings we had practised in England – it was every man for himself to get down safely as best he could. A heavy Hamilcar came in very steeply, when a tank shot out of the nose of the glider followed by the glider helplessly out of control. It crashed somewhere in the field, and I later learned the pilot who died was a man who lived two streets away from me in my native Northampton. A few of the gliders were burning, and their ammunition stores were exploding. So much was happening one could not absorb everything, except to carry out your own orders and ignore the seemingly chaotic background to it all.

Gradually the troops of the Light Infantry got their Jeeps out of the gliders and made their way to their own rendezvous, and the glider pilots came to our piece of the wood and commenced digging in. Dusk was now falling, and we settled into our positions for the night, wondering when and how the might of the German Army was to be thrown against us. Unbeknown to us, a small German counter-attack with tanks had already been thrown back. Darkness fell, and we stood-to in our hastily dug holes, apprehensive and alert – after all airborne troops are only lightly armed, and our defence against armoured troops was somewhat limited.

Gunfire broke out intermittently, but about 2 a.m. the sound of approaching aircraft was heard. Here was the expected German counter-attack with paratroops. The planes flew overhead, and dark shapes could be seen floating down towards us. No one opened fire. We just waited. About fifteen yards away from me I heard a heavy thud near a tree, and saw the billowing silk of a parachute sink slowly to the ground. I drew a bead on the spot with my rifle, and felt for the first available hand grenade. Nothing moved. I waited, and waited. I wanted to sneeze, then cough – but daren't. My nearby comrades were also silent. Did they know how we were fixed? At last a streak of light came into the sky, and gradually the dawn began to break. Now he must show himself! Still the form didn't move. I then decided to creep towards it, in the approved manner, and what did I find – a British container of something or other. I didn't even bother to open it.

Daylight brought the sound of heavy and light gunfire, and word reached us that German patrols were probing at us and very active in the nearby village. We set off on a small patrol through a tiny hamlet, but met no opposition.

Returning to our positions we waited for the next step of the operation. Our instructions, as glider pilots, were to return to England in the quickest possible manner in order to pilot further gliders to any other operation deemed necessary. We had landed our troops in the right position, and now waited to be relieved for our return.

A skirl of bagpipes gradually came towards us, and lo and behold, there was Lord Lovat strolling up the middle of the road swirling his walking stick. Following him, in Indian fashion, were the green-bereted Commandos who had landed on the beaches the previous day. 'Right-ho chaps, get yourselves back – we will take over here.' We needed no further encouragement, and in single file made our way across our landing zone, picking our way through the crashed gliders and remains of our landing. We reached the bridges of the Caen and Orne Canal (now named Pegasus bridge). There were ample traces of yesterday's battle for the bridge, and we were proud to see three Horsa gliders lying at the side of the canal just short of the bridge. Dead Germans littered the sides of the road, and we were reminded constantly with bullets that the fighting had not yet ended. We were warned that snipers abounded.

We began to meet the infantry coming from the direction of the beaches, then light tanks, then heavy Churchill tanks with heavy guns, flail equipment, and later lorries towing the artillery. Obviously the beach landing had been successful if this one-way traffic was anything to go by. We seemed to be walking right through the whole British Army.

One troublesome sniper shot a few of us and the infantry, and an examination of the surroundings seemed to point to his position being in a nearby church steeple. A passing Churchill tank was stopped and informed. His gun turret swung slowly towards the church steeple – one shell and the sniper and steeple were no more.

On we trudged until in the distance we could see barrage balloons flying in the sky – no doubt over the beach-head. This spurred us on. We snatched a few compo rations as we walked, although food seemed to have been far from our thoughts.

A short distance from the beach a German Focke-Wulf appeared in the sky and shot at everything and anything in a desperate solo assault. In what seemed to be seconds later, a squadron of Spitfires swept into view and appeared to queue up to shoot at the Focke-Wulf – we last saw him diving towards the ground, smoke belching from his tail.

On through the last village towards the beach – and what a sight to behold! Despite the sea getting up rough, there were ships of all sizes and design : battleships, cruisers, destroyers, troop carriers, lorry rafts, assault landing craft, tank landing craft with their doors open discharging tanks up the beaches like monsters coming out of the sea. In the far distance there were more troop carriers waiting to discharge their human cargoes.

The beaches showed signs of bitter struggles, and dead Germans were a common sight. Most pillboxes had been blasted apart, and tank obstructions lifted away as if by a giant hand. Gun flashes out to sea indicated that the Royal Navy was still bombarding targets inland until the artillery could establish itself in that role.

Our major told us to use our Airborne initiative and obtain any transport we could to get back across the Channel, and make our way back to our base.

Walking along the beach I saw a landing craft about to back out to sea. I hailed the officer and he agreed to my request to board. By now I was dreadfully tired, and the seas had increased. I waded out into the sea alongside this huge craft, and with my equipment weighing me down I had great difficulty in keeping my head above water, and was relieved to grasp a ladder and climb wearily aboard.

We were given the run of the ship, and settled down on the upper deck – tired and comparatively happy that we had done the job we had been trained for. Round about 3 p.m., when our air cover was apparently engaged elsewhere, a Focke-Wulf dived out of the cloud cover straight at us. I lay on the deck looking up at the aircraft dumbfounded. From beneath the plane a dark object detached itself and hurtled towards us. I leapt to my feet and crouched against the steel side of the ship, only to be lifted upwards as the bomb hit the sea about fifteen yards from the ship. Before the plane flew from our sight it was shot down by Spitfires.

The landing craft slipped backwards from the beach, and by about 5 p.m. it had joined a small convoy, and sailed westwards towards the American beach landings, and as darkness fell we headed out into the English Channel. The Commandos who had crossed the Channel in this ship had left many of their rations aboard, and thus enabled us to make up lost time in our eating schedules. A mist clamped down on us, and when I awoke in the early morning I was wet with sea mist. The sun came up, and after hours of sailing nowhere we entered Newhaven Harbour to a grand welcome from the natives. Our landing barge drew up against the steep vertical harbour walls, and immediately presented us tired mortals with the problem of climbing the ladders to the top with extreme difficulty. We were taken to a large mansion for a meal and a wash, transport was arranged, and in a few hours we were back on Salisbury Plain awaiting the next trip.

We were not needed to return to the D Day beaches, and were blissfully unaware that our next trip would not be so easy : Pegasus would be bound for Arnhem and a bridge too far.

Operation Overlord went according to plan, and did not produce the fear and frustration that we were later to experience at Arnhem. On this occasion our casualties were relatively light, and was not to be compared with our back-to-the-wall fighting at Arnhem, and later the privations and long marches in a bitter winter as prisoners of war in Poland and Germany. That is another story.

CHAPTER TWO

The Navies

Many navies took part in the D Day landings but of the 1,213 combatant vessels engaged 79% were British and Canadian. $16\frac{1}{2}\%$ were American and $4\frac{1}{2}\%$ of the total was made up of French, Norwegian, Dutch, Polish and Greek components. To these fell the task of bombarding the shore positions, escorting the landing craft, and giving close support after the landing. 4,126 landing craft were involved, and some 1,500 other ships.

In view of the fact that the Royal Navy had been steadily losing trained crews since 1939 it was an almost incredible feat to be able to find personnel to man the multiplicity of ships involved. Naval skills are not easily or quickly taught; the sea is a hard master and there is no substitute for experience. The fact that on D Day the sea was rough enough to make some experienced sailors sick should not be forgotten. Many of the boats were barely seaworthy when loaded with their awkward cargoes, and the Channel has the unenviable reputation of being one of the most unpredictable seas in the world when the weather is rough.

But of course no one outside the Navy thought for one moment it would not be able to do as much and more than was asked; perhaps a few inside had reservations but no trace of them showed.

*

From Mr J. M. Bossom
I was attached as an additional officer to the 263 LCL(L) Flotilla which was part of Force J on D Day, 6th June 1944. The flotilla, with others, was based in Newhaven and prior to D Day one of my jobs was to accept and deliver the top secret documents as they were issued from Allied Headquarters, near Portsmouth. They were brought from there by officers often at the dead of night and I had to distribute them to the commanding officers of the landing crafts lying in the harbour and obtain signatures for them. I was provided with an escort of

Royal Marines and we were all fully armed. I leave you to judge the sort of reaction one got when one was shaking a man at two o'clock in the morning and asking him to sign documents.

On D Day we landed on Sword Beach at Bernières-sur-Mer. I was attached for this operation to LCL(L) 165, commanded I believe by Lieutenant Hall. We embarked at Newhaven the KSLI* – 140 men and 140 bicycles, if my memory is correct. The planners believed that the army thus mobile would reach Caen on D Day and capture the town.

The landing craft was equipped with a kedge anchor, which was paid out over the stern as the approach was made to the beach. The object was that the kedge anchor was dropped about 200 yards from the point of impact and when unloading was completed the winch drew in the cable which enabled the landing craft to go into deeper water. We went in at a fair speed in order to give the troops as dry a landing as possible.

On reaching the beach, which we did at H plus 30 (we were sent in earlier because the operation was going so well), we were met by a bombardment of mortar shells coming from the fortified villas edging the beach. The Germans realised that a landing craft was almost powerless if the kedge anchor cable could be severed, and to this end they were using mortar shells with green phosphorous smoke. Our cable was one of those that they successfully cut.

While we were on the beach, the coxswain of our vessel sighted the point from which some of the mortar fire was coming and directed by voice adjacent landing craft oerlikon guns to concentrate their fire at the point from which the mortar fire was coming. This proved fairly effective.

I can remember clearly, at the starboard side of the craft, whilst we were on the beach, there was a knot of Commandos, who were obviously having a discussion about tactics. Jerry dropped a mortar bomb in the middle of this group and it disintegrated. One of the party involved staggered towards our vessel and asked if we could take him aboard. He was severely wounded in the face. We had had instructions not to pick anybody up but his condition was such that compassion overcame orders. He was brought aboard, taken into the CO's cabin, given morphine and a large dressing was put over his shattered face. We then withdrew from the beach and collected on the way, round one of the propeller shafts, the severed cable of the

*King's Shropshire Light Infantry.

anchor. This meant that effectively we had only one screw working.

All able-bodied ships were ordered back to the UK by Command Ship and we were ordered to rendezvous with another ship in the flotilla that had been badly damaged going on to the beach – we found out later this was due to Teller mines, it had staved in two of the troop-carrying quarters leaving a number of dead inside. We managed to effect a tow on this vessel and ourselves proceed back to the UK. Progress was necessarily very slow, we were limping along on one engine anyway and the tow was a serious drag. Our passage from the south of the Isle of Wight to Newhaven was at times more in reverse than forward due to the very strong tide running against us. Nevertheless, we eventually arrived off Newhaven where we beached the towed vessel before proceeding into harbour ourselves.

We had made arrangements for an ambulance to collect the wounded Commando and the stretcher bearers were waiting to come aboard. However, he refused such aid, stood up, saluted the captain and said, 'Thank you for all you have done, sir,' and marched on to the quay. Certainly one of the bravest men I have ever met.

I turned in at the shore base where the officers were quartered and slept for seventeen hours, then sailed again on another landing craft back to the beaches. My memory of this trip is not as vivid, except that when we arrived back at Newhaven we were in time to collect the full force of the storm that raged over the beaches. This kept us outside the harbour for a number of days.

*

From Commander C. F. Parker, DSC, Royal Navy (Retd)
I commanded HMS *Torrington*, a frigate, and was senior officer of the escort for a convoy of a dozen or more landing craft which all landed safely on Sword Beach at about 4.30 a.m. on the morning of D Day. The convoy left Newhaven the previous evening and I believe the landing craft contained mainly Canadian troops. The crossing was uneventful. Later in the morning about forty seriously wounded troops (paratroops, French and Belgians) were put on board and I returned to Portsmouth the same evening. All were still alive when we arrived at Portsmouth but I doubt if many survived for long. The big guns at Le Havre (shore batteries) opened up at us during the morning.

*

From Mr D. S. A. Gardner

My own part in the D Day landings was in the Royal Navy where I was a leading telegraphist and was assigned to the Fleet Gunnery Officer in the landing ship headquarters, HMS *Hilary*.

My task was to maintain contact with FOO parties ashore [Forward Observation Officers]. These parties comprised one officer of the Royal Artillery and two Naval telegraphists.

There were approximately 25 such parties and they did a marvellous job of spotting targets such as tank squadrons, lines of lorries etc. Information was sent back to the Fleet Gunnery Officer who assigned a warship and fire was directed on a grid pattern until the targets were destroyed.

As in invasions before it was a great success and I have often wondered whether the targets knew how the fire was drawn nearer and nearer.

I had done this same job at Palermo and Salerno so by the time the biggest D Day of all arrived I was well in practice for the task.

*

From Mr P. S. Evetts, former Lieutenant (E) RNVR

As a Lieutenant (E) RNVR, my duties were as Flotilla Engineer Officer in the 55th LCT Flotilla. This meant that I had very little to do from the time that our ten Mark IV LCTs had loaded their fifteen (or so) each Bren Carriers manned by the Durham Light Infantry. The remaining two LCTs (732 and 907) stayed at home in reserve. After the twenty-four hours' delay at anchor in Southampton Water I felt that this wait had enabled officers and men of both services to compare notes and understand each other's difficulties.

We left at about 1300 on 5th June; on rounding the Needles at 1450, my craft (LCT 1121) detonated a mine which did no damage but was the only warlike occurrence during the passage. I slept very well (fully-clothed), waking at about 5 a.m. In LCT 1121, Sub-Lieutenant D. M. Horner, RNVR (the CO) and our Flotilla Officer (Lieutenant D. R. Linn, RNVR) were on the bridge. Astern were 926, 922, 564 and 924. Abeam were 1122, 1120, 711, 923 and 565. Beyond was the biggest number of ships I had even seen in my life. Ahead was the dim outline of the French coast with flashes from guns or bombs.

The soldiers were preparing their vehicles and breakfasting on field rations. I felt rather guilty when the FO and I sat down to a cooked breakfast in the LCT's tiny wardroom. But of course the LCT's galley could cook for a crew of 12 to 14, but 80 or so soldiers could not have been given any facilities.

After our main course the FO said to me: 'Luck is in our favour, the weather has improved, and last but not least morale is very good. Do you agree?'

As I replied, 'Yes, sir,' I realised how lucky I was to have a very good working relationship with my FO. To the general reader it should be explained that the Executive Officer is in command, even though an Engineer was of equal rank and seniority. In some cases I can recall that Executive Officers and their Technical Officers were barely on speaking terms.

Everything seemed quiet as we approached the beach; in fact strangely so because some of us had expected very stiff resistance in the initial assault. For myself, I was apprehensive rather than afraid. I imagined that some terrible secret weapon might be used. As we beached, the ramp door was lowered, the vehicles were started up and orders were given to disembark (by whom *I* did not know). By this time I had joined the seamen in order to assist in closing the ramp door – a tedious process by handwinch. Shouts of goodwill emanated from naval men to all Army ranks; my own to our DLI* captain brought the reply: 'Thank God we've got off this rattletrap – we feel safer on dry land.' I felt exactly the opposite and was only too happy to realise that we had done the most important part of our job and were now on our return journey.

As we went astern off the beach the tide had ebbed a little and my thoughts went back to the nightmare worry of broken propellers, choked filters, lack of cooling water, overheated engines, cracked cylinder blocks. As we wound up the door I saw dark brown water and felt shudders as the stern thumped on the bottom. My poor screws! Go up, door!

With the FO's approval I had decided to allow each Petty Officer Motor Mechanic (one per LCT) to work out his own craft's mechanical problems; after all, his training foresaw this. However if problems beyond his ability or authority arose then it was my job to overcome these and/or advise my FO. Out of three LCT flotillas, I was the only FEO to make the passage because it had been decided at high level that two out of three should stay in the UK. Therefore I had the possibility of being asked to advise on thirty craft in all, i.e. 'U'

*Durham Light Infantry.

LCT squadron.

When we had arrived in the assembly area for the run back to UK I realised that some craft had broached to, some had been shelled and others had stopped for various reasons. Then my FO said in a firm voice, '564 has been badly holed and looks like sinking so I am going alongside. You will transfer and see what you can do.' Five minutes later I jumped aboard 564 and went straight into the engine room. The PO M/M told me that the bilge pumps could not cope with the inflow of water and suggested that, when the craft met the open sea, the usual bending of the boat would increase the inflow. I agreed and recommended the CO, Sub-Lieutenant B. M. Jones, RVNR, to stop one engine so that we could arrange for the inlet cooling water pipe to be disconnected from the inlet valve on the bottom and take its cooling water from inside the engine room. This worked and we got the boat back to Southampton on the morning of 7th June where 564 was beached and (if my memory serves me correctly) was still there on the mud in 1946.

All of us agreed that it was a great relief to be back home even though it meant another load for France. Some joker said, 'I'll bet Jerry will have his artillery on the beach next time.' In fact it was the bad weather of 18th–22nd June was the LCTs' enemy.

After reporting to my FO, I was able to spend a night with some friends in Chandlers Ford where the hot bath was most welcome.

Later our squadron moved to Portland in order to assist the build up of the US forces on the east side of the Cherbourg Peninsula.

On arrival I was accosted by our RN captain, complete with silver-knobbed walking stick. He ordered me to return to where I came from; my reaction was to compare him with a certain type of stage comedian! Fortunately a Commander (E) Moule, RN, intervened and told him that a complaint would be lodged with C-in-C if my duties were obstructed. The captain went on his way and one of my ratings said, 'That is the type of RN officer who gives the Service a bad name.'

After a few days I went over with a maintenance party in an American LST. On arrival near Carentan, we were given the job of patching up several LCTs marooned on the beach. The weather was perfect, we lived in a tented USN CB camp. The work went very well and we were able to see some of the countryside, even going as far as Bayeux before returning home for fourteen days' leave in late September.

On reflection it was an experience I wouldn't have missed and dare I say – one of the most pleasant operations during my service which started as an ERA in general service from 1939 onwards until 1943 when I joined CO as a sub-lieutenant (E). For all this I received a Mention in Despatches. Yet I got nothing for months of grilling convoy work with plenty of danger!

*

From Lieutenant-Commander F. P. U. Croker, RN (Retd)
I was present on D Day in Landing Ship (Tank) 361 as Secretary, First LST Flotilla. The commanding officer and flotilla commander was Commander A. B. Alison, R.N.

We left Spithead with the invasion fleet on the evening of 5th June 1944 and arrived off the British sector of the Normandy beaches at about 0900 on 6th, encountering no more opposition than a few shells, fired at extreme range from the German coastal battery on Cape de la Hève above Le Havre Happily these fell short, and we later watched the veteran battleship *Warspite* pounding this battery with her great 15-inch guns.

Apparently there had been some doubt whether the hulls of our LSTs, which had previously taken part in the landings and follow-ups in North Africa, Sicily, Salerno and Anzio, would stand the strain of much more beaching, and on this first trip to Normandy we carried amphibious lorries (DUKWs) on the tank deck and miscellaneous light transport, as usual, on the upper deck. (On subsequent trips, we *did* carry tanks and many other large and awkward vehicles such as bulldozers. We then sometimes beached near the top of the tide, where the beach gradient was steep enough, hauling off immediately after embarkation, and sometimes on a falling tide, drying out for disembarkation and re-floating on the next tide. This included beaching during the gale which occurred soon after D Day so it would seem that the fears for our hull strength were unfounded. Later again, we disembarked our vehicles in the Mulberry Harbour on to large pontoons anchored to the seabed by four massive posts at the corners, like a four-poster bed, and connected with the shore by a pontoon bridge.)

On D Day, however, we anchored about half a mile from the beach and swam the DUKWs ashore under their own power, from the tank ramp forward. We then offloaded the remaining transport on to 'Rhino' ferries. These were large pontoon rafts which we had towed across the Channel. After the departure of the DUKWs, the Rhinos were connected to the tank ramps and the upper deck transport struck down in the lift to the tank deck, from which it then reached the Rhinos via the ramps. The Rhinos were each propelled by two enormous outboard motors for their passage to the beach.

This was all accomplished successfully without any hitch, or disturbance by the enemy, and all we then had to do was wait our turn to go home for another load. During this waiting period, we had a grandstand view of the day's events and witnessed the arrival of the glider-borne assault, towed by Stirlings and Albemarles. Unhappily, on the return flight of these tugs, a Stirling was shot down by an LCT beached near the eastern end of the British sector. (This was a smaller vessel than the LST and, unlike the LSTs, came under the Combined Operations Command. I do not know who was operationally responsible for her on D Day, but she was in no way attached to the 1st LST Flotilla.) She had previously been hotly engaged with a German pillbox, and I could see streams of tracer flying in both directions. Suddenly, to my horror, she altered target to the Stirling, flying at about 2,000 feet, still firing tracer, all too accurately. I think that either the pilot must have been hit or his controls shot away, because the aircraft banked slowly to port and dived into the sea, blowing up on impact in a lurid sheet of orange fire. After thirty-five years, this recollection remains as vivid as if it had been yesterday. I *still* cannot think what possessed the LCT gunner. The Stirling was a four-engined bomber quite impossible to mistake for the FW Condor – the only German four-engined military aircraft. Battle fatigue is the most charitable explanation, but it may well have been poor aircraft recognition and worse fire discipline.

Of course, this was only one of many instances when Allied aircraft were fired on by Allied warships, and there were also numerous occasions when Allied ships were attacked by Allied aircraft. I remember, for example, when serving in HMS *Manchester* during the Norwegian Campaign of 1940, a long-nosed Blenheim diving out of a cloud and dropping a stick of bombs – fortunately well astern of us. There was no excuse for this, either, as there were no German warships with four triple turrets, as had *Manchester*. It is to be hoped that ship and aircraft recognition have improved since then – otherwise, all the Russians need do in a war with us is sit back and wait for the NATO forces to exterminate themselves. I am not entirely convinced that electronic recognition methods are infallible, and suspect that there is still a place for the Mark I eyeball, if only it can recognise what it sees.

After D Day, the 1st LST Flotilla (12 ships in all) continued to supply the Normandy beachhead, loading at a variety of ports as far away as the Thames estuary. When passing through the Dover Strait, we witnessed the onset of the V1 flying bomb campaign against Britain and were much puzzled by what appeared to be rapidly flying torches in the sky and by the distinctive stutter of their ramjet engines. A V1 only cost some £200 compared with £20,000 for the cheapest missile today, so it was a pretty cost-effective weapon.

After the Army breakthrough, we unloaded at ports further east, closer to the advancing troops, and eventually, at Antwerp. In November, it was decided to concentrate loading at Tilbury and other London docks, and the flotilla secretariats were disembarked at Tilbury. The only excitement for us then was the occasional V1 or V2, the nearest of which fell in Gravesend across the river.

I remember one day the arrival of LST 302 (Lieutenant Burne, DSC, RNR, also of the 1st Flotilla) proudly flying an unauthorised flag with the number '50' on it to indicate that she had completed fifty return trips to the Continent since D Day. There were a great many warships of all kinds which fought hard and well in defence of our merchant shipping and the seaborne supplies without which the war would certainly have been lost, but there was one ship above all others which made the active *winning* of that war possible – the LST, which provided the bulk of the military lift in all the major landings.

LST 361 was typical. We could do 9½ knots (11 mph) flat out, and to defend ourselves from the violence of the enemy we had one 3-inch gun (in some cases retrieved from museums) and a few smaller automatic weapons. Nevertheless, the flotilla never lost a ship, nor, I believe a man, in all the operations we took part in. The flotilla commander, one of the unsung heroes who rejoined the Navy for the war, was mentioned seven times in despatches. He and I were, I think, the only regular naval officers in the flotilla. The remaining COs, their officers, and most of their men were reservists, and the nation owes them much. We even had one enterprising Danish CO who had somehow secured an RNVR commission. They were the salt of the earth (or should it be 'the sea'?).

*

From Lieutenant-Commander M. S. Blois-Brooke, RNR (Retd)
At the time of the D Day landings I was a lieutenant (N) RNR in the LSI HMS *Queen Emma*. My captain was Commander Sandbach, RN. We did a great deal of training at Studland Bay – sailing from

Portsmouth. Our force was 'J' Force due to land troops at Juno Beach.

We had (I think) five cross-Channel ships adapted to carry LSAs. On one occasion, while training, I was told to give a lecture on the Channel tides – to the captains of these cross-Channel ships. (They were very kind and gave no sign that they had been sailing the Channel long before I was born!)

I had the operation orders and consequently knew where we were going four weeks before the actual date. Never have I guarded a vast book so keenly! The attack was due to take place on 5th June but was postponed twenty-four hours due to weather. This caused me some problems since I had worked out the tide, likely drift, etc., for the 5th – so all this had to be revised for twenty-four hours later. Those twenty-four hours were pretty dreadful. Our troops were loaded (I think Regina Rifles and Winnipeg Regiment) and these men had to be kept amused for the twenty-four hours). That was the First Lieutenant's job!

At last we sailed in single line ahead led by (I think) the Canadian Assault ship HMCS *Prince Rupert*, with her five civilians, and adapted ships. Half-way down the line came *Queen Emma*, with our five civilian ships. Later the line would be split into two columns, J1 led by *Prince Rupert* and J2 led by us. I cannot remember the exact time of sailing but I think *Prince Rupert*'s navigator and I agreed a time. The figure 2100 seems to ring a bell. We wanted to be able to steam fast enough to maintain steerage (when in the narrow swept channels) and yet not to arrive too early/late. On the day of sailing we had an 'air raid' over the assembled fleet at Spithead. It was *one* Ju88. He didn't last long!

Pass the Nab Tower, we headed for J buoy (later to be known by all as Piccadilly Circus – but as The Assembly Area in the Operations Orders).

Soon we were due to enter the central minefield (I forget what QZX number it was). We passed through this safely – the minesweepers had done a good job. Shortly after this first hazard, the time came for us to part company with *Prince Rupert* and go down our particular narrow swept channel followed by our brood of civilian ships. As a navigator I was now on my own! Forces J1 and J2 had split and we were leading J2.

It was growing light and the lighter it grew the more we steeled ourselves for the West Wall batteries to open fire. But nothing happened, not even a plane. This was too good to be true. Watching my watch – recently checked by the others – and adjusting our speed carefully, we finally dropped anchor exactly on time and exactly in position. Within minutes our leas were away and forming up with the others of our J2 division.

To the left of Juno Beach was Sword Beach and to the right was Gold Beaches. Their leas were also heading for their beaches.

My abiding impression of the whole day was, as soon as it grew light, the appalling number of church spires there were to be seen on the French shore. I had already encircled the churches I would use to fix our position, but daylight revealed so many I couldn't pick out my selected ones! I therefore had to rely a great deal upon, not only my DR but also the QH set which was *very* accurate. (I will not say what this was or how it worked.)

The weather was deteriorating rapidly and we saw our LCAs having a nasty time. These LCAs were manned by Royal Marines. Looking ashore through powerful Barr & Stroud binoculars we could see the actual landing, although every now and then a pall of smoke blotted out the sight. J2 beaches had been sub-divided into two and our LCAs attacked according to the beach allocated to them. There was a beach café (or some building) on the higher ground roughly between the two sub-divisions of our sector of Juno Beach.

We remained there for what seemed ages, and finally, at about 1500 we sailed for home carrying some wounded. Behind us Courseulles and Arromanches seemed to be shrouded with smoke. Having negotiated the narrow swept channel and the wider one at cautious speed, we then went out to J Buoy and thence to Portsmouth to land our wounded.

Shortly after that we were lent to the Americans who were having a pretty tough time at Utah and Omaha : but that is another story.

*

From Lieutenant-Commander J. Kane, RN (Retd.)
I was in HMS *Kingsmill*, a Brigade Headquarters ship in Gold Sector for Operation Overlord. While the whole event made an indelible impression on me, I do not believe that I have any particular personal impression to recount. The gigantic armada sailing into the unpromisingly rough channel weather, boldly bound for what had been the hostile enemy coast for the past four years was impressive in itself. The gay, laughing and cheering infantrymen of the first assault wave

of the Durham Light Infantry (50th Division), whom we led in as far as our own draft would allow. When overtaking us in their LCAs headed for the beach, they were not sitting down below their armoured sides as they should have been but standing and sitting on the gunwales waving and exchanging banter with the sailors as they overtook us. On D + 2, since all the key officers on board *Kingsmill* were 'doubled up' so that we could step into the shoes of our opposite numbers if the expected heavy casualties occurred, which happily they did not, I went ashore to view the army in action.

With a companion I thumbed a lift in a passing landing craft and then waded ashore with my shoes and socks in my hand and my trousers turned up and sat down on French sand to put on my foot-wear again while all around fully dressed and equipped reinforce-ments, many of them soaked to the waist from their leap into the sea from their larger landing craft, trudged past 'Berlin bound'. Then a lift in a halftrack past immense equipment, Allied equipment, parks, through leafy lanes and copses, through recently liberated Bayeux with infantry trudging along each verge of the road towards the front, each man with his head stuck into that very day's edition of the London *Daily Mirror*, surely the last word in quartermastering, to the most advanced units opposite German-held Tilly-sur-Seuilles. There we were struck by the calm composure of the Desert Rats (7th Armoured Division) upon whom we called. They were on the forward slope of a rise awaiting the infantry to catch up with them and walking around outside their armoured vehicles as if just await-ing the start of the next race at a point-to-point meeting.

'Jerry won't shoot at us, for if he so much as gives his position away we shall knock hell out of him and he knows it,' I was told upon enquiry.

An artillery spotter plane was lazily circling over the enemy-held wood a quarter of a mile away as if to emphasise the point.

However, it is what follows that prompted me to write in the first place. I, together with the other officers on the bridge of the *Kingsmill* at the time, witnessed in the early hours of D Day an event of great military importance, a gigantic mishap, that must have affected the entire battle and which has been carefully hushed up. I read Chester Wilmot's account as soon as it was published and even he with his nose for scandals had not spotted it, or if he had he had not men-tioned it.

It must have been about midnight when the *Kingsmill*, leading our several infantry assault ships, Glen Line ships with LCAs at their davits, was about to enter the German offshore minefields in channels that had already been swept by our minesweepers. There were many columns such as ours making the same approach. The problem was to lead our line into the correct swept channel. These were marked by dan buoys, each with its dim blue light fixed to the top of their slim wooden poles. The entrance to each channel was to be marked by an ML (motor launch) transmitting a distinctive signal letter in morse code that we were to be able to receive on our radar scope. But neither could we pick up any signal nor see any launch although some of the lines of illuminated dan buoys were visible stretching away into the night towards the French coast. But which line was ours? We stopped lolling in the now calmer sea with the infantry-laden Glen ships astern of us. But it was not only because of the lack of the anticipated signpost that we were stopped for a totally unexpected sight confronted us.

Crossing our bows and moving from west to east, that is proceeding up channel, when by this time being already in close proximity to the enemy-held coast every Allied vessel should have been on a southerly approach course, we saw a seemingly endless line of Tank Landing Craft. Obviously something had gone very wrong. On a shaded signal lantern we called them up and asked what unit they were. We received a coded sign in reply which we hurriedly identified from the voluminous orders that we had on board *Kingsmill*. They were an American unit. But the American assault was on our right, that is, to the west. On our left where these LCTs were heading there should not have been any American units. We called them up again and gently pointed out their navigational error. There must have been at least a hundred LCTs crossing our front in a solid line going up channel only a few cables distant from us as we lay stopped. Their reply to our query was a short one in which it was implied that we should attend to our own business.

Perhaps these intruders had swept away our motor launch? But we had no time to waste on the troubles of others and as soon as the last tank landing craft had passed on to the east we led the way into the nearest line of illuminated dan buoys towards our assault craft lowering position.

But this is not the end of my story about these strange American LCTs. During the afternoon of D Day as we lay at anchor in the Gold assault anchorage happy at the highly successful assault in our sector and listening to the radio reports from the army as they pushed inland, dozens of American LCTs began passing through our anchorage making their way singly and in twos and threes towards the west and coming from the direction of enemy-held Le Havre up channel. Several passed within a few yards of *Kingsmill* and I could see that they were all laden either with spick-and-span tanks and other armoured vehicles or fully loaded with hundreds of unfired rockets that were to have drenched the beaches with high explosive, as they had done so effectively on our front several hours earlier, a few moments before the first wave of infantrymen. Could these have been the self-same craft that had held us up as they crossed our bows in the opposite direction the preceding night? These had certainly not seen any action. Their absence at the most critical moment of the assault could in itself have been sufficient explanation for the bloody set-back that the US infantry had suffered on Omaha Beach.

*

From Lieutenant-Commander Hugh Spensley, RD, RNR

At the time of D Day, I was a 20-year-old sub-lieutenant RNVR serving in a landing ship tank. I had joined her in the Mediterranean the year before, having taken part in two previous D Days, those of the Toe of Italy and Salerno. In the early autumn of 1943 we sailed all the way out to Calcutta at our slow 10 to 12 knots for the projected landings on the Arakan Coast but, by the end of the year, it was decided that we should return to Britain for the invasion of Europe, wherever that might be.

An LST was, of course, one of the bigger invasion vessels with an enclosed tank deck reached through bow doors and a lowering ramp. Lighter vehicles could be carried on the upper deck by lift from the tank deck or by direct side loading. Our normal complement was five officers: a lieutenant-commander in command, a first lieutenant, a navigating officer, an engineer and myself as gunnery/signals officer together with a crew of about seventy. For the Normandy operation, however, we carried an extra watchkeeping officer and three doctors as, in addition to all the vehicles and troops that we carried on our southerly crossings, there were the wounded and prisoners whom we brought back.

Having arrived back in this country during February, we started the long wait interspersed with invasion exercises. I remember only two things about these exercises. One was code-named Trousers and the signal 'Trousers Down' signified 'Exercise Commence' while something equally suggestive indicated 'Exercise Complete'! My second reminiscence was of the final exercise off the coast of South Devon which by all accounts was the biggest disaster imaginable. Somehow, between the Army and ourselves, we put the follow-up ashore ahead of the assault forces and then the RAF came in late and bombed our own troops instead of the enemy. Our only encouragement was the old maxim that a poor dress rehearsal heralds an excellent first night.

One other item that remains in mind about this period of limbo was the request that came aboard for volunteers to become Bevin Boys* and go down the mines. I never did discover whether they would, at that stage, have taken trained seamen out of the ships to help dig the country's coal or whether they were, with subtlety, alerting us to those who might not have the stomach for what lay ahead, because not one of our crew volunteered to opt out of 'The Great Crusade'.

As the weeks rolled by, the ships and craft and Mulberry caissons increased in number all along the south coast and the day seemed to be not long off. Nowhere was this more apparent than in that great stretch of water protected by the Isle of Wight, the Solent, Spithead and Southampton Water.

About a week before the great day, we embarked the troops and their tanks and transport and the ships were sealed, apart from those of us who had to go ashore on official business. If my memory serves me right, we had the Guards Armoured Division and the Canadians for this first crossing and a superb body of men they were. By now we had opened the orders for Operation Neptune, so that all the corrections could be brought up to date, and in consequence knew our destination.

On the afternoon of 4th June a padre came aboard to conduct a brief service. I don't think I have ever heard 'Eternal Father Strong to Save' sung with such fervour and during the rest of the afternoon and early evening we could hear this hymn coming from ship after ship as he made his way round the assembled fleet. We then, of course, had to endure impatiently the one day's delay on account of the weather forecast but in the evening of the 5th we weighed anchor and formed up in station in our convoy. The invasion was on.

My first memory of D Day itself was in the twilight before dawn when hundreds of heavy bombers droned overhead on their way to pound the coastal defences. It was a reassuring sight to have such air supremacy, so different from the bloody beaches of Salerno. We

*Thus named because Ernest Bevin was Minister of Labour and National Service at that time.

reached Juno Beach at $H + 3$, that is, at about 9.30 a.m., and anchored off Courseulles where fires were still burning but where the assault troops had obviously penetrated inland to some depth. On this first visit it was planned that we should not beach until the mines and obstacles had been cleared. Instead we waited until afternoon for the Rhino ferries to come along and unload us.

It is interesting how many tides it can take to fill a hole blown in the sand by a mine. On one beaching, I well remember taking the depth at the end of our ramp and, when it had got down to the prescribed level, waving the first tank off. Just beyond the point of my sounding, there was one of these holes and the first tank to the surprise of all, not least the tank crew, almost disappeared beneath the waves. I don't believe that our little corner of the Navy was particularly popular at that moment. We had, of course, to wait for the next tide and rebeach.

It was interesting to see the gradual deterioration in the physique and bearing of the troops and prisoners whom we transported. On our first return run with prisoners we had the 12th SS Panzer Division, who like our Guards Armoured Division, were crack troops. By the time we were taking over the mobile laundries and bringing back labour corps conscripts it was, well – less impressive. Our treatment of our wounded and of the prisoners was of course somewhat different. We could carry about four hundred of the former mostly on stretchers roped together on the tank deck. In the unaccustomed medium of the sea and after what they had been through, poor souls, they were worried about how long the ship would stay afloat if she were hit. The correct answer should have been, 'not very long' but we were able to reassure them with a much more optimistic and wholly unrealistic assessment. When the prisoners, who were herded in eight hundred at a time, asked the same question we were less sympathetic and it was not unknown for us to fire off a few rounds of ack-ack to put the wind up them!

During the period as a depot ship there was very little that we had to do so we evolved our own diversions. We made an aquaplane and the ship's motor boat was fast enough to give us a very good run. I think that the soldiers entering for the first time what to them was the war theatre were somewhat puzzled seeing the Navy using the Mulberry Harbour as a lido. On one night I managed to persuade the CO of one of the MTBs, a Lieutenant Peter Vanneck, who over thirty years later was to become Lord Mayor of London, to take me out on one of his night patrols. It turned out to be about the liveliest night that I or they had experienced for we encountered a number of German explosive motor boats, small boats containing a hefty charge of explosive which the pilot aimed at a ship and then rolled over backwards out of it. One had to get fairly close to attack them and then they went up like a mine. That night our flotilla bagged six of which our score was two.

My final reminiscence of this period was the fall of Paris and my captain giving me three days leave of absence. I hitch-hiked with a variety of armoured cars, trucks and Army motor cycles reaching that great city for my first, most memorable visit, about ten days after its liberation and our welcome was overwhelming. Judging by their reactions, I was the first British naval officer they had seen and I often wonder how near I was to being the first in the city altogether.

*

From Mr E. A. Neale

Casting one's mind back over thirty-five years has shown me that some things are as vivid as when they first happened, whilst others have faded or have been forgotten completely.

June 6th 1944 was not a very good day weatherwise, being very wet, with gale force winds, and deteriorating rapidly, not the sort of weather to make a landing on a beach. The invasion had already been delayed and it was now or never, bad weather or not.

Our ship was HMS *Glenearn*, a converted cargo ship carrying two flotillas of Landing Craft Assault, manned by Royal Marine crews: coxswain, stoker and two deckhands (myself and another). In our case being sub-flotilla craft we carried a Royal Marine sergeant as SF leader.

The rendezvous point was about six miles from the French coast, our designated landing point 'Sword Beach' near to a small town or village called Ouistreham, our landing time 0730.

As we left Southampton Water we felt the full force of the weather, waves were about thirty to thirty-five feet high and the ship, although 29,000 tons, was thrown about like a cork. The Army personnel were housed up for'ard in holds converted to carry the troops, and not all that roomy. The weather was not getting any better and it wasn't long before the troops were feeling the effects, as indeed were some of us.

Anchoring off at our allotted place we attempted to lower the craft having safely boarded the troops. The waves running the length of the ship lifted the craft up on their davit cables, letting them drop back with a jarring thud as they passed under them. The troops were not in a very fit state due to the rough crossing thus far and this did nothing to alleviate their discomfort, indeed it made life very hazardous for all concerned. I had all my work cut out trying to release the after hook without severing my hands, to think much about what was going on at the time. After managing to launch the craft the troops had received a real soaking and all in all we were a sorry-looking bunch. The pre-training for the Normandy landings had been very intensive, being carried out at dawn over a long period, so that to me it was just another exercise, at the time. The landing craft were flat-bottomed, flat-nosed craft with a very shallow draft and the wind and waves were making it very difficult to make headway; every wave thudded into the front of the craft causing it to shudder from stem to stern and water just cascaded over the front into the well of the boat. We carried about thirty Army personnel in three lines, one port and starboard, and one midships. My colleague was up for'ard with the sergeant; I was sitting on the rear deck space with my back against the kedge anchor reel holding a stripped Lewis gun across my knees.

The first realisation that anything was different was when the first salvo of 16-inch shells screamed overhead like banshees out of hell from a Dreadnought somewhere to our rear. The shock to my system was indescribable. At about the same time we were coming alongside a rocket carrier as it launched its rockets in banks of about twenty; the noise was deafening. We watched them exploding along the beach in patterns. Things had been quiet until then but suddenly Jerry started to return the fire, sporadic at first; I heard someone in the craft say 'O God'. Many of the lads had been sick during the journey and the stench in the craft was fairly high. It is strange how emotions transfer themselves. I heard someone sobbing and felt the urge to do the same, but just then machine-guns started to fire and you could hear the bullets whipping by and I did not stay up top to stop any of them, quickly dropping into the well of the craft for protection.

We hit the beach shortly afterwards, the ramp door was dropped and the steel doors opened to reveal about twenty to thirty yards of water-covered beach for the lads to negotiate. It was the intention to land on a neap tide to shorten the distance and make for a dry landing but due to delay the tide was receding rapidly. The German opposition by this time was becoming intensified and we began to get heavy mortar fire. The lads left the craft knee deep in water holding their rifles above their heads. I saw several men stagger and fall and can remember thinking 'God help you poor bastards . . .' Teller mines were visible fixed to metal stanchions above the water, and the mortar fire was beginning to get too close for comfort.

Having disembarked the troops, the cox called for 'Full Astern' and it was then we discovered we were beached well and truly on a sandbar, and no amount of engine power was making any impression. Suddenly there was an explosion in front of us and the bow of the craft reared up in the air and the boat began swinging broadside on to the beach. I began to feel panic as fear welled up inside me and I had visions of being literally blown out of the water. Another explosion erupted very near us and suddenly I realised that we were afloat. The stoker put the engines in reverse but only one engine responded, but at least we were free and able to move away from the beach which by now was chaotic, the noise was deafening as shells rained down on the beach and in the water all around us, as Jerry began to throw everything he could at us.

Our craft had been damaged below the water line and we were shipping water very fast; the sergeant was on the rotary hand pump whilst my colleague and I were frantically baling out with whatever would hold water. This was it, I thought. This is where it is all going to end. I felt the tears rolling down my face and was weeping quite unashamedly, working in an automatic fashion. I felt totally isolated from my companions and completely resigned myself to the fact that I was going to die. I suddenly became aware of shouting and, looking towards the sound, realised that we were passing a control vessel and someone on the deck was calling us through a loud hailer, instructing us to return to the beach. I remember the sergeant shouting back, 'Get . . . ed, you stupid bastard,' and I was laughing and crying hysterically, in fact we all became a little unhinged, forgetting completely our plight.

I have never considered myself a religious person, but it seemed that in that moment I knew I was going to be all right. We carried on for some distance but were not making any headway when out of the blue our flotilla leader hove into sight to see where we had got to, threw us a rope and took us in tow back to our mother ship, the most welcome sight on earth or water. Once back on board I was overcome with exhaustion and can recall that things were happening around me as if in a dream. I saw severed limbs and feet in buckets being thrown over the side of the ship and thought to myself how pink and clean they looked without any feelings of repugnance.

It transpired afterwards that we, although in the first wave, had been the only flotilla in our group to have returned safely to the ship without loss of life or craft.

I know that for me my experience changed my whole attitude to life and death. I have seen death and returned. Life has become very precious and I have resolved to enjoy every minute I am privileged to remain.

*

From Mr J. N. Cocker
I was in the Royal Navy, a petty officer motor mechanic on a Tank Landing Craft (LCT) 2302.

We landed in France on Omaha Beach with the Americans on D Day morning. We did actually drop anchor at 3.30 a.m. quite a few miles out, at about 6.30 a.m We moved in closer awaiting the signal to go in which didn't actually come until 10.30.

A few miles behind us cruisers and battleships were pounding shells inland behind the beaches and one name I remember particularly was a brand-new cruiser called the *Black Prince* that did a wonderful job. I heard soldiers later say that they would love to shake the hands of the skipper and crew of this ship for the wonderful job they did of silencing the enemy and softening up behind the beach.

On the beach was one large house, empty now of course, and three or four concrete pillbox gun emplacements. There were also small (4 feet long) remote-controlled tanks that hadn't the chance to do anything but were obviously meant to be filled with explosive.

Our beach was in a bay and the Germans were holding both sides so were able to shell the beach. On D Day afternoon the RAF came over to bomb them out of it, then dozens of gliders passed over and landed inland. This seemed to have the desired effect of cutting down the frequency of the shelling. At this very early stage I had the terrible fear that perhaps we wouldn't make it and would all be thrown back into the sea, but after a couple of days when we realised what a huge and vast operation it all was we gained in confidence and never doubted the outcome.

One day we were transporting wounded from the beach to a hospital ship a few miles out and in the bows we had six or eight Germans – one of them, an officer, spoke very good English. He showed us photographs of his wife and family, and I asked him what he thought of the landing, to which he replied : 'You are in now, in two weeks you will be out again.' It did seem very strange and in a way frightening to be talking to Germans after five years of fighting them. I got the same feeling when we walked along the beach, there were barbed wire 'cages' full of German prisoners looking very sullen and angry. You felt as though you daren't turn your back on them in case they broke out and turned the tables on you so to speak.

I will never forget the most frightening experience we had. It was a couple of days after D Day. We had beached to unload American troops with Jeeps etc., when the Germans started shelling the length of the beach. The beachmaster ordered all craft to get away at full speed, so we started to heave in on the electric winch of the kedge-anchor to pull us off the beach, but it would only work at about one-third of the normal speed. *All* the other craft had got away and we were the only one remaining, the shells were getting closer and closer as they got their sights on us. I was in the wheel-house and fully expected the next shell to land right on my tin hat. It was a terrible feeling being unable to move, absolutely helpless. Finally, after what seemed hours, the seaman watching over the stern called up to the bridge 'Cable straight up and down, sir.' Then it was full astern on engines, hard astarboard, then emergency full ahead and away we scampered – what a relief! We got quite a few shrapnel holes, and the First Lieutenant found that a piece had come through the bulkhead of the wardroom, gone straight through his cupboard, his suitcase and his brand-new greatcoat which was inside it.

We did admire and really feel sorry for the poor troops we were landing. I remember wondering where and how they would sleep at night – if at all. At least we had our home with us, our own bunks, washing and eating facilities etc., and they were going to be in for such a hell of a rough time, to say the least.

We worked for two weeks, running between the big ships anchored a couple of miles out and the beach, unloading their cargo of troops, jeeps, tanks, etc. One of the last trips we made was to land two or three large mobile laundries before we ran on to an iron stake on the beach which holed and flooded one of the engine room hatchways, so we had to return to Weymouth for repairs – and we weren't sorry either!

Quite a tension had built up over two weeks working from the beaches, due to shelling, strafing, aerial torpedoes and lack of sleep etc., and if anyone slammed a door one would almost jump out of one's skin. Looking back it was a tremendous experience, one that I am very proud to have been part of and would hate to have missed.

*

From Mr J. S. French

I took part in the D Day landings, having previously landed at Sicily, Salerno, and Anzio. I was a leading signalman on LST 364, and we arrived off the beach-head at Arromanches at about 1000.

The unloading procedure was different from that in the Mediterranean landings in so far that whereas in the Med we could run up the beach at any hour of the day (there being no rise and fall of the tide), the intention at Normandy was that we should anchor off the beaches and motorised rafts were to edge up and secure to our open bows and the tanks and troops be driven on to the rafts. Unfortunately the run of the current made contact very difficult and unloading very slow and dangerous; in fact one tank drove off the ramp into the sea with the loss of the tank and crew. Eventually one exasperated captain decided to run up on the beach and unload in the traditional manner. We all thought he was mad as it was obvious that the tide would leave him high and dry before unloading was completed, and make him a sitting target for enemy aircraft. However, the beaches were secure and the remainder of the landing craft followed suit and we kedged off when the tide came in six hours later. Nevertheless we were subject to machine gunning from fighters by day and bombed at night-time.

One incident, not connected with the actual landing, sticks in my memory. We were anchored in the Solent prior to departure and the ships were sealed for about two days before we sailed. However, D Day was postponed for twenty-four hours, which necessitated informing all ships by motor launch. In our case an officer and seaman went into Portsmouth by motorboat; the officer to collect orders and the seaman to man the launch. Arrived at Portsmouth, the seaman promptly deserted, but was picked up by a patrol and returned to the ship within hours of sailing. Commander 'X' ordered the man to be handcuffed to the guardrail on the main deck and we put to sea with the seaman in that exposed position. His meals were brought to him and placed on the deck. Anybody who spoke to him incurred the wrath of the commander. Meanwhile the ship's carpenter was ordered to erect a kind of shelter, like a small sentry box, which was secured to the upper deck and again the seaman was handcuffed to this structure. He did two trips like this and was later sent ashore under escort.

*

From Lieutenant-Commander T. T. Euman, RN

As the commanding officer of one of the minesweepers which swept the channel to Normandy my recollection of D Day remains the most vivid of any event that I took part in during the whole war.

We passed the boom at Portsmouth at 1300 on D − 1 and I had butterflies in my stomach! I then had to read out to my ship's company what they had to do if taken POW − which cheered me up.

After dark as we settled down to our sweeping I seemed to lose the butterflies and everything went smoothly. What did fascinate me was the German flak as our airborne boys went in.

At H − 1 hours we had to anchor clear of the channel we had just swept and our main anxiety then was what would be flung at us from the shore batteries when daylight arrived, as we were only three or four miles from the shore. However, it was a complete anti-climax, as we only had a few shots come our way.

So we settled down to a grandstand view of the vast armada as it came pounding down the swept channels, then all the landing craft going in. I must say my heart went out to them, especially the Landing Craft (Personnel) which had crossed the Channel on their own. It wasn't rough by our standards, but they certainly had a pretty grim time.

To add to this amazing sight were the cruisers and destroyers bombarding shore batteries and, I imagine, pre-arranged targets.

*

From Mr G. Pugh, who was at that time a 19-year-old midshipman RNVR serving as first lieutenant on LCI(L) 374

We sailed at 0700 on D Day, LSTs and LCIs together. We had taken our troops aboard the day before, who were a Beach Organisation group in the armada of thousands of which had anchored in the Solent overnight.

Everyone was afraid of a postponement due to high seas, but to our relief we saw the carriers and the assault troops beginning to move off late on D − 1 and knew then that things were starting.

The ramps were tested and I put on my battle order. We were told to go to White beach which we did and touched down about 1900 in six feet of water, made worse by surf. In order to try and get the troops ashore in less depth, we beached and unbeached six times, being sniped at from a pill-box on shore and once a FW190 came down and dive-bombed the beach, demolishing a few already ruined houses.

After we had put the troops ashore in dribs and drabs our engine went on us and we found ourselves unable to go astern. Another LCI coming on to the beach ripped our 5-ton starboard ramp off like matchwood and put a hole in the side. We dropped the hook 300 yards offshore and called up every possible boat we could see and at last a flotilla of LCMs came up and took off the remainder of our troops for us. We then detached ourselves from the flotilla and reported to the SOFC, who told us to anchor close to him which left us a mile off shore so we prepared for the night to come.

Jerry was now shelling the beaches but the *Rodney* and *Frobisher* were pouring stuff in at them. At dusk came the airborne troops in their gliders towed by Dakotas and DC3s and it was an awe-inspiring sight to watch them detach themselves from the tow and go down to land five or six miles inland. There were literally hundreds of them, stretching from above the beach out to way beyond the horizon. A little later we had a bomb 50 feet away from us, which started our water tank leaking like a sieve due to the terrific concussion.

Round about eleven that night things became rather hot and we closed up at action station. We shot down a Jerry which came swooping down towards us with twin searchlights blazing in each wing. The flak was terrific and the plane slowly disintegrated into a burning mass and crashed into the sea about one hundred yards ahead of us, lighting up the force with a terrific pool of burning oil which fortunately didn't last too long.

Shortly after another plane was shot down into the sea, so close to us that pieces of burning fabric rained down upon us like hail.

The next day was wet early but cleared up later. The Rhino ferries were working like mad, unloading LSTs. This day the enemy had a battery firing on the beach from inland. The cargo ships were just beginning to arrive and a number of them were blown up close to the beach to make a breakwater.

That night was much quieter but there was some activity with E-boats and the area further west seemed to be having quite a tough time. On Thursday the bombardment from our ship was renewed with doubled intensity. Numerous dog fights and perpetual action stations were the order of the day.

Friday afternoon was good fun. The rocket ships closed in and laid waste the shore with terrific ferocity and were shelled doing it.

We had two near misses from shells that afternoon and were shaken up rather.

That evening we were sent back to UK with two hundred Dutch and British seamen who had manned the old Dutch cruiser *Sumatra*, which had been sunk as a blockship.

There are a few incidents that I would like to record. When we were three-quarters of the way across we passed about one hundred small craft, all milling round, something akin to a terrific traffic jam, with the boats' klaxons blaring to complete the illusion. They were apparently lost and, when we passed, their leader yelled out 'Which is the way to France?', whereupon we answered 'Follow us' and they took up their cruising order as I went on. After we had left the beach we found that the screws were out of order so I said I would go down and take a look. Down I went in my short trunks, with shells and God knows what going off, so I can say I've bathed off the French beaches anyway. I also had my hair cut by a marine and it was hard for him not to cut me each time a bomb or shell dropped. I was very thankful when it was all over but he made a very good job of it.

Another well remembered evening, the Wednesday I think, when we were lying at anchor off the beach, a 10,000-ton merchantman came into our stern and just crushed it like a matchbox but no leaks developed.

We arrived back in UK after six days lying off the beach more or less a floating hulk, but they patched us up and we were soon back on the job again.

This account was written shortly after D Day.

*

From Lieutenant-Commander S. E. Glover, OBE, MBE, DSC
I was the gunnery officer and first lieutenant of the cruiser HMS *Orion* of Force K which supported the landing at Gold Beach and opened fire on my appointed target, a gun battery, at 5.21 a.m. on the morning of D Day. Being positioned on the east flank directly opposite Arromanches, I was able between shoots to observe the landing and the bulldozers at work to clear a way for vehicles and also to view the early stages of the build up of the harbour. I was then moved to the west flank next to Omaha and was able to see what happened to the US forces on landing. To visualise what is happening during the course of an action, when one's concentration

is thoroughly absorbed is most difficult.

We had on board with us the war correspondent named Harrison of the *News of the World,* who seemed to be enjoying himself with what he saw during our five days at the beachhead, during which time we had worn out our 6-inch guns or 152-mm and it was necessary to withdraw and have new gun liners fitted and then to proceed back to the Med to prepare for the South of France landing, which my ship led in at San Tropez.

The signals which we received during our bombardment at Normandy are as follows :

From Commander 2nd Army to all stations
Orion doing excellent shooting, engaging panzer tanks and concentration of troops at top range 24,000 yards.

From FOB to BCW Bulolo
Request Orion supporting fire Juvigny crossroads. Big Sunny says well done good shooting this afternoon.

From HMS Emerald to Orion
Nice work, I wish we had a few more yards of range.

From BCW to Orion
50th Div Tactical HQ, Good shooting, congratulations.

From HMS Ajax to Orion
Congratulations on your good shooting yesterday.

From HQ Bulolo
Heartiest congratulations on your great shooting.

From Admiral Phillip Vian
Additional reports of good shooting earlier received, the 2nd Army Cmdr has expressed to me supreme satisfaction himself this morning.

From SOG to all stations
Enemy troops in 8171, Enemy tanks reported 8369. Enemy holding Tilly-sur-Seulles, Enemy para troops reported area Vended 8665, Own troops 8075, 7777 and 8075. Orion excellent shooting panzers and concentrations of troops at top range.

Having been at the landings at Anzio and up to two weeks before the Normandy operation, we had become quite accustomed to supporting land forces.

*

From Mr Jock Irvine
I did not take part in the actual D Day landings but as a signalman on board the Polish Hunt class destroyer *Krakowiak*, I was two miles off the Normandy coast before those taking part in the landings.

The *Krakowiak* with three other Hunt class destroyers had acted as escort to protect two trawler minesweepers and two buoy layers, also trawlers, who were sweeping and marking a mine-free channel for all ships to use, both then and subsequently. We had started from the Solent the previous evening just before dusk and when dawn broke and I looked astern I saw more ships than I have ever seen, before or since. The sea seemed to be covered. One extraordinary sight was the view we then had of HM cruiser *Belfast*, at least a mile ahead of us, bombarding enemy positions ashore with all she had, as we were also doing. How she got there before us we never knew.

As we four destroyers steamed, dead slow, in line abreast towards the coast, firing our main armament of 4-inch guns, the enemy coastal batteries were returning our fire and I remember watching a series of splashes from their shells, each one approaching the port bow of our ship nearer than the last, until one spout of water arose only ten yards from our bows (it was my baptism of fire). The yeoman of signals, a veteran of Dunkirk, said: 'You'll have to do better than that, Jerry.' We then pulled out of line and, describing a circle, came back in again. We saw no more water-spouts. The impression I got was that the German resistance, at least from their coastal artillery, was rather half-hearted.

Later that evening as we slowly steamed along the coast near the small Port au Bessin, two German machine-gunners were observed on a sloping ledge, which led from their cave to the cliff top. They were carrying the machine-gun and ammunition box. One of our 4-inch guns fired and hit the cliff just below them. As our yeoman put it later, 'Jesse Owens* wasn't in it.' They certainly wasted no time disappearing over the cliff top. We had to return to Portsmouth as we had exhausted our supply of ammunition.

*Famous Olympic sprinter.

*

From Commander J. C. Turnbull, CEng, FIEE, RN (Retd)
I was electrical officer to the flag officer, Force S (Rear-Admiral
A. G. Talbot, DSO) and our job was to assault the beaches at
Ouistreham, at the mouth of the River Orne, the most easterly of
the landing beaches. Our HQ ship was HMS *Largs*, a converted
French banana-carrying ship. From mid-April we had been operating
from a shore HQ in Portsmouth and I had been living in the Royal
Portsmouth Corinthian Yacht Club in Southam. I only went on
board HMS *Largs* a day or two before D Day.

The day before we were due to sail I had to go up to the stores
in the Meon Valley to collect some special mine detection equipment
for the assault craft. (I don't think it was ever used.) The roads were
jammed with tanks and vehicles, all converging on the loading points
and I was late getting back. I had just got back on board when
Churchill, Smuts, Ernest Bevin and the C-in-C Portsmouth (Admiral
Sir Charles Little) came out of Admiral Talbot's cabin and went
ashore. They had come to wish us luck. Churchill looked very old
and solemn and went very slowly down the brow to the C-in-C's
car. Smuts nipped down like a two-year-old and Bevin lumbered
down like an amiable elephant. Churchill stopped at the door of the
car, turned to face the ship, and raised his hat. He stood for a
moment, then got in and they drove away. The ship's company and
staff were lining the rails; no one spoke, no one cheered, we all stood
there in silence. We had all been warned that we stood little chance
of coming back (50% dead, Admiral Talbot told me) and I think
we all felt the wings of the Angel of Death over us. It was a very
moving moment.

The invasion was, of course, delayed 24 hours, so we were at
anchor out in Spithead, off Fort Gilkicker, for longer than expected.
I had divided my twelve electrical officers between Fort Gilkicker,
Portsmouth Dockyard and the craft squadrons and landing parties.
I had now nothing to do but wait.

At last we were told 'It's on' and all day on 5th June the landing
craft came chugging past us on their way to the concentration areas.
The Solent and Spithead were covered with vessels of all sorts, a
vast armada and an astounding sight. As the landing craft passed
us we flew the signal 'Tally-ho. Drive on' (one of Admiral Talbot's
favourite expressions!) This drews cheers from many craft and one
reply 'There's an eternity of rest to follow'. One flotilla of craft

with a Highland regiment embarked, went by with the pipes playing. Everyone was keyed up; we knew that this was the greatest invasion ever undertaken. We were the last to go, at 2100, with the big infantry assault ships. We were to steam right through the lot to arrive off the beaches first, to direct operations.

I never expected to sleep, but I did. I had a rather hard and narrow settee in the cabin of the ship's own electrical officer. We were a very crowded ship and life was rather uncomfortable. I was up very early (H-Hour was 0730) and I went up to the lower bridge with the chief yeoman of signals, who was an old shipmate of mine. As it grew slightly lighter we could see, away to port, on a parallel course, the battleships, cruisers and destroyers protecting our flank. It was murky, blowing fresh and with a nasty top on the sea. Low clouds scudded overhead and it looked very unpleasant. Suddenly, away to port, there was a flash and a heavy explosion. The Norwegian destroyer *Sford* had been torpedoed (by an E-boat as we subsequently heard). A moment later the chief yeoman and I saw a torpedo track on our port bow.

He said, 'What do we do, sir?'

I said, 'I think we'll move to the other rail.'

So we walked over to starboard and saw the track vanishing over there. Then we both burst out laughing at the stupid idea that we would have been safer to starboard if we'd been hit! The 'fish' could only have missed us by a few yards. The bridge saw it too and made a sharp alteration of course, but I don't think it made any difference.

During the night we had heard the aircraft going over with the Airborne Division but had seen nothing. Now, as we neared the French coast, we saw and heard the guns of the destroyers (which had been escorting the minesweepers clearing our channel) starting to bombard the beach defences. The battleships and cruisers also started to open up on the defences east of the River Orne.

About the time of the torpedo incident the chaplain held a Communion Service which many of us attended. We were all a bit tense. We expected the German defences to be very strong and we couldn't believe that they would be taken by surprise. HMS *Largs*, moreover, was a sitting duck; she had no weapons other than a few light, close-range AA guns.

We were being 'homed' on to the beach by a beacon operated by a midget submarine. This craft had been lying submerged off the beach for three days, with the crew going out at night taking the mines off underwater obstacles!

We arrived at last off the beaches in a sort of half-light, and anchored about a mile off shore, with the assault ships astern of us. They at once began to load their Landing Craft (Assault) (LCAs) with troops and these came plunging past us through steep, breaking seas, on their way to the beach. We had Major-General Rennie, Black Watch, commanding the Third Division, on board and he was upon the bridge with Admiral Talbot. As the craft swept by a bugler stood up in one of the leading ones and sounded 'General Salute'. General Rennie was delighted. I believed at the time that the leading craft contained men from the Royal Warwickshire Regiment but I later heard that they may have been from another unit. Our force landed the whole Third Division.

For some time after the landing craft went in nothing seemed to happen. Visibility was still poor and though we could hear a lot of firing, nothing came near us. About 0900 the Admiral became impatient and decided to go closer in. We weighed anchor and went in a position about 750 yards from the beach. The clouds began to lift and the wind and sea moderated and we began to see something of the activity ashore.

Shortly after we moved, the midget submarine surfaced and came alongside us. The two-man crew came on board for a bath and breakfast. They were in high spirits and had done a splendid job. The old warships and merchant ships which were to form our artificial harbour (the Gooseberry) were also brought into position, just east of our anchorage and sunk. They included the old French battleship *Colbert*, the Dutch cruiser *Sumatra*, and a British D class cruiser. The upper deck of the *Colbert* was well above high water mark and the beach organisation made themselves very comfortable in the rather plush wardroom and upper deck cabins. There was an emergency diesel generator on the upper deck and we got this working and connected to give them light and power.

During the morning we began to get a few German planes over the beaches and some heavy guns in a fort on Cap d'Antifer, across the Baie de la Seine, began to shell the anchorage. The RAF soon fixed the German planes and we never had any more daylight raids, though there was much mine-laying at night. We asked HMS *Ramillies* to attend to the fort. She came steaming through the anchorage and turned slowly and majestically to port and fired two or three ranging shots. Having got the range, she fired three, 15-inch broadsides (eight 15-inch guns a time) and the fort vanished in a cloud of smoke and dust. We never heard another squeak from it.

Ashore we could hear firing and some houses were burning and tanks were pouring on to the beaches. I saw a herd of cows stampeding across a field in front of some of them. The warships were firing over our heads at targets inland, but there was little in the way of a battle to see. During the forenoon the first batch of prisoners came on board to be interrogated by our intelligence officer. He was a remarkable man, a Belgian cavalry officer who had escaped and had become a lieutenant RNVR! His name was Hendrik van Riel but his identity card and disc named him Lieutenant Henry Vann, in case he was captured. He had made several daring landings in France and Belgium before the invasion. He told us that very few of the troops in the beach defences of our sector were Germans and that most of the prisoners were Austrians and Ukranians and that there were even a few, so-called 'Free Indians'! They certainly looked a poor lot.

My officers were all well organised and there was nothing for me to do after lunch, so the padre, one of the doctors and I and one or two others, got deckchairs and binoculars and sat on the boat deck watching the goings on, for all the world like spectators at Cowes. It was all slightly unreal and rather an anti-climax. It was only later in the week that German field batteries got back into the woods on the low hills east of the Orne and shelled the anchorage, giving us an unpleasant time. They had an artillery officer spotting for them from the top floor of a house on the beach. This was marked, 'Achtung! Minen!' and our soldiers didn't go into it for about three weeks, when they found him, very comfortably ensconced with ample food and drink.

Later in the evening a big airborne force arrived in gliders and landed inland from our beach. We sat there with a grandstand view as hundreds of planes came over and the gliders cast off and landed. A few planes were shot down but most got away safely. The gliders landed, out of our sight, behind a low ridge.

NOTE. – We spent a month off the beaches and I moved over to HMS Albatross for a time and then back to the Largs. We were supposed to be repairing landing craft but, in fact, did very little. Craft were, generally, either write-offs or able to get back across the Channel and the big gale later in the month and the German shelling stopped a lot of the work. I ended up doing watches as a duty officer, in the operations room of HMS Largs.

I recently read the official history of 3 Division and find that it differs in detail from what I wrote. However, I think we are in agreement on essentials.

*

From Mr D. S. Hawkey, ex-Lieutenant RNVR
On D Day I was in command of LCT 513 and was leader of the 20th LCT Flotilla. Since its formation the 20th had been used for training of every description. We had helped in the training of innumerable army units, we did the trials for the idea of using guns in landing craft in the initial assault. We were involved in the trials of the DD tanks as well as seeking out and testing new beaches to be used in assault training. We were not sent to the Mediterranean as most of our contemporaries were for the invasion of Italy, and so it could be said that although we lacked combat experience we were probably among the best trained of the LCT flotillas.

Our beach was Juno and H-Hour was about 6.30. As we sailed in it was obvious that we were going to be the first ashore on that sector whereas, according to plan, the AVREs should have been there to clear the beach obstacles. There was a fairly strong cross-beach tide running which made beaching difficult. A lot of the obstacles (mainly tetrahedrons with mines or shells attached) were beginning to be covered by the water so what we tried to do was to pick a touchdown spot between two obstacles and get in there before we were carried too far sideways by the sea. This took a good deal of concentration and judgement and had the opposition been greater would have proved to be very difficult. I was lucky enough to get on the beach, unload, and get off again but unfortunately many of the other LCTs hit the obstacles and were badly damaged as a consequence. All the time we were on the beach the only opposition we encountered were what seemed like mortar shells landing around us.

In pulling off the beach I found that one of the tetrahedrons, complete with shell, was entangled in my landing ramp extensions and was being held in position by its own weight. I tried all ways to get rid of it but it would not budge. All this time I was being flashed by various assault ships to come alongside to help with disembarkation but it would have been a tricky operation and I decided against it. As our next job was to take part in the build-up shuttle service I thought the best thing I could do was to get back to Portsmouth, get rid of the obstacle and get another load. On the way back we rigged a wire to the ramp extension with the idea of taking the weight off and shaking the obstacle free but it didn't work and the whole thing came inboard, the detonator of the shell breaking off without exploding.

On arrival off Gilkicker a launch came alongside and Richard North of the BBC asked me if I would like to go to a studio in Fareham to record my experiences which I did.

Back on board we were given another load and sailed with the next convoy that evening. This then became our regular routine, going over at night, unloading, sailing back next day and loading again. One night at sailing time we had engine trouble and by the time we were ready the convoy had gone, so we went over on our own and only learned later that the convoy we should have been with was attacked by E-boats.

So life went on until we were eventually taken off the shuttle service to become part of Force N for the landing on Walcheren Island at the mouth of the Scheldt. That was to prove very different from our experiences in Normandy, but is another story.

CHAPTER THREE

On the Beach - the Sappers and Others

Many people will be surprised to hear that the first troops to enter a
battle are sometimes members of the Corps of Royal Engineers,
known as 'the Sappers'. In the long history of military engineering
certain soldiers have specialised in the art of making saps – long
approach trenches – and also mining under walls and fortifications
prior to blowing them up. In modern war the task of the Sappers is
to find a way through enemy minefields, an extremely hazardous task.
The Sappers did this most successfully at the battle of Alamein
(among others) and on D Day they had an even more formidable
task in clearing paths across the beaches. The task also included
destroying obstacles which would have hindered the advance and for
this they were equipped with AVREs (Avvryes, as they were called).
An AVRE was a heavy tank, even more heavily armoured, which
would launch a huge amount of explosive from a short distance on
to an obstacle. In accomplishing this, and other tasks, such as
attaching demolition charges to various fortifications, the Sappers
were exposed to the full force of enemy fire. Their hazardous tasks
demanded not merely great courage but also skill, patience and
coolness under exceptionally unnerving conditions. But they had
them all.

*

From Mr P. G. Barton
As a member (rank of lance-corporal) of 1034 Port Operating Company, RE, part of No 7 Beach Group, I took part in those landings.
Ours was a seaborne landing on Juno Beach, and as I had the
misfortune to be blown off the landing craft, thanks to the craft
making contact with a mine, my impressions were far from jolly
to say the least.

Having said that, the overall impression gained prior to the incident mentioned was, as I now recall, one of awe at the sheer size of

the undertaking and the vast numbers of ships and fire-power employed. As I also remember, I had a great pride in taking part in the operation, and a firm conviction that it would be successful.

*

From Mr S. R. Sharman
Somewhere in a field near Littlehampton, or perhaps Silverstone, without disclosure by name where we might land, the briefing began a month or more before it happened. Photographs were shown of the Caen Canal, River Orne. You could see a German soldier looking up on one photograph and the high banks of the River Orne and Caen Canal, a problem we were to overcome.

As the craft made its way toward the beach one could see a warship opening fire on targets inland, broadside on, a most impressive sight. The waiting whilst the ship made its way inshore was taken up with getting everybody up on deck, as soon as the ramps came down. There was much harassment from the American sailors to get us off and get away. I remember some shells landing near the left-hand side of the ship and on entering the water complete with an inflated lifebelt being helped by a member of the Beach Group Pioneer Corps, then the run up the beach meeting all kinds of personnel, some with a mixture of Army and Navy clothing, with radio sets and odd equipment. Noise from artillery, amphibious tanks shedding trunking which allowed the exhaust to escape and prevent water getting into the engine, a terrific bang; after the explosion the trunking fell to the ground.

On the walk from the beach to Bénouville we met prisoners who wanted to surrender.

At the arrival in Bénouville I stood near a soldier, a Commando in a prone position firing a Bren gun. The situation became real and I realised that the Germans were not far away. We were met by a major from the 17th Field Company who made us aware that there were snipers about. We were detailed to search the church in Bénouville but found the belfry door closed and we did not go into the tower. Whilst we were sheltering in the school playground in the early afternoon, supplies were being dropped by Douglas aircraft. We saw a machine-gun being fired from the tower by a German soldier. You could see his arm bent to an upright position, holding the gun and firing into the air. Someone must have fired at the tower with something heavier than machine-gun fire, because the masonry was scarred. They came down and gave themselves up, I believe.

Behind the wall where we were sheltering a Sapper was making tea on a little stove called a Tommy Cooker which was fired by a small round tablet. The tea was made with compressed dried milk, sugar and chlorinated water. Still, it was a cup of tea. Suddenly some low-flying aircraft appeared and in the panic the tea was kicked over and a near fight ensued.

I remember my first experience in handling a dead person, an Airborne lad. Civilians had looked after him and he had died in their bed. We took him away, wrapped up in a sheet, on a door. The major previously mentioned got killed. He died that day from wounds, poor fellow.

George Dransfield, a driver, supporting his officer in the search for snipers, was killed and buried in the churchyard later on. It is somewhat difficult now to separate the first and second days and to put certain thoughts out of one's mind: the three tanks which were destroyed by 88-mm shells at close range, a dead German lying there with no boots on. I could not believe it was true, this was my first reaction.

The Airborne had done their job in taking the bridge but some of the soldiers coming back over the Pegasus Bridge for rest expressed uncertainty about their task.

Second Platoon 5 Section's job was to supply drinking water. Canvas water tanks were erected and water taken from the canal. The canvas water tanks were damaged by shell fire; clots of mud and clay were used to prevent the water from escaping.

Maybe it was the consequence of Dunkirk and previous successes of the German Army that there was much uncertainty and apprehension. We were joined by another Royal Engineer company and I was impressed by the efficiency with which they carried out their allotted task to help in the erection of the bridge across the Caen Canal.

Because of the high banks the centre piers were built of angle irons called Christchurch Cribs, placed on pontoons bringing the bridge to bank level. This had been worked out in England at Goole, Yorkshire, on the rivers Ouse and Humber. The bridges of the Orne and Caen Canal were similar, save that the river Orne was wider and tidal. Both bridges worked. So complete were the details, that a stone-crushing machine was landed in our first days in Bénouville. It crushed stones at night, grading them into smaller and larger pieces for the approaches of the bridges, using stone from quarries in the Caen area. So complete were the preparations for our task in hand.

The arrival of the blankets, which must have come after the first week, took place late in the evening. It was decided that we sleep in the grounds of the Hôpital Maternité, and being late and somewhat subject to a leg-pulling prank by my fellow Sappers I followed a white tape into a wooded part of the hospital grounds, the tape being put down to help in the dark, but alas somebody had made the tape lead to a heap of discarded baby enamel pots, thrown away because they had holes in, quite a heap, and I remember scrambling amongst them, bewildered in the dark. The noise produced much laughter. I never knew who did it.

We did not encounter too many enemy aircraft but more than most writers mention. Lieutenant White was wounded by an anti-personnel bomb one evening, and shelling kept on. The whole front was hinged from a place called Cabourg. I remember the CQMS and his vehicles, including one which belonged to my section, being destroyed one night by 88-mm shellfire, and Driver W. Twidle being killed trying to rescue his vehicle. The noise from the ammunition, mostly 303s, went on for some time in the night.

Whilst maintaining the bridges we had built, we had the experience of seeing explosives being floated down the River Orne with the outgoing tide, fortunately not damaging the bridge.

We used to stand to for four hours each night instead of two which I think now was a great mistake. It is true that one gets a longer and undisturbed rest, but what tiredness!

I remember being on a burial party in the Bénouville churchyard where we buried Driver G. Dransfield and two Airborne lads. Our Major L. E. Upton conducted the service, being alerted afterwards to the reports of the uncertain situation at the front by an Airborne sergeant.

It was interesting to me to see the folding bicycles and what must have been the forerunner of the now-familiar scooter, used by the Airborne. Some of my fellow Sappers were reluctant to give them back when requested some weeks later.

I returned to the area in 1965 to find that the Pegasus Bridge across the Caen Canal has been widened and many parts of the banks have been made higher. The people around the hospital in Bénouville who were children then are grown up with families now. The concierge and his wife recognised me and made me welcome. The café at the Pegasus Bridge has been made into a little museum with pictures of Churchill and many war souvenirs.

Between the sights of the Caen Canal and River Orne bridges was a small cross, the grave of a flying officer from the Canadian Air Force, I believe, aged 21, shot down by gunfire. Parts of the plane were scattered there and the machine-gun from the plane was mounted on the end of a piece of wood, about four inches by three in thickness, an improvisation which could be considered dangerous but was used against enemy aircraft that came near the bridge.

I close these notes now, but not forgetting the fear and apprehension and sadness.

*

From the Diary of 234 Field Company RE
Tuesday, 6th June, D Day
We hove in sight of the Normandy beaches, and our AVOCH training became a reality. A calm crossing after weighing anchor at 2130 hours 5th June. A grey dawn, which gradually turned stormy. Assault craft away on a pitching sea at 0600 hours. The bombing and bombardment of the French coast was visible from 0400 hours. The *Rodney, Repulse, Warspite* and other battleships opened up. The first wave of wounded were brought back to the boats at 1000 hours. Great difficulty was experienced in hitching up the assault craft again, owing to a heavy swell. After scrambling down nets or being lowered over the side in slings, we went ashore in LCTs. Several attempts were made to land, for although the beaches were quiet, the obstacles were many. A 'duck' was blown sky-high to starboard. The landing was made in water varying 2 to 4 feet in depth, near Courseulles and Gray-sur-Mer. The civilians were there with open arms to greet us – in actual fact a dishevelled mob of bedraggled wretches collected from amongst the ruins and stood stupefied. A few odd snipers were encountered in the Banville area. 1 Platoon was held up by an enemy strongpoint. 2 Platoon encountered some Canadians coming in the opposite direction. The task of route and verge clearance in the area of Gray-sur-Mer, Tierceville, Banville and Reviers went without a hitch. 'Smudge' Smith of 1 Platoon brought in eight German prisoners – apparently without a fight.

Company HQ failed to land and anchored off the beaches near Gray-sur-Mer.

The priority was for tanks, and in consequence our platoons

received no transport. The night was one of ack-ack fire, with its streams of red fire disappearing into the heavens. The beaches were bombed, but on the whole the night was reasonably quiet – in fact, very few men did much in the way of digging in. Our experience of war was far lighter than we had ever expected.

Wednesday, 7th June, D + 1
Major Hughes' assault landed, complete with Recce Sergeant and two bicycles, early in the morning. Remainder of Company HQ plus transport were ashore by eventide. There was a meeting of the clans near Reviers bridge, during which the convoy and all officers were nearly wiped out by bombs. Platoons were very thankful to see their transport arrive.

Sapper Cairns was sniped or hit by shrapnel whilst on guard. He was buried next day, at the top of the hill, in a field by the road from Reviers to Amblie. Platoons were employed on route clearance and maintenance. 1 Platoon moved near Creully whilst Company HQ, 2 and 3 Platoons stayed in the area of Reviers. 3 Platoon Officer and Recce Party recced for two waterpoints for military and refugees, and passed near an isolated enemy post covering a deep gorge. We trod stealthily with guns at the alert. Heavy air raids at night and much flak. We dug in a little deeper.

*

From former Driver E. G. Sargeant, 73rd Field Company RE
The memories are still with all who took part. Memories of underwater marines in skin suits floating dead in the sea. Memories of soldiers with the African Ribbon on their chests lying dead on the beach.

We were part of a mixed bag of vehicles on a landing craft. Our vehicle was an armoured half-track carrying plastic explosives, etc., for beach obstacle clearance and medical equipment, stretchers, etc., for first aid on the beaches.

In October 1940 I volunteered as a driver in response to a radio appeal for drivers for the Corps of Royal Engineers. Due to my civilian experience I was made medical orderly to the company, a job which I did all through up to the break up of the company.

We sailed from Southampton and what a sight with dawn breaking to see a vast sea of ships of all kinds with warships flanking. Our craft was well over halfway across when we hit trouble with engine failure due to water in the fuel tanks. What a sensation to be wallowing helplessly in the sea, machine-guns were mounted on the rails for protection against attack. We were lucky to evade any trouble other than a mine floating free, but it was a relief to hear the engines roar to life. Away we went, full speed ahead – someone did a good job.

We passed sections of Mulberry Harbour being towed across, this as it turned out was to be just left of our landing point. Land in sight, a certain Sapper (no names, no pack drill) should have done the job of mounting a Bren gun to give covering fire, but he had been stretched out on one of my sling stretchers since leaving Southampton in a state of hopeless fear. I set up the Bren gun for him.

We were then running into beach. Our run was not good, we were still in fairly deep sea. Anyhow down went the ramp. The first to go off was our friend, the Bren-carrier and gun (someone made a blunder to put it mildly). He left the gun in the sea at the bottom of the ramp. Driver Skipsy was next to go with our half-track, he tried to avoid the gun so to get off we slid off sideways from the ramp, the sea was lapping above the screen. We seemed to be doing fine with our water-proofed engine when, alas, it cut out dead. Being too 'hot' a perch for staying on, we grabbed small pack and rifle and into the sea we went.

We got ashore with God's help and made for cover. We had been issued with 'goods' rubber to put certain items in and so protect them from water. I then realised that I still had my watch on my wrist and wet cigarettes in my pocket.

On the beach was a bulldozer at work. This had a winch equipment and Skipsy and I approached the driver and asked for his help to recover the half-track as we badly needed the explosives and medical kit. With his co-operation Skipsy and I waded in with the winch rope, which we attached to the half-track, which still housed our terrified Sapper. We got the vehicle ashore and made use of its contents and one reflects on the risk we took from sniper, mines, etc.

Towards evening we looked around for some cover for the night and I and a good many more dug ourselves fox-holes and got our heads down. All night long there was the roar of engines with material, tanks, etc., being pushed into the bridgehead, and the noise of aircraft, machine-guns, shells filled the air.

As morning came I had actually dozed off for quite a nap. D + 1 saw an early start by Driver Skipsy on repairing the half-track, then with a sudden few thumps we were under shell fire again. At that time a group of senior military personnel were doing a tour of inspection, and they took quick cover by the half-track. We dived for ditch cover, and I can still see the look on their faces as Skipsy said to them, 'You picked a B . . . . good cover – it's still loaded with quite a quantity of explosives.'

One particular incident which sticks in the mind was of Sapper Heatley and his pal Sapper Uttley. Before land was sighted Heatley took his watch, ring, etc., and passed them to Uttley saying, 'Take these home to my mother, 1 shall not be coming home.' He was eighteen years old and was shot almost before he had hit the beach.

*

From Mr K. Hollis
I belonged to the 62(9) Field Squadron Royal Engineers and came back from the desert having been in all the major battles from El Alamein to Tunis. I was wounded at Alamein on the minefields and later joined my unit at Mersa Matruh.

We were chosen to go on the landings on D Day on Sword beach, Lion-sur-Mer. I would be the first to wade ashore two minutes after AVRE tanks had landed and they would be available to assist us in removing beach obstacles after we had disarmed mines, etc. from them.

We set off from Portsmouth at 5 p.m. on 5th June and I wondered what and where I would be the following evening. After being in previous actions I always felt that if I could get through the initial fire and all went well, I could survive. Until late that evening we wrote letters and smoked, talked, anything to keep our thoughts off the coming hours. (We were on Liberty ships, with the LCAs hanging on the side and the 120 of us were on two different ships with infantry – in other words, 'all the eggs were not in one basket'.)

I eventually fell asleep – quite remarkable really – and I awoke to a tannoy which said, 'Good morning, everybody, it is now three o'clock and reveille and it's a nice day' – my thoughts were, I wonder if he's coming with us? I now felt a calm excitement and went up top to see where we were. Eventually we could see the coast in the distance – sinister and now and then red glows. I then thought of the paratroops who would now be going to the bridge over the Orne, some two or three miles from where we would land.

The time came for us to get in our LCAs and I can remember the numbers were 145 and 147. We clambered in with our special equipment and packs with eight 3-lb charges of plastic HE to use in demolishing the obstacles. We set off and were due to land at approximately 7.20 – everyone was seasick and the thought was just to get off and out of this misery. I stood up with my officer and peered over the top of the ramp. The rocket ships had unloaded their frightening salvos and the haze and smoke hung menacingly about the beach. By now I could see the beach and just beyond was the sea front and houses with their attics. At this stage some of my pals in the other LCAs were ordered to jump overboard and swim to the obstacles and remove teller mines and shells.

We hit the beach and were met with withering machine-gun fire; the sand was spurting up in front of us. I jumped into the water waist high and now our unit of some 120 was supposedly in line along the shore. I realised our desperate position and together with my eight Sappers (I was a lance corporal) knelt in the water under the cover of the partly submerged obstacles. Most of the RD assault tanks (AVRE) were knocked out. I shouted to make for the two end tanks, as we were on the extreme right flank of the beach. As we ran, one of my team, Arthur Jasper, shouted 'Frank's hit.' We ran back in the open but Frank Dick (who had shared my bunk on the ship – you know the type, top and bottom) had been shot and had died instantly, there was nothing we could do. We ran for our lives for the safety of one of the tanks and even then the other tank got hit.

At this stage I felt some confusion. More people were coming ashore and the tide was moving us up – I wondered if we would make it; it was now obvious that the mines and obstacles would have to be cleared when the sea had gone back. (Incidentally, about twelve of us had trained to go under the water in Davis apparatus suits to blow up obstacles. Alas, not all the plans went right and the suits went back in the LCAs and we never had to do that task.)

So many things seemed to be happening now and it was as if the incoming invasion couldn't get off the beach. The sniper was still there. Then I saw an officer wounded, we picked him up, got a stretcher off a tank and ran with him and put him under cover. I looked round and saw my pal Geoff Hewitt climbing on a partly submerged 'Element C' obstacle (a sort of gate 10 feet by 10 feet with a support ramp), calmly disarming teller mines which were attached to them.

It must now have been late morning and I was beginning to feel that luck was on my side. At this stage we were now under the front road with the houses some 30 feet away; the sniper was still there and he fired away at everything and everybody.

The tide gradually receded and now we had the task of disarming the mines and removing the obstacles. I went with three of my team to a row of obstacles with shells on them pointing out to sea. I decided to do the disarming – I was not brave, I just felt I wanted to be responsible for my own actions. There was always fear when doing this, wondering just how easy it was going to be. However, I disarmed four of them and when I was unscrewing the arming head off the next there was a hiss – Oh, my God, I thought, this is it – I dropped down, the others behind me did the same and asked 'What's up, Ken?' I began to reason and think. Nothing happened and then I thought that it must have been air released after I had broken the sealing compound on the igniter. A minute passed and my courage began to return. I had the feeling that I had mastered the mystery and I think that afterwards I crazily disarmed a dozen or so more.

Something then said stop and we went and lay down under the cover of a beached LCT. There was always reaction after doing this work and I felt – how many more of those must be disarmed? There must be bloody millions of them, there's no end to them. All the way in the desert and now this lot.

It was late afternoon and a rollcall was taken. We had suffered heavy casualties and in our unit history it was noted that the 629 was dead.

The next wave of Airborne arrived and we had the feeling that with a sight like this we must be making headway. These air armadas were terrific morale boosters. On releasing their gliders the planes flew very low over us on their return home and incredibly two were shot down by a sniper who was still in his position. I just looked in disbelief as his tracers went into the planes – one a Stirling and the other a Halifax, if I remember correctly. Later he was taken prisoner and the fear of immediate small arms fire disappeared. Eventually night came and we remained under the beach front.

I think I should mention that in the days that followed more of our unit were killed and our CO asked us to form up in a field off the beach. The order was given to the depleted number that senior sappers should become lance corporals – lance corporals and corporals to lance sergeants. About one week later we were reinforced with some fifty or seventy officers and men.

D Day and the days afterwards had cost three officers and eighteen other ranks killed, two officers and forty-two other ranks wounded and four other ranks missing. It was a terribly tragic loss, many old faces were no longer seen about the leaguer area. The old 9th was dead.

*

From former Driver A. O. Palser, 246 Field Company, RE
My personal emotions and feelings on knowing I would be amongst the first British troops to land in France started a few years before the actual Day. During the chaotic exercises and seeing the Heath Robinson equipment and the lives lost in practice made me wonder if we would ever leave Britain. However, when I was put in the concentration camp near the south coast, shown photographs and briefed individually on my particular task, and listened to Monty giving his talk and explanation of the operation, I felt confident and optimistic as to how easy it would be.

Mid-day 4th June, I reversed my scout car into its position on LCT 304 (I believe) as I had done so many times before, and felt proud that at last we were off. Then we sailed out to join a sea so full of craft that my optimism increased; if we were not blown out of the water by aircraft I felt it would be no worse than an exercise off the coast of Scotland. We sailed all night and were surprised the following morning to arrive back off Gosport to refuel the craft and learn that D Day had been postponed twenty-four hours.

We sailed out again and I marvelled that so many craft could fill the English Channel without a visit from enemy aircraft. Another day and night were spent sailing and finally as dawn began to break the captain told us we were going in, and he would be putting us off on time H + 45 minutes. The barrage of shells from what seemed to me must have been every ship in the Allied Navy started firing so low overhead that my main worry was if a few fell short, but this reinforced my optimism that any Germans could not possibly survive.

Suddenly as the mist lifted I saw the shore – the houses exactly like those photographs I had seen during briefing. It gave me a feeling of having been there before. Suddenly the ramp dropped and the leading vehicles moved off. I followed but found on touching land I was in deeper water than expected. A sergeant standing above me in a small turret told me to stop and reverse as I would have run over a number of dead sailors. In humanity this was the only thing to do but, not being able to see as my visor was still below water, unfortunately I became fouled up in the wreck of another vehicle. I could not move and could do nothing but grab the Bren gun and ammunition, get out and wait until the tide had receded.

I made my way up the beach and was shocked to see we had made so little progress. The Germans had survived the shelling and were returning fire very accurately. During a heavy barrage I dug in alongside a number of sailors who had lost their craft, feeling very despondent at my own effort. A shell landed in water a few yards away and all my feelings of disappointment disappeared for, as the water turned colour from the exploded shell and the smell of burnt explosive wafted over us, the young naval officer alongside me shouted : 'Gas.' His chaps put on their masks, but I had left mine in my scout car so, hoping the naval lad was wrong, I resigned myself to the inevitable, said the Lord's Prayer, and waited. Much to my surprise no one else in the vicinity was wearing a mask.

When the tide receded my car was pulled out on to dry land and I spent some hours changing oils and doing everything I could to get it going. This was not to be for after immersion the electrics had been ruined and would need complete renewal. With nothing to do except wait until I could contact my unit, I spent the day dodging shells and beating out the fires they created. It was a long time before the beach began to clear and our troops were able to move inland. The Germans refused to give in and were able to shell the beach – well marked by our own balloon barrage until someone realised this. Then with the lack of enemy aircraft, it was hauled down.

It was a long day. During the evening the shelling eased and I breathed more freely. Then the sky filled with aircraft and spilled out thousands of multi-coloured parachutes and cast-off gliders landed a few miles inland, and my confidence was restored. Before dusk I was picked up and taken to my unit and was shocked to learn that we had not made our objective of Caen, the Airborne landings had taken place in a battle area and all hell was going on around us. We had suffered many casualties. A sleepless night was spent on the outskirts of Ranville and everyone was dug in to protect their own patch. D + 1 dawned and I had a replacement vehicle and started the job I came to do, to drive the officer commanding on his various reconnaissances, a lonely job which meant visiting sections of our own units clearing minefields and supporting infantry. I spent every night for weeks in front of our infantry, just waiting in the vehicle whilst the officer inspected the area, my only contact being the crackling of a '19' radio set tuned to the base frequency. I used to repeat in my mind the night's password in case I forgot it and would then be shot up by our own infantry on our return. We usually got back to base in time to take part in the dawn 'stand to'.

This was a very depressing period and troops were being hammered constantly, every attack being costly in lives and materials to gain a few yards. Rumours were rife and most of us were physically and mentally worn out. We heard of the American advances, which did not improve our morale for at that stage the strategy had not been explained to us. Both British and Canadians were receiving a very bad 'press'. We had no answer to a Tiger tank, their 88 mm could outgun our Shermans and their multi-barrel mortars were creating havoc amongst our troops. The Germans holding high ground on two sides of us could watch every move we made and with such a heavy concentration of troops and equipment in a very small area I felt that were the Germans to make an all-out effort we could have been routed and driven back into the sea.

I felt very despondent during this period. I believe the 3rd British and 3rd Canadian casualties were the highest of any infantry divisions, and even the prisoners we were taking and the damage we were inflicting did not make me feel any happier or hopeful of success while so many of our chaps were going down. About a month after landing we began to prepare for the attack on Caen. One evening the drone of aircraft was heard. They were flying very low and I witnessed the RAF bomb Caen in perfect formation until the dust from their effort almost choked us and visibility was practically nil. The following morning I entered Caen to find that the Germans had departed. From then on life improved. We were a month behind on target, but the ease with which we were able to move about and advance to Belgium restored my faith and optimism that the war would soon be over. I still did not think of the tenacity with which the Germans fought, especially as we approached the German border. A small number of Germans left behind our lines caused havoc sniping, a tank and small unit strategically placed could hold up an army. However, this is another story.

*

From Mr K. Cockersell

I was with the HQ 1 Corps Troops RE. As we neared France, I well remember there was a card school going on on deck and the lads were so intent on their cards they took scant notice of the Normandy coast that was looming up.

We rushed the coast in our LCT but on each occasion when the craft shuddered to a standstill the water was too deep to enable the lorries, although waterproofed, to disembark. It was eventually decided that we should anchor off shore until the tide was right on the next day.

All was well for a time because the Germans would not come near in the daytime. However during the night all hell was let loose and we and other boats were bombed from the air. I was below deck and eventually there was the most ear-splitting crash I have ever known. I remember thinking, 'This is it' and my colleagues and I made our way up the ladder on to the deck. This was completely enveloped in smoke and I was convinced that at any time the order would be given to jump overboard. Somehow I made my way to the stern and to my utter relief discovered that the smoke was caused by a smoke screen that was enveloping the boat.

Just before dawn when things were comparatively quiet, a plane came over and the Americans on our LCT really let him have it with tracer bullets. The pilot twisted, turned and did all he could to avoid the bullets and then I realised, as also did the gunners, that it was an Allied plane they were firing at. You recall the planes were striped for D Day. Fortunately this one got away.

The ear-splitting crash I mentioned earlier was a direct hit by a bomb that went through the decks and came to rest on the tarpaulin of a truck, one of many carried in the LCT, with mines and explosives of all kinds. The bomb was eventually very, very gingerly placed on a stretcher and dumped in the sea.

We were told that in all probability the bomb could have been filled with sand, as the Germans were compelling some of the French to fill bombs. Had it exploded you can imagine what would have happened to all the mines and explosives on the craft. The LCT and everybody on it would have disappeared and I shouldn't be writing this note!

*

From Mr E. Randle
I was involved with 246 Field Company RE of the 3rd British Infantry Division landing on Queen beach with the 8th Brigade.

I quite easily remember the fact that I had eaten very little for the twenty-four hours before landing and had been very sick whilst crossing, but when our LCT beached at last — after some hesitation about getting ashore as the LCT next to us rammed us after being hit by shells from the shore – the weakness and sickness just disappeared and no further thought was given to it. I don't remember much about getting off the beach after being pinned down for a while, but it felt better to be on terra firma again and walking on the road, although Jerry was still pelting us with shells and other fire. This wasn't for long, it seemed, once we started moving in.

Though the weather was foul, it was an impressive and confidence-giving sight to see the huge armada crossing the Channel. By afternoon another sight was the further gliders and Airborne troops landing near the River Orne. I was surprised to see part of the German Army consisted of Poles and that their transport included horse-carts.

*

From Mr R. F. Ellis, ex-246th Field Company RE, 3rd Division
I think we were all apprehensive as to what was going to happen when the landing craft ramp came down, I think most of us expected machine-gun fire to meet us. Although time was immaterial to us, it may have been around 6.30 a.m When the ramp came down – we never got our feet wet – we saw the first wave (South Lancashires) just clearing the road which ran parallel to the beaches. All we met was the odd hand-grenade, mortar or sniper. I understand that later arrivals, that is thirty minutes or so later, had a tougher time when the enemy mortars had ranged up on the beaches, by that time the village of Colleville had fallen and we were attacking the platoon objective 'Hillman'. Prisoners were already being shepherded back to the beaches and the local people who greeted us appeared to be under the impression that it was just another raid and not the real thing. I suppose we all felt a certain amount of fear at the time but we were all too busy to realise it. There was certainly no humour before or after the landing; everybody was deadly serious and we kept our thoughts to ourselves.

As I said before, time was immaterial, so I have no idea how long it took to take 'Hillman'. I remember the three of us, Engineers, were called in to clear a path through the minefield surrounding the strongpoint. I recall one of our chaps being hit and being trapped by Spandau m.g. fire with the bullets ricocheting off a small mound that I was lucky enough to fall behind. (In peace-time I suppose they call it field-craft.) Eventually I taped a path through the minefield. As I withdrew I distinctly remember the perspiration running from my head and the terrible dryness of mouth and throat – once again, was it fear? If it was, I was too busy to think about it until afterwards. I must say I experienced more fear sitting in a foxhole when shells were falling, simply because I had nothing to do.

I should point out that, because we worked as two- and three-man teams being attached to various platoons of the South Lancs and Suffolk Regiments in the bridgehead, we saw action on all the Sword fronts, including mine-laying at night and night reconnaissance.

The days following the landing are hazy. I recall the Orne, Troarn, supplying the paras with water at St Aubin-sur-Mer, some of the later happenings. The first two or three days were spent consolidating our positions within the mile or so bridgehead. We were pleased to hear that famous divisions like the Polar Bear (49th) and Highland (51st) were landing on the second and third days, also the news that Montgomery had arrived; we then knew that the bridgehead was fairly secure.

I have condensed most of the actions. It is difficult when it comes to putting it down on paper, some actions will never be forgotten with every detail imprinted on one's mind. The unit suffered losses, with so much steel flying around casualties were inevitable. I still recall the names of close friends who never lived to see the outcome of their efforts.

*

From Mr W. J. Walsh, ex-Sapper RE

Coming up from below decks and looking out we saw land some four miles ahead. Of the conflict we saw very little at that range.

We received our instructions from the beach at last, or so we thought. As our craft inched its way forward, consternation ran wild again on the beach and some shell found its mark on ammunition. We received a command to turn about which we proceeded to do.

Looking out towards the west we saw what appeared to be the surfacing of dolphins or small whales and someone shouted out 'Shells'. These splashes grew uncomfortably near and a feeling of utter helplessness grew upon me. I felt it was time I made contact with my maker and I prayed that nothing would hit us.

We were prepared for mines from below. We knew we couldn't sink but if one of those shells hit us we were done for – with all this transport aboard it would have become a floating inferno. In training we had all been taken to the swimming baths and those of us who couldn't swim had lessons but, even so, with all our equipment, rifles, not to mention boots, how could we swim if we were driven off into the water? At last, however, miraculously spared, we had fresh instructions from the beach to come in and disembark. We jumped off and found ourselves in waist-high water but somehow managed to hold our firearms up to keep them dry. I have very little recollection of getting wet or of how long it took me to dry out. I had arrived safe, that was all that mattered. Our section scrambled up the beach, keeping to the areas marked out with white tape, as there could still be mines for the unwary.

The Germans, unlike wartime Britain, had not removed the road signs and I observed I was in Lion-sur-Mer. Forming up in some sort of order we then marched up a dusty road to the next village, Hermanville. We didn't know the extent of the bridgehead – we were, it seems, not far from the Airborne Division at Ouistreham and the Caen Canal.

*

From Lieutenant-Commander H. M. Irwin RNVR (Retd): a Naval Assault Group

I had command of nine Landing Craft Assault (Hedgerows) for the landing of King Beach Gold Area. These were the ordinary small Landing Craft Assault fitted with spigot bombs to blow up the beach obstacles before the Duplex Drive tanks touched down. The crew consisted of three ratings and one sub-lieutenant to each craft. At the time I was a lieutenant RNVR, having been in Atlantic convoys 1940, a Q ship after being sunk in 1941, a cruiser up in the Denmark Straits, the invasion of North Africa, Sicily and Salerno in Landing Craft.

Our Landing Craft were supposed to be towed across the Channel by Landing Craft Tanks or Landing Craft Flak (Anti-Aircraft). One of my craft of nine turned back after passing the Needles due to an obstruction to the propellers. Another was towed under during the night with loss through drowning of the whole crew. I always remember the officer, Sub-Lieutenant Knox, had bought a new kapok type life jacket whilst we wore service issue! Another craft with Sub-Lieutenant Ashton (an Australian who should have returned home but chose to stay on) was rammed off the beach. He and two others were drowned and their graves are in the Military Cemetery, Bayeux. This left me with six craft. In the area of my opposite number he did not get one craft to the beach.

It is all a long story. I made my own way after we were half-way across the Channel as my towing LCT fortunately had engine trouble. On my return to base in UK I found that the towing shackles were in a bad state and I am sure therefore I could have been towed under.

The sight of the enemy flak was a wonderful sight — we were wet through, no food — and we knew then that land, even though enemy-held, was on the horizon. We saw an aircraft shot down, it slowly dropped to earth in the darkness as if it were a balloon which had caught fire.

At dawn we passed the bombarding vessels (cruisers) and those not working the guns cheered us as we passed by. This was my moment of fear. I had seen blood shed at Salerno. Why had I volunteered for the job, etc etc.! Then we passed the destroyers and on towards the beach. At a given moment we proceeded ahead of the LCTs carrying the flail tanks 'AVREs'. The DD tanks were not to go on their own.

The army were taking off the camouflage netting. A few shells fell near us but I wondered if they were our own fall shorts.

The beach appeared ahead. The sky was cloudy and the sea rough. Our bombardment was coming down from the hinterland to the beach. Ashton was rammed. I closed the steel hatch and then, when a few yards from the beach, I worked the ripple switch. Our bombs went off with a terrific bang ahead. Two bombs remained in the craft. Hard aport and the LCT beached. The first tank moved out. Amazing, unbelievable, not a shot fired! All was quiet for a minute or two — nobody on the beach but one tank. An explosion as the water-proofing was disposed of. Her flails started. Then black smoke came from the tank as she was hit and it caught fire. This was H − 1 minute.

Our job was placing sticky bombs on top of Teller mines on top of beach obstacles. We were hit by tracer from a gun emplacement manned by Poles under German orders. An LCE came up and blew it up. (I have pictures of this which I took with my camera.)

The East Yorks landed and rushed up the beach. We were 150 yards away and saw it all. One man wounded. Just like a rabbit, up, down, up and crawled to the sea wall. The Germans on top of the sea wall were chucking hand grenades over the wall on to the soldiers (ours) below.

The tide came up. We could do no more. We turned seawards. It took us about three hours to cover a distance of approximately four to five miles, to be lifted on to a specific large LSI (Landing Ship Infantry). In this time we lost two more craft but no loss of life.

From Mr G. C. Brown (SBCPO (M) Retd)

As a SPCPO in charge of a party of twenty-seven, including sick berth staff, seamen and Royal Marines, I had been drafted from RNB Chatham to one of the LST craft lying off Gosport. The cabin I shared with the coxswain had two holes in its bulkhead where two 88-mm shells had passed through on a similar assault at Salerno, following the victory in North Africa. Does lightning strike in the same place twice?

After several postponements waiting for the better weather conditions, we finally set sail in the early hours of 6th June with a contingent of REME, together with their various vehicles and equipment, and towing part of the Rhino ferry for the Mulberry Harbour.

In charge of the medical party was a surgeon lieutenant-commander RN and there were two surgeon lieutenants. The tank space bulkheads were lined, in two tiers, with narrow stretcher supports. At the port side aft of the tank space a canvas screened 'operating theatre' was erected and medical stores placed in several crates were easily available at strategic points in the tank space. These arrangements were made after the tank space had been evacuated.

As we made a slow 10 knots across the Channel, aircraft roared overhead and excited tension mounted. I had several requests from soldiers for 'sea-sick' tablets and queries as to how violent our landing would be when we ran on to the beach. One soldier asked me for cigarettes, and for a tin of 50 Players gave me a battledress which I still use for painting.

As it became lighter one could see we were but one of a huge armada of ships of many kinds which stretched as far as the eye could see. Near the coast we passed a battleship and, further inshore, others firing salvos over our heads, screeching and whining, into the French coast; several screamed back at us from the coast.

Our destination proved to be Arromanches in the Juno sector and as we glided gently on to the beach I saw for the first time one of our miniature submarines, manned by two men, surface almost alongside the LST.

The second wave of the assault had landed. As soon as the ramp was lowered, vehicles and troops moved off ashore. This proved to be the signal for the enemy occupying houses along the promenade to open fire and in reply a nearby ship armed with rocket launchers opened up; the result was devastating and the enemy fire was silenced.

There were isolated instances of enemy attack by shells and dive bombers and we did sustain slight damage. A couple of bombers dived into the beach to the west of us. Later, during a quieter period, the Surgeon Lieutenant Commander suggested I accompany him to the nearest information post and we made our way there through the white-taped safety lane which had been cleared of mines. I learned later that the object of this trip was to suggest that casualties be directed to our LST.

About 6 pm there was the increasing roar of approaching aircraft and from the west of us we saw sweeping inshore and wheeling along the coastline towards us the 6th Airborne Division in Wellington bombers of the RAF, some towing gliders. They advanced across our bows and flew on just to the west of Caen, where they turned inland and released their gliders. Others proceeded to bomb the Caen area and the enemy put up a block barrage over Caen which looked like a large black brick in the sky as the shells exploded. We watched anxiously and saw all too many aircraft at first trailing just a thin wisp of smoke, which increased as many of them turned inshore again to crash in flames. One or two came down in the sea around us and we did have a few RAF crew aboard who were picked up.

In the early hours of D2, 7th June, I was awakened and informed that casualties were coming aboard, and all hands were on the tank space to receive them. The amphibious craft transporting them came up the ramp and into the tank space to unload.

I remember that when I was taking a nominal list, one of the first I spoke to was an Army padre. He seemed pleased when I asked his religion – for the record. Another I remember was a senior officer of a famous northern regiment who came aboard carrying a sten gun and a black and white rabbit in his arms. He was most distressed at the large number of casualties his men sustained during their assault on Caen, which had been expected to fall on the first day.

We finally collected 364 casualties, 144 were on the racks around the bulkheads, other stretcher cases were roped together on the tank space deck, to avoid pitch and roll. The remainder were walking wounded, including civilian women and children and a few POWs – one blond youth I recall was very pleased to be aboard.

The surgeons operated for fourteen hours. One soldier had a foot amputated, but mostly treatment was a matter of wound toilet, apart from the more unfortunate requiring major surgery. All had to be documented and labelled with details of treatment given, morphia etc., and whether fit to travel to a distant hospital. Some time that night we commenced the return trip to Gosport, where the Army took over.

I had collected a number of guns, hand grenades and ammunition, and amongst them was the sten gun of the officer with the rabbit. There was a telescopic sight attached to his gun and before he would leave the ship he demanded his gun. I found the gun, but the telescopic sight was missing! However, on instructions from the First Lieutenant, the sight was uncovered and the officer with gun and rabbit proceeded ashore.

We had one death, that of a RAMC corporal.

After unloading, my first job was to order stores to replenish stocks in preparation for our next trip to the beaches. But before that however the ship was put alongside and a hole in the ship's side, which we had collected during the dive bombing, was repaired with cement packed inside a wooden frame built around the hole inboard.

Whilst this was going on, I heard what I thought to be an electric drill being operated on the damaged hull. It turned out to be a V2 flying bomb – another first for me – and the end of D Day plus one.

*

An account sent with an indecipherable signature, and no address
On the 3rd or 4th June the 4th Commando rejoined us and settled in their messdeck. By this time we were well acquainted with each other and good friends. As you know, there was a delay of twenty-four hours due to bad weather, so that it wasn't until the night of the 5th that we were briefed on the task before us. This was very thorough, complete with photos of the defences etc.

The average age of the boats' crews was about twenty, all of us were experienced in the handling of small landing craft and felt more at home on them than on dry land. We all realised that this was the greatest adventure of all and were very keen, so much so that money was offered by those not chosen for crew to obtain a place.

At about 6 a.m. the *Astrid* anchored about 9 miles to the north of Ouistreham, at the mouth of the Orne. We took aboard about thirty soldiers each and were lowered into a very heavy sea. A flat-bottomed LCA was not a good craft to be in when the weather was rough. However, with a following sea we didn't anticipate any difficulty. Our emotions by this time were confused, to say the least. We were scared, have no doubt about it, but overlaid on that was a feeling of awe at the sights and sounds around us. We went through lines of heavy cruisers which were sending their shells whistling over the top of us. Above were 500 Lancaster bombers which were dropping their loads on the defences. Rocket ships were discharging hundreds of anti-personnel missiles. Before us was what appeared to me one long volcano stretching along the coast to the west as far as the eye could see.

At a given signal we altered formation and our eight boats went into line abreast and we went for the shore. At that time the bombardment slackened and the smoke cleared. It was low water and we could see thousands of stakes in the shallows each with a mine on top. As was to be expected the waves became shorter in length and greater in height and it was obvious that landing would be difficult. After the bombardment we had not expected much opposition.

I should explain that we were not the first 'wave' in. That dubious honour had gone to a few LCTs carrying special heavily armoured tanks and beach clearing parties who were supposed to deactivate the mines. As far as I could see they had only limited success and they were all knocked out and burning. The Germans were very brave and somehow or other had survived. They opened up with machine-guns, quick-firing mortars and 88-mm guns. We made a bad landing and ended up resting against one of the mine-tipped stakes, which obviously didn't go off. We lowered the small ramp in the bows and the soldiers made a run for it.

We considered we had discharged our responsibility to them and turned our minds to saving our boat and ourselves. We went full astern and managed to disengage from the obstacle, turned about and headed back to the ship. This was by no means easy as we were now heading straight into the heavy seas. This was about 7.50 in the morning. We started taking water immediately. Our formation had been broken and each boat was on its own – shells, I believe from Le Havre direction, were landing all around.

We four crew members, all ratings, took it in turns to bale out, and we reduced speed to a minimum. We were helped by the presence of two bottles of Navy rum which we had not touched on the way in. When about a mile off the beach we came across one of our other boats which had been hit and was sinking. We tried towing her but that was useless, so we took our friends aboard and cast their boat adrift. This was a great help as we could now double our baling efforts, and they brought their own rum. We then slogged on to the north, baling and drinking, through this vast armada. It took us until 1300 hours to get back to the *Astrid*, eight boats left and five came back, and we didn't have a single casualty.

As for my impressions of that great day – we had seen the impossible on a scale that was unbelievable. And what do I feel now?

Sorrow that all those years of struggle and misery were for nothing, the fear that 1939 is not so far away.

*

From Mr S. J. Osborne
As the name implies, the LCFs were designed for action against dive bombers. The armament of LCF36 was four single barrel pom poms and ten oerlikon casemates. The oerlikons were later changed to twin guns and when all guns were in action the ship was a solid sheet of flame.

The LCF36 craft followed the first wave of troops in to the beach and fired whilst the troops ran up the beach. This was very successful and worked according to plan.

The LCF also had to form the inshore part of the 'Trout' line with LCSs, LCGs, destroyers, gun boats and motor launches which acted as rescue craft. This 'Trout' line was formed to keep the enemy from the anchorage and to deal with the V weapons. We got very used to this owing to our heavy armament. We had not been told about the ships being very top heavy which, no doubt, was the cause of the high casualty rate. They would turn over very easily after a hit, trapping most personnel underneath.

The original plan was to act as AA ships against dive bombers, but this was only effected for one or two days, at the actual invasion of the beaches. Then all ships, including the AA ships which were specially detailed to protect the headquarters ship – the converted *Bulolo* – were forbidden to fire at aircraft. As a result *Bulolo* was attacked by dive bombers – FW190s I think – and I saw the bridge set on fire. This was extinguished by the crew.

Signalling: All the war we were issued with code books with weighted covers etc. and forbidden to use the radio except in dire emergency. At the invasion, however, the radio was used several times a day and only plain language was used. Black light signalling was used (infra red was highly secret in those days and never used by us).

Food: American K rations were issued. These were very good and contained chocolate, boiled sweets and cigarettes, as well as food. The odd thing was that everyone went white as sheets after living on them for a long time. I recall that even *rotten* vegetables were craved for.

Shelling, of which we had a good bit, did not trouble us much as the shells which missed, in our case, landing in the sea with a harmless plop. The small arms fire from the enemy on the shore made a noise like angry wasps and caused us to worry very much.

The actual assault was easy as we had done our working up at Cruden Bay, being based at Invergordon under bad conditions. So the real thing was not too bad. During the latter part of the invasion when the ship was part of the Trout Line the personnel were frightened at first but after having got out of a few difficult situations the officers and ship's company became a very efficient fighting machine and, I think, enjoyed their task. The reaction came later.

We were able to destroy a good few V weapons during the nights.

Great confidence was instilled in all by the false start. In this the confusion was so great you could have walked from the Isle of Wight to the mainland on solid ships. We thought if the enemy missed this golden opportunity to bomb us, which they did, they never could or would.

During the gale which blew for about a week following the initial landing, about which little was said, I recall a destroyer drifting into the Mulberry harbour with engines stopped and becoming a wreck on the beach and no one taking any notice. During this time the Channel seemed to be littered with ships drifting up and down with the tide like paper bags.

*

From Mr R. J. Mellen, former AVRE Operator, 82 Assault Squadron RE

Our tank, a Churchill AVRE, with two others, an armoured bulldozer and a flail tank, loaded on a LCT, left Southampton at 2000 hours on Sunday, 4th June. As a Hampshire man I knew the coastline well. We passed well-known landmarks, the tower at Lee-on-Solent, Portsmouth Harbour, the War Memorial at Southsea and, as it grew darker, the cliffs at Beachy Head. A group of us stood at the side of what was no more than a flat-bottomed barge. We were very quiet, thinking should we ever see England again?

We prepared to land at 0650 on 6th June on Jig Green beach near Le Hamel. Our tank had been waterproofed and was carrying a bridge. As the driver, I took it down the ramp into the sea. Most of us were suffering from sea sickness. We bottomed in about six feet of water, which meant my only way of seeing, via the periscope, was blocked by the sea water. I seemed to drive for hours totally blind, although it was only a few seconds. Suddenly my periscope began to clear and I could see a sandy beach dotted with gun emplacements and tank traps. The roar of engines and the sound of exploding shells seemed insignificant now we were on dry land. There was a babble of shouts from the crew, my seasickness disappeared. We had arrived.

A few nights later we were holding one side of Caen airfield, with German troops on the other side. Tank crews had to have one man on duty ready to man the gun at all times. My 'stag' was around midnight. It was very dark, and I had wandered about fifty yards from the tank. I heard a plane overhead and, to my surprise, he dropped a parachute flare. This lit up the area brighter than day, which left me in a very exposed position. German machine-guns opened up, I have never been so afraid in my life. The time I took to get to the safety of the tank would, I am sure, have beaten any of the great sprinters of the past.

We were on reserve, parked under trees in a potato field. Each night the last man on guard had to dig a few roots of potatoes, to help our rations which were still the one day packet variety. Duty this night fell on our wireless operator. I was tank cook and when I woke I asked for the potatoes. The reply was, 'I dug up a whole row without finding one.' On looking I found he had gone to the far end of the field and dug up a row of 6-to 8-inches high runner beans.

*

From Mr V. J. Galliano
An individual's memory of his experiences as a participant and eye-witness of an aspect of the momentous happenings of the D Day landings in Normandy, must necessarily be of a sketchy nature. When recalling these events thirty-five years later, the sharpness of even the most vivid impressions is bound to have become somewhat blurred. It would have been easy to look up reference books to clarify points, but this seemed to be analogous to the touching up by another hand of an original drawing, thus losing its validity.

In the following notes therefore consideration has been given to the spontaneity of expressing whatever image remains, with the hope that enough facts emerge to make the re-telling worthwhile. Certainly no account of personal involvement can be seen in proper perspective without a brief mention of the preparation preceding D Day.

As a lecturer and trained member of a camouflage unit of 21st Army Group HQ, I was attached to No 9 Beach Group then being formed in a large camp in the vicinity of Winchester. There was much work to be done and arrangements were made immediately at top level for lectures to be given and practical field work to be carried out.

Everyone and everything in the camp seemed to buzz with life. It was a hive of purposeful activity coupled strangely with calm anticipation. At that time no one knew the date or place of the much discussed invasion. There were the inevitable rumours which everyone suspected of coming from the most secret and sensitive areas of the camp, but those fictional flutterings soon dispersed in the cold practicality of work and the busy atmosphere engendered from it.

Then quite suddenly I was summoned to a meeting. This had more than a whiff of utmost urgency about it. At once I met other members of a team with whom I was to work for the next few days under closest security; an armed guard in fact. We were to make a model of No 9 Beach Group landing area in Normandy. The 12 feet by 12 feet model had to be accurate, especially as the personnel of the various units were to be brief from it.

Liaison with the Navy, RAF reconnaissance and our Intelligence unit was essential. A mosaic of photographs from all angles came in plentiful supply. Up-to-the-minute information of enemy defences was readily available.

Nothing of course was provided for making the model, so our first task was to gather from around the camp the simple, almost primitive, materials required – wood, sand, paper, flour, wire – and it was a masterpiece of discretion and improvisation. When has the latter not been a *tour de force* of HM Forces? No elaborate description of the various artifices conjured up in the process of collecting this strange miscellany is either necessary or appropriate here. Suffice it to say that our purpose was eventually achieved without a whisper of a leakage of the information then available to us, in spite of much vigorous probing and persistent questioning from the more suspicious individuals whose assistance we solicited.

Returning overladen – for our fatigue party was a small one – with what must have appeared to be a most incongruous assortment of articles, to the place of our first rendezvous, a hideous, badly-camouflaged hut, we were unceremoniously bundled into it and summarily told to get cracking. This segmental corrugation known as a Nissen hut was to be our living, sleeping, working and eating quarters – a virtual prison until the job was finished.

Already photographs and maps had been released. Naturally our immediate curiosity was to discover exactly where the landing area was to be. We had not long to wait. A map was produced with distinctive boundaries marked on it. These were the now well-known beach areas of Gold, Juno and Sword. Our particular concern was the stretch of beach at Ver-sur-mer, between Courseulles and Arromanches.

I remember well the outstanding landmarks, focal points of much importance, in the first photographs I saw of the locality. I have only a vague recollection of their exact siting. There was the pale-toned ribbon of road, leading at right angles from the coastline and up a slight incline with fields on one side and a copse to the right, as it was seen from the sea. The white silhouette of the lighthouse, the pink walls of a château near the beach and several concrete monstrosities, obvious gun emplacements, one of which was enormous. All of these could be taken in at a glance.

Eventually, with the aid of excellent close-up photographs of various details, the model was finished and the personnel of all units of the Beach Group was briefed for their hazardous adventure of storming the beaches, always provided the extremely uncertain and risky business of the Channel crossing was accomplished.

News then came of the approximate date of D Day and from thence onwards there was a mass movement of troops seemingly in every type of vehicle imaginable, in a patchwork of convoys to Southampton where, to be brief, we embarked.

Here I must refer to what surely was a most unusual, if not unique, experience. Once installed down under on the lower deck of an LST with its all American crew, I had some limited time to continue my work as a portraitist. I was not an official war artist, consequently there was no chance of serious painting over an extended period and I therefore seized every opportunity to sketch or draw, according to the time available.

No sooner had the members of the crew discovered an artist in their midst and one prepared to do a likeness, just for the slight frustration of sitting still for a time, than a queue began to form and took such formidable proportions one feared that essential posts in the ship were not being manned! Still a few portraits were done, evidently to the sitters' satisfaction, and I was assured that the drawings would be safely sent or taken home when the chance arose. I often wonder how many of those sketches reached their destination.

No such enthusiasm came from 'our' men, whose cultural interests if any, already dulled by the impending prospects, were utterly swamped by the stark reality of seasickness. This was evidenced by the ghastly pallor of faces which filed past the 'studio', seemingly in quick succession, to disappear silently into the dark recesses of the lower deck to find an outlet or some convenient spot from which to relieve their distress. I hesitate to offer an explanation for the procession, except a psychological one, as I felt no movement of the ship that I can recall which could give rise in itself to the acute ailment. Fortunately I am not subject to the complaint.

The significant moment for 'us' to weigh anchor was delayed for a couple of days, thus giving a breathing space and time for a few more sketches, a little personal satisfaction and even a limited joy.

Inevitably, however, the joy came abruptly to an end. Although below deck and having somewhat impaired hearing — certainly as a result of being an AA gunner during the blitz — I could hear the steady drone of what was quickly realised to be wave after wave of heavy aircraft, probably loaded bombers, throbbing their purposeful way through the night and morning of 5th and 6th June respectively. I waited. As there were no resounding cracks, crunches or ominous thumps, I guessed the planes were ours and heading south. Luckily the conjecture was correct. Still, it was action stations for the crew. At once I realised that 'This was it'.

Then a most incongruous thing happened: I dozed off. It must have been for quite some time because upon resuming consciousness I discovered we were on the move. I suppose for the first time in this context, my thoughts turned to submarines and torpedoes. Where was the enemy? When would the attack come? Would we get across? Without incident? Hardly to be credited! I wonder what it's like in the drink? How long would survivors be in the water? All these questions and more came flooding into my mind.

Surprisingly the crossing was without incident. That is, up to within a mile of the Normandy coast, by which time I was steadily hacking my way towards the upper-deck through dozens of equally active, well-armed, khaki-clad bodies in full kit. It was during the eager scramble for the light of day and fresh air that the familiar rumblings of distant gunfire broke through all other noises attending the movement of army personnel and its impedimenta.

On reaching the main deck I was sharply brought to a realisation of the extent, intensity and indeed ferocity of the bombardment from our warships covering the landings, which were already well advanced. At once I seized a vantage point from which I could get the best possible view. It was truly an astonishing sight. The sea was a mass of ships. My first reaction to this vast, well-nigh stupefying conglomeration, was its vulnerability to attack. It was soon evident however that the few pockets of resistance left behind by the enemy, because of the speedy thrust of our first assault, were of little consequence and would not impede our progress. The *Belfast* was pounding away over our heads and with the general softening up of enemy defences in our sector, it was not surprising that resistance was negligible.

Scanning the beaches with field glasses, I was astonished to observe the exact resemblance of the scene before me to the model we had made, in spite of the devastation wrought in the area by sustained bombings and naval guns, the conspicuous landmarks were undamaged. I saw too an occasional flash presumably from the 88 mm (spotted in the aerial photograph), now used as an anti-tank gun. The most horrific sight I witnessed was the action of one of our flamethrowers attacking a troublesome force occupying a small château adjacent to the beach. A couple of bursts from that fiery dragon sent the dwelling up in rolling volumes of smoke and flame. A few seconds later I could see through the gaps which were once windows a raging furnace within.

By this time we were getting near to the beach and ready to disembark. Flails were in operations and there was much evidence of their invaluable work. One of them had been knocked out and a few tanks, leaning like the Tower of Pisa, were lying helplessly crippled; there was no sign of their crews.

At last I got ashore and, contrary to expectations, made a dry landing. Thankful to have my feet on terra firma, I was careful to tread on previously made tracks until I joined a large contingent furiously digging in on the perimeter of the sandy beach, which was by then a relatively safe area. The process of entrenching was all too frequently interrupted by an ear-splitting blast of a whistle warning us to take cover before nearby mines on various obstructions were exploded by the pioneer corps.

Troops were pouring in: it was a human flood. Several remarks echoed my thoughts exactly, that with the necessary changes the scene resembled rush-hour at Piccadilly Circus. We observed this influx until dusk when we had to leave the beach, cross the coastal road and move to the cover of a small copse for the night. Here two of us found a convenient trench, poignantly reminiscent of a grave but affording speedy and welcome protection which ironically may well have saved our lives. Lying on my back at the bottom of the pit, tin hat covering my face, I tried to doze off but there wasn't a chance. Directly our fighters returned to base after dark the Jerry planes came out and at regular intervals throughout the night we were heavily strafed and from the sound of it the trees received the punishment!

In the middle of all this a message was sent round to the effect that if a Very light was seen (I forget the colour), everyone had to stand-to ready to repulse a counter-attack from a Panzer division. It is doubtful whether a vivid imagination is a good thing on such occasions and I failed to see what possible use I could be or what I would do if a Tiger tank suddenly loomed up and passed near or over our pit; a burial chamber in truth. Luckily, no attack was forthcoming. As if that wasn't enough, I received an order to go back to the beach and find our Jeep and driver. It was clear moonlight and, apart from the menace of air attack, there was a formidable section of enemy gunners on the other side of the copse about a hundred yards from our position and a number of snipers who had already given a good account of themselves. Add to these hazards that of the mined verges of the road which meant walking down the middle of it, making an excellent target, and the impossibility of finding anything like personal allocations on a beach swarming with men, equipment and vehicles; it seemed sheer lunacy to attempt the undertaking. I did not delay my return to the wood where, more by luck than judgement, I arrived unscathed at the same spot and speedily slid into my protective sanctuary.

Shortly after we received another severe drenching from machine-gun and cannon fire delivered at what must have been fairly low level. It sounded like a vicious hailstorm through the trees. I couldn't see the other chap and, as there was no sound or stir from his direction, I gathered he was either asleep, scared or dead. I decided on the most optimistic of these possibilities and it turned out to be the right one. It might seem odd that anyone could sleep under such circumstances, but it is well to remember that we had to snatch what sleep we could, when and where possible. I too managed something of a nap.

When I awoke it was daylight and as there was no chance of attack from enemy planes while our fighters were on the prowl, I, along with the rest of the company, ventured out from the bowels of the earth to prepare breakfast. I made the tea and was just about to enjoy it and some oatmeal heated up in a billy-can when a DUKW suddenly loomed up from apparently nowhere and, obviously out of control, headed straight in my direction, jerkily careered over my breakfast 'table', sending everything flying. Luckily I saw it in time to take evasive action, otherwise I would not have survived and the incident would probably have been officially recorded as 'Killed on

Active Service'. It was a near thing. The recalcitrant vehicle with its vital load of supplies was brought to a halt by the stubborn resistance of a tree-trunk nearby.

I soon had the water boiling again and in a rough and ready sort of way, somewhat more watchfully, got on with the first meal of the day.

I was not to remain in that wood. After another excursion to the beach, this time successful, the Jeep and driver being at the appointed place, we drove off for a short distance inland to a thickly planted orchard where a miniature earthwork was already being prepared by members of the pioneer corps. This was to be our *pied-à-terre* for some time to come.

It was our second day in Normandy and of course the beachhead was very vulnerable. Everyone was eagerly waiting for the heavy stuff to come in. I am sure others felt as I did, an inward relief and more secure to see large contingents of men, equipment and supplies coming in.

I selected my plot in this new refuge and then went on reconnaissance further inland where there were several jobs to be done. Among these was the concealment of a large number of dumps of petrol, vital supplies, deployed over a wide area on open ground; they were sitting targets. To my knowledge none of these was ever destroyed either by raids or sabotage. It is tempting to think that this was the direct result of our unit's conscientious activity rather than the enemy's inactivity; I shall never know.

Certainly German fighter aircraft were conspicuously active at night and regularly sprayed the orchard and other similar places of natural cover with machine-gun fire. Sleep was difficult under these circumstances, but I managed to nod occasionally. During the many less somnolent periods I was aware of the poor chap next to me who was shaking like a leaf in a stiff breeze. There was nothing I could do. I thought the fellow far more intelligent than I and that he fully realised the true danger of the situation. A few days later he was so ill that he had to return to Blighty. I never saw him again.

There were day raids too but these were rare because of Allied air vigilance. On one occasion, I had just returned from a slightly hazardous journey, when I had a front-row view of a Republic Thunderbolt in hot pursuit of an Me109, practically at tree-top height. Both of them were going all out, firing their guns and, as they passed overhead, they banked steeply and I caught a glimpse of the pilots' heads. I tried to imagine the expression on their faces. Far

1. *Feldmarschall* Erwin Rommel visits a newly constructed gun battery, a part of the Atlantic Wall defences, in 1944.

2. Beach obstructions being constructed on the French coastline. Note the *Tellermine* secured to the post.

3. German gun crew manning a captured French 75 mm gun on the coast at Fécamp.

4. German workers working on Normandy Beach defences scatter as an Allied photo reconnaissance aircraft makes a low level pass.

4. Supreme Commander, General Eisenhower, poses in front of a map of Europe. With him is Air Chief Marshal Dowding, Air Chief Marshal Tedder and General Montgomery.

5. Landing craft are loaded up for the cross Channel trip to Normandy.

6. American GIs embark on a transport in Devon.

7. Boston bombers set off to 'soften up' the coastal defences.

8. The Supreme Commander, General Eisenhower, visits men of the 101st Airborne 'Screaming Eagles' just prior to them taking off to be dropped on the right flank of the landing beaches.

9. Major General Gale gives some last minute instructions to British para-troops shortly before their departure to be dropped on the left flank.

10. Allied gliders landing in France.

11. Major John Howard's glider, at what would become known as 'Pegasus Bridge'. The Oxfordshire & Buckinghamshire Light Infantry were ordered to capture and then hold the bridge until relieved by Lord Lovatt's 1st Special Service Brigade.

12. American landing craft heading for UTAH Beach.

13. 1st Special Service Brigade, Commandos, landing on SWORD Beach. They were to relieve men of the 2nd Battalion Oxfordshire & Buckinghamshire Light Infantry who had landed by glider and captured the bridge over the Caen Canal.

14. Americans landing on OMAHA under heavy fire.

15 and 16. HMS *Ramillies* (top) and HMS *Rodney* (above) were among the Allied warships providing a powerful bombarding force in support of the landings.

17. British infantry moving off the beach.

18. German prisoners are gathered on the beaches for shipping to England.

19. 'Mulberry' Harbour off the coast at Arromanches. Sections of this temporary harbour are still in existence today after sixty years of battering by the sea.

20. Sherman belonging to 13/18th Hussars at the airlanding fields.

21. Rocket firing Typhoons operating from a field in Normandy.

22. A violent storm from 19 to 22 June wrecked the American 'Mulberry' off OMAHA. As a result the damaged British 'Mulberry' at Arromanches had to handle twice the amount of traffic.

23. Allied bombers attacked German strongpoints around Caen.

24. German troops man their field gun position on the cliffs above Arromanches.

25. After the invasion the same position in the hands of the Hampshire Regiment.

26. A lull in the battle at Audrieu and a Tommy plays a game of Solitaire, watched over by his pal.

27. A 5.5 inch gun in action at Audrieu.

28. An unofficial photograph. Winston Churchill with Brigadier Calvert-Jones at C Troop OP, Point 103, 21 July 1944. This was Churchill's first personal view of the enemy in World War II. He is watching an artillery concentration fall upon the Germans along the Tilly Villers Bocage Road.

29. 0700 hours at the OP. But not very peaceful. Five minutes later they were being sniped at. During the day they were frequently mortared and the Troop Commander was killed.

30. Soldiers of the Hampshires have just entered Arromanches (see page 282) and are being served Calvados. Mme Bernadette de Renouf whose reflections appear on page 280-4 is standing behind the Frenchman's right shoulder.

31. The grave of Captain R. J. Crofts in Bayeux cemetery. When his tank approached a gate he said, 'A farmer's son should open gates not break them'. He jumped down and opened the gate but in doing so stepped on a mine and was killed.

clearer were their planes' markings and camouflage. I had hoped to see the all too familiar symbol of evil now, the swastika on the fin, being justifiably torn to shreds by machine-gun fire, but up to that point there was no such luck. Most of the men who were variously busy around the orchard during this sudden aerial intrusion speedily dived for cover, others mysteriously vanished. In truth it was a bit too close for comfort. Still, fascinated by the drama of the combat and whether I would see its end, I became rooted to the spot. Of course the planes had gone almost as soon as they were seen, with no more ado for the casual observer than a disturbing roar and a few enigmatic puffs of smoke. I overheard one derogatory remark about my apparent foolhardiness. It would however have been useless to explain to the gentleman concerned – for the irreverence was shared with a small coterie which had subsequently assembled nearby – that my absorbing interest in this encounter was the result of a familiarity and knowledge of aircraft developed as an instructor at an aircraft recognition school for the three Services and by being the co-author of a book on aircraft recognition. I therefore felt some justification for the so-called rashness. Instinctively I knew that the angle at which the planes were flying, quite apart from their preoccupation with each other, ensured that there was no way their fire would affect us directly. Even the chance of a ricocheting bullet was extremely remote in that setting. Risky? All things being considered, that was laughable. Still, I said nothing.

Pockets of resistance were still holding out against persistent attacks. The one nearest our original position in the copse was giving most trouble and we were constantly kept on the alert for the odd sniper or stray patrol. Many rumours circulated of shots being fired at our men as they went about their work, but certainly I had not heard any desultory firing from that area nor had I seen a German soldier since landing.

This anomaly however was soon to be adjusted and with credit. Batches of prisoners started to arrive from the various sectors of the front and walked in very disorderly, almost slovenly columns, remnants which expressed defeat in every step and difficult to reconcile with a once proud, disciplined and indomitable army of the Third Reich as publicised in all the media for the world to see and, indeed, for some of the world to experience. I noticed with surprise that scattered in an arbitrary fashion among the captives were a large number of extremely young lads who were no doubt as disillusioned as the rest of the men, but manifestly more aggressive and impudent

than their true situation warranted. As they trudged along the dusty
road in the heat of the mid-day sun, I suppose they gave no thought
to the fact that they were lucky to be alive and uninjured.

The next few days went by rather more slowly than the preceding
ones, or so it seemed, but we were by no means complacent. I had
time for a few sketches which I hoped to develop later. These studies
were not records of the general scene but wholly symbolic and concerned man as formed of the clay which was at once his strength and
his weakness. None of these sketches was satisfactory, consequently I
destroyed them. Of the portraits done at this time, some possibly
survived. One of these stands out in my memory. It was of a sergeant
of the Pioneer Corps, who had prepared one large earth dwelling and
was sharing it with us and some of his men. In one of his rare free
moments which coincided with one of mine, he sat for his portrait.
He seemed well pleased with it and asked me to send it to his wife
if anything happened to him; a wise precaution as he was doing an
extremely dangerous job, that of clearing minefields. Certainly, it
seems that he had a premonition, for he was killed the next day. I
carried out his request and sent the portrait to his home, but I have
no idea whether it ever arrived.

An excursion to Carpiquet village and airfield was unpleasantly
memorable. The small, now hollow buildings that had once formed
the village were practically reduced to rubble and every footstep I
took raised a white dust cloud that covered boots and uniform, a
glance at which recalled the appearance of an industrious miller's
outfit at the end of a busy day at the mill. The sickly sweetish stench
of corpses pervaded the air and as I passed another heap of masonry
I expected to see one or more bodies rotting in the hot sun; I did not
see one anywhere in that place. In a sense this unfulfilled expectation
made the situation even more eerie. Mortar shells were still exploding
at intervals in the immediate vicinity, so I considered that a hasty
exit was expedient and I decided to leave that crumbled relic and
with it the death-charged atmosphere it engendered.

On my way back to the orchard I witnessed several dogfights at a
fairly high altitude. As the planes dived, climbed and rolled, it was
quite impossible to distinguish one from another without field glasses
which I did not have with me on that occasion. I saw also a dump
of khaki equipment cast aside under the trees just off the road. It
was topped by bullet-holed steel helmets with blood-soaked chinstraps
– a gruesome and gory sight.

It would be inconsistent with a generally optimistic outlook, stemming from a Christian philosophy, to end these notes with anything but a quite uplifting experience. First it is necessary to point out that although there had been a steady influx of troops, equipment and stores to and through the beachhead, it was still vulnerable to a sustained massive counter-attack by an opposition comprising many divisions which were known to be building up in the area. Every new British contingent then arriving was an additional source of encouragement and security. Usually these troops came and went by our position quietly with no more than a sympathetic glance or understanding nod from bystanders who happened to be there at the time. There was, however, one exception.

I was working with a small group of volunteers on the concealment of a relatively large carport at HQ, when I heard the distant but distinct sound of a bagpipe. At the sound grew in volume it became obvious that although the piper had not yet come into view he must be on the road which led from the beach and passed our HQ. The penetrating tone of the pipe got nearer and nearer and, as it approached our HQ, a number of the personnel came from the building along with other sundry individuals from around the precincts, to see what was going on. Soon I sighted the piper leading what eventually turned out to be platoon after platoon of infantrymen in two widely spaced files marching in broken step. Whether or not it was the custom of that particular regiment to march with a single piper in full throttle, as it were, I have no idea, but the reaction of those who heard him was readily manifest by letting forth a great cheer as he went by.

I could not attempt to describe the full effect the sound of that pipe had on me but certainly it was as stirring as it was a most unusual experience.

Just as the Union Flag, Regimental Colours and the Drum have far reaching power and meaning as symbols, so the Bagpipe is all important too as a symbol. It was a symbol of the cause to overcome an evil that I saw and heard the pipe that day.

CHAPTER FOUR

The Armoured Corps

Once the landings began men from a variety of different units scrambled, swam or drove ashore. It is therefore impossible to make a sequence of arrival. However, armoured units fit in neatly at this point. Many of these regiments are described somewhat puzzlingly – to ears unaccustomed to military terms and tradition – as cavalry. Cavalry no longer go to battle on horses but proudly retain (when possible) their former titles, such as dragoons, hussars, or lancers, although they have exactly the same tanks, weapons and tactics as their brothers in the Royal Tank Regiment. The latter are very well aware that they themselves were the pioneers of this type of warfare (as the Royal Tank Corps) but the cavalry feel that their particular tradition of dash and vivacity make them pre-eminently suited to it also. The only rivalry which exists between cavalry regiment and tank regiment then is the very healthy one of efficiency.

Many of the cavalry units in the forefront of the battle were not regular units at all but territorial forces which in peacetime had attracted lively young men with a fondness for horses and an interest in military skills. When war came these units were mechanised for a variety of purposes. Some were equipped with tanks, others were converted to signals or artillery. However, they keenly preserved their former designation and were the yeomanry, the rangers or the dragoons of their individual tradition. The standard of recruit in these voluntary units was very high and moulded by enthusiastic training they were soon found to be supremely fitted for dangerous and difficult tasks. After the war, the survivors reverted to their peacetime tasks of estate agent, solicitor, farmer, etc. For example, the writer of the first account, who was then Captain B. W. G. Rose, was a musician and Fellow of an Oxford college who also happened to be a good horseman. During World War II he fought in the Western Desert, in the Italian Campaign (where he was wounded) and landed on D Day. After the war he returned to Oxford and his College Fellowship and has continued a very successful musical career. Like many others, he never talks about his part in the war and it was difficult to extract any memories from him. Such men regarded the war as an interruption in their normal career to which they returned when the task of winning it had been completed.

Readers will note a somewhat lighthearted note in some of these accounts. It was just as well to be lighthearted if you were in a tank. It was noisy, hot, uncomfortable and, as you were surrounded on all sides by high-explosive, your fate if the tank was 'knocked out' was probably to be fried to death.

*

From Dr B. W. G. Rose, OBE, MA, DMus, FRCO

Alas, by now my memories are pretty vague, but the first thing which comes to mind is the mixture of Bostic and contraceptives! Once we arrived in our concentration area by the river Orwell near Harwich the mucky business of waterproofing all our vehicles began, and some bright chap suggested that the most effective way of waterproofing the injectors in our tank engines was the *capote anglaise*.* The manufacturers of these objects must have been mightily surprised by the sudden and great demand for these things! In the tank park, day after day, we became covered in Bostic – everything and everybody smelt of Bostic, and at the end of the day came the awful business of trying to remove Bostic from oneself and one's clothing. I suppose this was good psychology, because when the day came to drive the vehicles on to the landing craft we were delighted. As adjutant of the regiment I was particularly pleased to have a bonfire of the loads of bumf which an operation of this magnitude and complexity had necessitated.

Well, the great armada eventually moved slowly southward, and we could see the booms on either side which had been laid by the Navy and through which the minesweepers had cleared the passage. It will be remembered that the weather was not ideal, and General Eisenhower had to make the awesome decision of whether or not to call the whole thing off. The sea was choppy, and about half-way across our craft began to drift over to the port boom. Major Carr and I were on the bridge and, although rather alarmed by our proximity to the boom, were hesitant to mention this to the captain. Eventually however we had no alternative, but by then it was too late as the craft's screw was tangled up in the boom. The flap was on, and the captain,

*French letter.

instead of giving orders to his crew to go overboard and sort out the mess, whipped off his clothes and did the job himself! When we were eventually free we had the difficult job of finding the regiment, but this we did, so the next job was the landing. I will not bore you with the general picture because this is all documented in Andrew Graham's *Sharpshooters at War* but I must refer here to the skipper's promise that he would push the bows up on to the beach. Once a tank had been waterproofed one could not use the steering gear, as all the moving parts were sealed against sea water, hence it was vital that the craft should go full ahead. Alas, our skipper for all his confidence lost his way, and we finished up broadside! By dint of superb driving and patient control, our drivers managed to get all our tanks on to the beach.

When we could not break through Tilly-sur-Seulles, Montgomery sent the 4th CLY right through to Villers-Bocage where we were ambushed by the 12th Panzer Lehr Division. All the tanks of our leading squadron were destroyed by a couple of Tigers, and most of HQ suffered the same fate. Even Chester Wilmot (*Struggle for Europe*) has a paragraph on the last action of our tank because we fired point blank at the side of a Tiger at about 8-foot range with our Cromwell's 75-pounder and the shell bounced off the side. Soon afterwards we were hit by the Tiger with a very different result! After we had been captured we were able to see the place where our shot had landed – it had merely smoothed the rough surface of the hull.

That was D+5 and roughly the end of my war. It all seems centuries ago!

*

From Mr M. E. Mawson
In the 13/18 Royal Hussars our role was to learn the use of swimming tanks, based on set piece assault. We trained throughout 1943 in East Anglia, then at Gosport, and finally the north-east of Scotland, then back to Gosport for embarkation. The tactical training was extended, repetitive and dull, but a few weeks in Normandy soon made me realise that our then CO taught us most thoroughly, to say the least. I was also lucky inasmuch as while two sabre squadrons were run by officers who were, as far as I could see, prone to think of their rank and file more as marching and kit-inspecting material, my own asked the best of us, set a remarkable example, and left us to get on with our own duties.

To go back to technical training: this involved launching the vehicles from landing craft ramps – at which we became remarkably proficient in all seas, for which the vehicles had not been designed. To look today at their flimsy flotation structure in the museum at Bovington, it is hard to believe possible what was done with them.

One period of training was with a version of the Davis submarine escape apparatus – a fascinating saga. Originally we were seated in an old tank turret at the bottom of a deep pit and thousands of gallons of water were poured on top of us. We had just a few seconds to don apparatus and surface.

There was much need to experiment with tank stability because of the necessity of loading as much ammunition as possible, plus a variety of supplies to contribute to our well-being. I even had a small shelf welded in my turret for Penguin books. Waterproof pocket escape kits became the fashion and Admiral Ramsay (who commanded the whole show) had a brainwave that each tank should have an inflatable rubber dinghy – and to this I owe my D Day life, as I am a non-swimmer.

Day by day the Solent and Spithead became more tightly packed with vessels and the day came when I posted home my pyjamas, wondering if I would see them again. We were given our last outing before being sealed in our base. This was a highly emotional afternoon, which I remember well. There was not much in the shops, but everybody working in them in Gosport High Street seemed to know very well what was up and we could have carried away their entire stock for nothing. This was the only occasion I have ever had anything free from Woolworths!

Finally embarkation – like any other loading time save for the highly charged atmosphere. Then there was the long week-end wait for the 'off'. At least, as we were neatly tucked inside the boom, I was not sea-sick. This began after the start when I adopted my normal resigned horizontal position on the deck and just prayed for any sort of landfall because, strangely enough, the moment I was launched in the small swimming tank I was always fine. In the very early hours of D Day the Navy presented us with strong tea-cum-rum – we had known them a long time and I think they were quite worried over our immediate future. The question had been raised as to whether we would swim in a very rough sea or go in on the craft all the way. I still feel that our then CO (so soon himself to be killed) knew exactly what our feelings would be if we did not actually launch. It is incredible the trained confidence we had in nearly fifty tons of metal and explosives held just above the water surface by a mixture of canvas and pram struts. It was not misplaced – there were mishaps and casualties, but these did not come from faulty material or training. The code word 'Floater' was received with relief – it meant that we were to be in our own little maritime element.

The run-in over the last few miles was wonderful – nothing happening at all, except that as the light became stronger we could see the entire ocean was covered by lines of vessels, elbow to elbow and seemingly stretching back to the UK, and all rolling remorselessly along. Anything that faltered just had to be run down; due to slow speed one of our tanks was overtaken in the rough water and the occupant only survived because a rope was flung to him accurately from a passing ship when he was at his last gasp. I realise now that all this might that I was gazing at awe-struck was the last fling of the empire, before the intellectual know-it-alls dismembered it.

Then my personal environment began to be uncomfortable. Despite the solid curtain of British ammunition whizzing over us, we touched land, dropped our front screen and, I believe, let off a round or two, but the breakers from the fast incoming tide immediately swamped us. The water came up and reached the turret top just about the same time as we did. We threw out the inflatable dinghy, remembered to retain hold of the ripcord and to our joy, after an eternity, it swelled up and in we got in rather undignified haste. Mortar shells were plopping all around and in front were all the underwater devices with explosives on them, towards which we were drifting. We were using our helmets as balers. Around the obstacles were poor devils drowning as they tried to neutralise the booby-traps in the rough sea. Curiously enough, this rising tide saved me – it carried the dinghy right over the fused obstacles and on to the beach and also, I suppose, it had quenched the mortars, thus saving us from blast or splinters.

Once we were on the beach we covered the open ground very quickly, in spite of our wet and weak limbs. We reached the scrub at the top and here my memory fades. I know we found ourselves on the extreme left, near the Orne Canal and that just further east was a mined tank landing craft aground with a figure flat on the sand just by it. This proved to be a rating with one, or possibly two feet missing, but still conscious. As we had earlier taken heed of our ever canny young troop leader's advice to divide the contents of the first aid box among us, we had plenty of morphia syringes. So we gave him morphia – I hope with good effect – and then searched along the beach for succour. We got a stretcher with which we tottered back to the injured rating and here let me say that ever since I have regarded the toughest task in a war to be that of a stretcher-bearer. I shall never know how we managed to carry that rating between four of us, yet they did all this in just pairs.

By this time the immediate hornet's nest had quietened down – in fact I know now that the assault was well inland. The beach was crowded with later technical arrivals and follow-ups. We found a patch cleared of mines in the scrub, dug a trench and roofed it in with the anti-sea shields being thrown off by arriving Bren carriers, and settled down to await events. During the sunny late afternoon I walked right out over the beach left by the receded tide to one of our tanks which had not made it and got some tinned food. I passed the corpse of a member of my unit and recollected rather soberly how I had felt hard done by in the early hours.

*

From Mr R. Cadogan, FRICS
(The first part is an extract from a letter written to his mother shortly afterwards. Mr Cadogan says: 'I was then a shy and impressionable nineteen-year-old and reading it over now makes me wince! But I was brought up on the popular literature of the thirties – 'Boy's Own Paper', 'Greyfriars', etc., so perhaps the style is understandable!)

The shore was very near now – the first assault craft had touched down, and the infantry were storming the beaches as they had done so many times in practice on the shores of Scotland. Wonderful men, those infantry – to me they represent the finest fighting men in the world.

We made good progress, the tank behaving magnificently in a sea which would have daunted many a larger craft, leave alone a tank! Never in our wildest hopes had we thought it possible that they would stand up to such a sea.

By now, the shore was about two hundred yards away and some of the tanks had already touched down, deflating their canvases as they beached. We were close behind a tank which, beaching suddenly, had the misfortune to run on a mine. The canvas collapsed and water poured through a jagged hole in the canvas. The crew, as calmly as though they were on an exercise, climbed out on to the deck of another tank which had pulled alongside.

We were not so lucky. We beached, but by a stroke of ill luck we hit an anti-tank obstruction. The driver slammed it in reverse, and we backed a couple of yards, but too far. With our canvas already deflated, the sea just poured in, naturally stopping the engine. So there we were – finished – before even starting! Still, as our orders were to destroy any houses left standing in the village we just stayed put, and kept the gun firing. But soon the water was halfway up the inside of the turret, so we had no option but to 'bale out' on to the back of the tank.

We carried an inflatable dinghy with us, and we had relied on this for such an emergency. Needless to say, the shore was now about two hundred yards away. However we were to be sadly disillusioned. A piece of shrapnel had neatly taken the top off the oxygen bottle rendering it absolutely useless. This placed us in a very cheerful position!

We had one thing to fall back on – our rubber lifebelts. I must say none of us felt particularly cheerful and we little knew then that only three of us out of our crew of five were destined to reach the shore.

So there was nothing else for it but to abandon our tank, which was by now almost completely submerged. I don't think we fully realised the seriousness of the situation. Death was hovering very near, and men were being killed on the beaches which we were heading for.

I was obsessed with one thought – I must get to the shore alive! I was lucky, but our operator was never seen again. He was one of the many who paid the price of D Day. The driver was picked up and taken back to England more dead than alive. I managed to keep afloat and at last, to my great joy, my feet felt sand underfoot. I staggered out, just about all in, but I was alive . . .

Later on D Day, a friend and I procured a couple of bicycles and cycled down to the beach to see if anything could be salvaged from our wrecked tanks, which by now were high and dry on the beach with all kinds of flotsam – wrecked landing craft, guns, lifebelts, all kinds of things. It was quiet on the beach as the great mass of follow up craft had not yet arrived, but we didn't stay long as one had the prickly feeling that it would be shelled any time, and later it was. Riding back, near a crossroads, I came across the body of an infantry-man who had been killed that morning – his leg had been blown off and lay near his head covered with flies. I remember feeling quite sick at the sight, which unfortunately became commonplace in the days to come.

During the day I passed the survivors of tanks of the Staffordshire Yeomanry who had been blown up on a hill outside Hermanville. They passed like zombies with burnt uniforms and staring eyes, oblivious to their surroundings. At that time I had never seen anyone badly shocked before and their appearance and burnt hands and faces frightened me when I thought of the days ahead, going into action and perhaps suffering as they were.

Later in the day it became apparent that a number of men of the regiment had been killed or were missing in the landings and I think I realised for the first time that one could get killed or badly wounded – a singularly depressing thought!

Strangely enough this mood of despondency didn't last and one became excited at the thought of going into action after such a disastrous start to the day. The next day new tanks arrived and I joined a new crew. There was so much work to do refitting the tank that there was no time to think of other things.

Everything was still terribly unreal, and although we had lived out on exercises in the past it was still a novel experience to dig a hole in an orchard and climb into it to sleep. I did hear of a chap in another squadron who was injured by a cow who fell on him whilst digging his fox hole.

The smell of rotting animal flesh was appalling and as the weather grew hot again unburied German bodies stank too. I came across the body of a German soldier who had been killed by a wound in the neck which was crawling and heaving with maggots. Needless to say he was buried with rapidity.

We had casualties too, from sneak mortar attacks which would come without warning and kill or badly wound one's friends. Even then at the very beginning of the campaign it seemed that the odds were very heavily stacked against survival.

*

From Mr A. V. Tribble
At 5 a.m. not many of the tank crews of 'C' Squadron, 13th/18th Royal Hussars (Queen Mary's Own) on the tank landing craft were eating their breakfast of porridge, fried tinned sausages and tea, which was being cooked with difficulty in a sheltered part of the ship

free from the strong wind. This was due to sea-sickness which had turned their previously tanned faces to a shade of pale yellow. The tops of the waves of the grey-green sea were flecked with white, the overcast sky was a lighter grey and later the coastline of Normandy was seen, with some smoke rising as a result of the Naval bombardment prior to the landing.

As we approached nearer to the coast, more shipping activity was evident, with heavily laden troops clambering down the nets on the ships' sides into assault landing craft which were rising and falling dangerously in a heavy sea. Our friends in 'A' and 'B' Squadrons, who were in duplex drive swimming Sherman tanks, had been launched into the rough sea a considerable distance from the coast, and were going round in a circle before lining up for their final assault on the enemy-held beaches. At the rear, yellow flashes could be seen from the big guns of the Navy ranged on inland targets but these later subsided before the final assault of all the various types of landing craft.

We were approaching land faster now and the front ramp of the tank landing craft was lowered, making visible a small depth of sandy beach, it being high tide. Rolls of barbed wire had been laid against the partly grass covered sand dunes and beyond the open farm land commenced. There were no buildings nor any sign of Germans on this isolated flat part of the coast. Dull orange circular flashes, about the size of a football, surrounded by puffs of light grey smoke were visible in the air just six feet above the beach.

Soon, ten minutes after H-Hour, the beach was close enough for the first tank, commanded by Sergeant 'Dibs' Diver, later killed in Normandy, to go down the ramp and wade ashore in about five feet of rough sea. Along the shore were several other landing craft disgorging their tanks, there being nineteen in our squadron, and soon all the vessels were withdrawing from the beach, except the one next to us which had yellow flames and black smoke coming from the far side. No doubt it had hit an undersea Teller mine which had not been cleared earlier in the day by the frogmen.

To our surprise the beach was deserted without any signs of the military police in their Jeeps, as it had been planned that they would direct the tanks along the beach with signboards, indicating the safe exits through the coastal minefields, with the aid of large rolls of white tape. Major Sir D. Cotter DSO gave an order over the wireless for the two captains of 'HQ' Troop to move in their tanks along the beach in opposite directions, to find the exit. Soon it was located, a quarter of a mile westwards at the seaside village of Lion-sur-Mer where there was much activity with infantry and vehicles moving forward. A Churchill flail tank for mine clearing was burning furiously on the promenade and we saw our first Germans on the beach, in their long grey overcoats and full peaked caps, awaiting shipment to England as prisoners.

As we moved forward down a side street yellow flames were licking the open window and curtains of an upstairs room in a house, and the furniture inside was alight. Before long we came to the open country and all the squadron tanks were harboured in a large field where the first tea on land was brewed. The first objective had the code name 'Hillman', a German underground concrete command post with a fortress above ground, surrounded by mines, barbed wire and trenches. In the distance heads and shoulders of enemy troops, carrying wooden packing cases no doubt containing ammunition, could be seen passing along the trenches, but at this early stage we were not given permission to open fire at such long range and our own infantry were ahead. These troops were the Warwickshire Regiment of the 3rd Infantry Division, the late Field Marshal Lord Montgomery's regiment and old division.

We soon moved on again and for the next five hours supported the infantry by firing high explosive and machine gunning the enemy held position, until the Germans surrendered at four o'clock in the afternoon. There were many casualties on both sides but only one of our squadron tanks was knocked out of action. Many of the swimming tanks of 'A' and 'B' Squadrons were sunk in the heavy sea and some of the crews drowned.

*

From former Lieutenant Stuart Hills, MC, C Squadron, Sherwood Rangers
When dawn first broke we found ourselves rather disconcertingly in the lead, and apart from the other landing craft bearing the rest of the squadron there was not another ship in sight. However, as it became lighter, and vision clearer, we could see, over the very rough and very grey sea, hundreds of ships of every description.

As we closed in to the shore the larger ships came in closer from behind and we could see the infantry preparing to board the smaller craft in which they were to make the assault. At the same time the fighter bombers started to come over, and the Royal Navy opened up from behind. Every now and then there were terrific explosions from the shore which was soon a large haze of smoke and small fires and I remember so distinctly that I experienced the same 'stomach sensation' which I always used to suffer from before going in to bat.

It was now apparent that we were to launch from a short distance, and last minute preparations were taking place on board. There seemed to be very little opposition coming back from the shore at that time, except for a few odd shells which raised columns of water high in the air. When we were about a thousand yards out the landing craft bearing the flails came past us as it was their job to beach their tanks which were to make gaps in the beach mines for the infantry and ourselves. B Squadron, over on our right (under Major Hanson-Lawson) were up in line with us, and shortly afterwards I saw them drop their ramps. Major Stephen Mitchell's craft, which Bill Enderby and I were watching, never did, and later we learned that during the night their craft had collided with another, damaging its bows and ramp, so that they eventually had to beach. All I could hear over the air was some other station netting in and Stephen's furious cries of 'Get off the mucking air, I'm trying to fight a battle.' After a short consultation therefore, Captain Bill Enderby gave the order to move and we prepared to launch.

We were now about 700 yards from the shore and as the ramp was lowered I could see two of the flails brewing up just to my front, and I could not help wondering what had caused them to be knocked over and to catch fire and whether our tanks would meet the same fate when we reached the shore. However, the very intricate operation of launching my tank from the craft into the very unpleasantly choppy sea soon drove away any further speculation as to what would happen when we reached the shore – the immediate problem was holding all my attention.

We were just going down the ramp when I noticed that the hawsers weren't quite tight and this took several minutes to rectify. During this time I had to sit on the top of the ramp, a huge white target for any German gunner who liked to take pot luck. Sure enough the shots soon came, one on the side of the ramp and the other on our starboard beam, the latter wounding Sergeant Sidaway. Without more ado I gave my driver the order to go, and down the ramp we went. The screen was very flimsy in the rough sea and water poured in everywhere. I gave a few technical orders to try and save the day, but when I saw that things were hopeless, I gave the order to bale out. I can only imagine that the first shell which landed was our undoing and that it must have holed one of the bottom plates. Corporal Footitt pressed the button on our rubber dinghy which inflated automatically, and Trooper Kirman, the only non-swimmer, put it over the side. I scrambled inside the turret to get my map-case out, but we were going down so fast that I had no time to retrieve it, and in my haste to get out again I tore the headphones out of the set altogether. I followed Troopers Reddish and Storey over the side and a few seconds later our tank 'Bardin Collos' disappeared into the murky depths.

Even during those hectic and exacting moments I could not help wondering what Old Father Neptune would think about the sudden appearance of a tank on the sea bottom. My next feeling as is often the case when no one has been hurt, was one of annoyance at losing my kit, but it soon became evident to all of us that our position was not over-entrancing. We were now about 500 yards out, and by this time the German gunners seemed to have woken up a bit, and there was a certain amount of stuff flying about. Moreover there was a strong current running from west to east which we were unable to combat, our hands being the only means of propulsion. Our chances of reaching the shore therefore were about nil. The rubber dinghy was extremely small. We were wet and cramped – in fact the only hope was that we would be picked up. I looked back on our own landing craft and saw that things had developed rather badly there too. SSM Robson was sinking fast, likewise Sergeant Sidaway (I later discovered that owing to his wound he himself was unable to go and that Trooper Mitchell had taken over command – a highly commendable performance). I could see nothing of Captain Bill Enderby or Sergeant Saunders. They did, however, both eventually reach the shore where Captain Enderby was wounded.

Soon after we managed to hail an LCG which came over to pick us up, and we were bracketed by high-explosive as we climbed on board. The skipper moved away rather fast, but I noticed he had time to take our dinghy as well.

The Navy, as always, treated us magnificently, and we breakfasted on whisky and Mars bars – an admirable combination.

We were on deck the whole morning, running up and down close to the shore, firing a 6-pounder and twin oerlikons, so, at the end of the day, we did feel we had at least helped a little to speed up the landing, and by mid-afternoon everything was comparatively quiet. Darkness brought a few German bombers but they were met by a heavy concentration of ack-ack and very soon disappeared.

The next day was much calmer altogether and we were transported to another ship closer in shore. There I borrowed another dinghy and rather ignominiously invaded the Continent in that!

Certainly those responsible for morale and confidence had done a wonderful job in so far as the uninitiated-to-battle were concerned. As a youngster I had no doubts at all that we would succeed and may I give one example of over-confidence – bordering on stupidity – to illustrate this. Before launching my DD tank off the landing craft, knowing almost certainly – due to damage and the rough sea – that we would capsize and sink, I was confident enough not to don a Mae West and to think that, even in the event of our dinghy not inflating, I would be capable of 'swimming' the one non-swimmer in my crew to the shore some 700 yards away. In battledress, boots, gaiters, revolver etc. I would barely have covered ten yards on my own – much less assisting a non-swimmer as well. Fortunately, however, as described above, the dinghy did inflate under the hand of my battle-encrusted corporal who had fought with the regiment in the Middle East, so my overconfidence – stupidity – call it what you like, did not materialise.

I think the only explanation is that, because our training had made us supremely fit and supremely confident, degrees of common sense and elementary standards of safety went straight out of the window. A bit like the Charge of the Light Brigade perhaps – not bravery, just ignorance and stupidity.

One learned as one went along – if one was lucky enough to survive – but, in becoming more canny, perhaps one's edge was dulled and it was then that one needed to be brave! A change in one's outlook and feelings also came about with a sudden rush on the evening of D Day when news of casualties among one's friends started to come in. I suppose I grew up in the course of one day.

*

From Mrs A. Herbert-Smith
This is a verbatim account by my brother of his D Day landing. He was a corporal (I think) in a tank regiment. He was very reticent normally about his war experience, particularly about Alamein and later his entry into Belsen, but occasionally he would open up a bit and when I asked him about Normandy I took his account down in shorthand. Alas, he was an invalid from a year or so after the war finished and after years of pain and suffering, died two years ago.

After the Africa bit – we were in Alamein and never washed or had our clothes off for six weeks – God the stink!

The D Day business? Well, I was at Aldershot and one Saturday they gave us all our pay in French money. Ay, ay, we thought, something's up – all very hush-hush but it didn't need a genius to know where we were going. Top brass stupidity to imagine it could be kept quiet. They gave us ten bob each as well – we were supposed to buy cleaning stuff with it. Anyway, off we went to the pub in Aldershot and needless to say the ten bobs were soon gone. The French money they gave us was all new stuff with the French flag superimposed and on the back: 'Guaranteed by HM Government'. Well, I thought, no Froggie is going to accept this paper rubbish, so we flogged it all in the pub to the Aldershot civilians and drank the proceeds.

The next morning reveille was at 5 a.m. Believe me, there were some thick heads that morning. We knew that the balloon was about to go up, so we'd all had a booze up the night before. Off we set in our lumbering tanks up to London and they'd closed some of the roads through the middle of London. We rumbled on till we came to the Southend road and all stopped on the grass bit down the middle. We all had to strip off and put on special louse-resistant underwear – shabby and a bit smelly too – left over from 1918 probably. We spent a very uncomfortable night sleeping by the tanks and the next morning drove into the docks and then on to an MTB. There were dozens of them there and ours was crewed by Yanks. The front dropped down and the tanks bumped aboard. They fed us on board and we just hung around till a bit later when off we set down river. They gave us a barrage balloon to hook on to and there we were, just like kids with balloons at Henley Regatta, going down the river, each MTB with its balloon overhead. Out we steamed into the Thames Estuary and to my surprise we turned left. We slept that night in beds that let down from the walls (or superstructure or whatever) next to the tanks. It was pretty uncomfortable but I can sleep anywhere.

When we woke up in the morning there was green sea all round and was I bad! I only have to look at the water and I'm off, so I spent my time in bed. The next day – still sea all round and the third day. We all wondered where we were going. On the fourth morning our sergeant woke up and shouted, 'Land, land, I can see land.' So we all trundled up on deck and sure enough there were towering white cliffs in the distance.

'Bloody Norway again – must be after four days at sea.'

Can't be, I thought, tanks wouldn't be any use in Norway and we were a tank regiment. So, 'If that's not the bloody Isle of Wight, I'll eat my hat,' said I.

I was howled down – 'Four days to the IOW, don't be bloody daft.'

Then the unmistakable Needles appeared out of the early morning mist. 'Now who's daft?' I asked.

And, as the mist lifted, there we were, dozens of MTBs, some supporting corvettes and destroyers, going along a narrow, obviously mineswept path bordered by flags on each side. One of the MTBs had something wrong with its steering and was going round and round in circles. We left a corvette on guard duty and on we went. Talk about move! We went off like greyhounds at a terrific pace and in no time at all sighted the coast of what we now knew to be Normandy. It was unbelievable. In my naïvety I had thought our convoy was the only one but the sea was black with ships all making for the coast. From the coasts came bursts of fire. Our engines stopped some way out and they sounded the depth and we were hitched on to a chain and so we did the last bit on a pulley system. We could see blokes already on the beaches, tanks, guns, the lot, and the noise was indescribable. We went on but we grounded and even then had to wait till the tide receded so that we only had seven feet of water to get through. They opened the front and out we went, infantry and tanks, through the water.

They were already burying some poor buggers in the sand. Behind us our warships were letting fly with their enormous guns. God knows what they were aiming at. And do you know, one of the first things I saw was a Sherman tank with three bloody great holes through it. Crikey, I thought, so old Monty was having us on. He told us at Alamein that the gun hadn't been invented that could pierce a Sherman – well it certainly had now, as we could clearly see.

We went up that beach grinding slowly along in the sand, a target for the enormous Jerry guns we could see on top of the dunes. The infantry were suffering terrific casualties but we were urged on and on and gradually we overcame the opposition, taking some prisoners, and then looking around to see what was happening. It was impossible to see really – everywhere was sand, fumes, smoke and noise. It looked as if the Yanks on our left were getting a merciless pounding. We old Alamein sweats knew what to expect – they didn't.

The boss was a funny chap with a twisted sense of humour. We got on well as he came from Devon farming stock and I am a country man. Most of the kids were townies and were bloody hopeless when we had to make our way through the countryside, sleeping out under the stars and grabbing vegetables and extras where we could . . .

*

An extract from the diary of Major Tim Wheway MC, commander of C Squadron, 22nd Dragoons and of 'Timforce'

6th June 1944 D Day
Reveille 0500 hours. Troops all very sick and much to ill to feel excited. It was quite an effort to get them on their feet and none desired breakfast. Dry land dead or alive seemed to be all that mattered.

0630: HMS *Rodney* and accompanying cruisers, destroyers and rocket-ships open fire off French coast. Some rockets fall short and hit LCTs.

0700: We are looking for our gapping places through glasses. Houses on the sea front seem untouched by aircraft bombing and naval shells. There is an ominous yellow stillness the whole length of the shore. Enemy coastal batteries now open up on us, several LCTs are hit and we pass one destroyer sinking. The LSTs have now put down their LCAs and the infantry are heading for the shore in these, the seas are heavy and toss them about like corks. The noise is terrific.

0710: The DDs are floated, but owing to rough seas one by one they sink. We then realise it will depend on the flails to give the close support fire. We get into our tanks and seal down the hatches.

0720: The LCTs go full speed ahead and it is a race for the shore. We land at 0725 hours and the impact nearly shoots the tanks through the doors. The flails stream out in 3 feet of water, followed by the AVREs. We are met by terrific shell, mortar and 88 and 75 AP and small arms fire at 300 yards range. The LCT with our CO, Colonel Cox 5th ARE, is hit. Leading flail on the ship manages to get off but Corporal Brotherton is killed and crew wounded of the second and also Colonel Cox is killed. Several tanks are hit as the landing craft doors go down. Mines are sighted on top of the wooden beach obstacles. We go as far as possible in the water to be able to use our guns effectively and then open fire on concrete gun emplace-ments, houses and dug-in infantry. Tanks are brewing up right and left. We then proceed flailing our gaps, but no mines are encountered so speed up and get within fifty yards of our gapping places and open fire right into the slots of gun emplacements. One flail tank strikes a sunken obstacle with a mine on it and the bottom is blown in. Lieutenant Robertson's has a direct hit on the flail's arms, knocking them off. Lieutenant Allen has three 88 mm AP straight through into the turret and all but one of the crew are killed. Wounded and burnt personnel succeed in getting into the sea and are picked up by an LCA. Corporal Agnew's tank has three AP through the engine and brews up. Trooper Jennings is wounded in getting the driver's hatch undone. An 88 AP goes straight into the front of Sergeant Cochran's tank, killing the operator, Trooper Kemp, and wounding Sergeant Cochran and Trooper Mckinnon. Some flails now start gapping and the East Yorks and the South Lancs are now streaming up the beach covered by fire from the beach clearing flails. The AVREs follow the flails and the Bridging AVREs dropped their bridges, but the crews jump out to make them fast and in doing so are killed or wounded and the tanks receive direct hits and are brewed up. German soldiers rush from the houses shouting and firing as they come and soon the beach is strewn with the dead and wounded of our own and enemy troops.

The beach clearance flails are now waiting for the 629 REs to assist them in clearing the beach. Captain Wheway and Lieutenant Sadler get out of their tanks and attempt to contact them. Shells and mortars are falling thick and fast, but no one realises the danger of them until Trooper Hogg is killed by his tank. A lieutenant of 629 is eventually found and he states he is the only officer left and their casualties are so heavy they cannot assist us, so clearance flails proceed up the beach and commence gapping defences where they can to clear the congestion on the beach. Sergeant Turner and Corporal Aird returned to the beach after having successfully made their gaps and flailed their laterals, small arms and shell fire is still intense and both Sergeant Turner and Corporal Aird are killed by snipers' bullets. After two hours' fierce fighting enemy resistance is wiped out and the lanes are made and the laterals are clear and the surviving flails are back on the shore. We gather there between two houses where there are numerous weapon trenches and tunnels running under the houses and on searching these got twenty POWs, some from under the tanks.

$H + 3\frac{1}{2}$: 27th Armoured Brigade (two squadrons 13/28th, Staffs

Yeomanry) with Major Clifford and Captain Barraclough landed and also SPs, RAMC, and the Suffolks, Lincolns, RUR and KOSBs. The beach is now only 25 yards wide with high tide and the congestion is terrific and the flail crews were kept busy keeping the lanes clear and directing the landing troops on to the centre line. The whole area is still being heavily shelled and mortared from enemy positions two miles inland. By this time the armour is fighting its way forward with the infantry and at H + 5 the beaches are reasonably clear with the exception of burnt out tanks and wreckage.

Available flails are gathered together and proceed with the ERY and flail the assembly area. Only 11 out of 26 flails are fit to go on. We are then warned by Commando officer that 300 yards up the road is an anti-tank gun which has already knocked out 4 AVREs and that his company is withdrawing, having nearly been wiped out. It is impossible to get tanks into a position to get at this gun because of large minefields and houses. We then forked left through assembly area and contacted Brigadier Prior-Palmer (27 Armoured Brigade) to assist in going forward with the 13/18th to take over from the 6th Airborne on the Ouistreham Canal. This was not possible as fierce fighting was taking place round Hermanville and we were told to take up positions and be prepared to fight to the last. Snipers were very active and Spandau bursts from the left flank kept us well under cover. As dusk falls we go into close harbour with one company of Lincolns between us and the enemy on our right flank, the left flank being an unknown quantity. It was not until five days later the village on our right was cleared by 51st HD.

We hold a check on our casualties and find we have five tanks knocked out, five missing and five still on the beach under Lieutenant Mundy who was still being troubled with snipers and was attempting to get his tanks going again, some having assemblies blown off and some with tracks broken. That night they were heavily bombed by enemy aircraft and having set up A/A posts gave good account of themselves.

Killed = 9   Wounded = 8   Missing = 25.

Enemy guns knocked out = ten 75 & 88, two 50-mm.

General Rennie, 3rd British Division Commander, congratulated the flails on the magnificent show they had put up and stated that if it had not been for them he doubted if the landing would have succeeded on this strongly held front which was so vital to the whole operation, being the strongly fortified and held left flank. Meanwhile the AVREs had distinguished themselves and with eleven tanks of

79 Squadron succeeded in getting the bridge at Ouistreham. 77th Squadron also successfully battling forward with only four tanks left. Their casualties were extremely heavy, somewhere in the region of 70 per cent tanks, and 60 per cent personnel; they were extremely brave men.

June 7th 1944 D + 1:

News came through that our forces had captured the two large enemy strongpoints and also Colleville-sur-Orne and were moving on to St Aubin d'Arquenay. The Staffs Yeomanry making good progress and fighting hard on high ground above Plumetot.

Guide from 27th Armoured Brigade at 0230 hours guided us through Hermanville to Brigade Harbour. Crossed in front of enemy patrol as we turned into Hermanville but owing to darkness and not knowing whereabouts of own troops could not engage, Stood by under 27th Armoured Brigade as gun tanks. Only four flails still in action.

0800 hours: Lieutenant Sadler left to flail minefield in front of strong-point at Colleville-sur-Orne to rescue 13/18th tank.

0900 hours: Eight enemy Junkers bombed us, causing casualties in 13/18th HQ. Also sniping from church tower in Hermanville which we ranged our guns on and eventually blasted out.

1000 hours: Major Clifford, Captain Barraclough with five missing tanks and twenty-five missing personnel joined us, also one squadron of the Westminster Dragoons. The five tanks (commanders – Lieutenant Knapp, Sergeant Wood, Sergeant Johnson, Corporal Rains, Corporal Aplin) had successfully made their gaps and joined up with the Staffs Yeomanry and had been fighting all day and night with Major Clifford and Captain Barraclough and one squadron WDs. Lieutenant Knapp had one 75 AP through his jib on crossing the lateral on D Day.

The following are Major Wheway's additional recollections:
At about 10 a.m. on D Day Pat Sadler and I were searching a bistro on the road at the back of the sea front at Ouistreham, when a very smart and beautiful French girl came walking down the road, very self-possessed, smiled and said *'Bonjour, Messieurs.'* We were too dumbfounded to say anything but *'Bonjour, Madame,'* and she walked

on amidst all hell let loose, bombs, shells etc. quite unharmed and disappeared from sight.

Later, attached to 3rd RTR, I picked up two little French girls in the middle of the battlefield and put them in the bottom of my tank. They were about seven years old. After some two hours I saw a Red Cross ambulance returning from picking up wounded and luckily got them to take the children to safety.

*

From Major Peter Selerie, Sherwood Rangers Yeomanry
On beaching we solved the mystery of the black patches on the aerial photographs supplied by the RAF. They were boggy areas and already one or two tanks had fallen foul of them. I ordered the drivers to engage emergency low gear and we managed to negotiate this hazard.

There was quite a shambles on the beach. The flail tanks which were supposed to clear the main exit lane through the minefield had been knocked out. Fortunately, an extremely brave Sapper officer offered to clear a secondary lane manually. We gave him and his small party covering fire. Out of the squadron's nineteen original tanks, only five were still mobile and I ordered the first two, closely followed by the remaining three, down the lane. We were engaged by an anti-tank gun firing from a concrete casemate. He scored a hit on the leading tank, destroying the gun mantlet on the front of the turret. With all five tank guns however we managed to silence him. We then turned on to the road leading to Le Hamel. Pausing on the outskirts to check on enemy defences, we were overtaken by one of the AVRE Churchill tanks armed with a petard that looked like a short and very wicked piece of drainpipe sticking out of the turret. The sergeant in command said that he was the sole survivor of his troop and asked for instructions. I told him to follow our five tanks, remarking, as far as I remembered them, in the words of the Iron Duke – 'I don't know what effect you will have on the enemy, but by God you terrify me!'

When we entered Le Hamel it appeared that the main enemy fire was coming from a large tall many-storeyed house. I ordered the Churchill tank forward to demolish the house with the petard, which had a very short range. Maximum covering fire was given by the Sherman tanks' 77 mms and machine-guns. The petard fired and something like a small flying dustbin hit the house just above the front door. It collapsed like a pack of cards, spilling the defenders with their machine-guns, anti-tank weapons and an avalanche of bricks into the courtyard.

Having reached the open country on the far side, I looked back for the 1st Hampshires, our infantry who should have landed behind us. We were just about to press on to our next objective, which was to attack the enemy coastal guns lying west of Arromanches from the rear, when the leading platoon of the Hampshires emerged from Le Hamel. They had in fact been landed over a mile further down the coast.

The coastal batteries were taken and the infantry began to marshal the prisoners. There were virtually no Germans below the rank of sergeant and the bulk of the troops were the most varied collection of nationalities – Poles, Ukrainians, Russians and some with Mongolian features, who looked as if they hailed from the steppes of Asia.

It was now our task to spearhead the advance of a battalion of another infantry brigade, namely the 59th, in their advance down the La Rosière road to Bayeux. Another of our squadrons was performing the same role with a battalion of the Essex Regiment on the Ryes road.

By nightfall we were within two to three miles of Bayeux. It was deemed advisable not to attempt to enter the town until first light and so around 22.00 hours we leaguered on the road with infantry outposts in front and on the flanks. It was heartening to find that thanks to the marvellous work on the part of Beach Recovery and our own fitters and tank crews, we had been joined by another seven tanks, making the squadron strength twelve. I learned later that our irrecoverable tank casualties had been three drowned and four 'brewed up'.

Early on the morning of D + 1 we entered Bayeux, encountering on the way a machine-gun nest and sundry snipers. There were cheers from the local inhabitants as we drove through the town. One driver – doubtless with his eye on one of the many pretty Bayeux girls – misjudged a corner and knocked down part of a house. In one street where we had to slow down a girl threw me a bunch of flowers but, unlike the good actor, I failed to catch them!

We now pressed on to capture the St Léger feature south-east of Bayeux. It was here that we caught our first glimpse of German tanks since the end of the war in Africa. There were about three or four of them and they withdrew southwards before we could engage them. Subsequently we learned that the enemy had thrown together a series of veteran training cadres to form the crack Panzer Lehr Division.

In addition the 12th SS (Hitlerjugend) Division was moving up on our front. Our old desert adversaries – the 21st Panzer Division – were also reported as being near Caen.

The 8th June (D + 2), saw the formation of a mobile column under the command of our brigadier, consisting of the 8th Armoured Brigade, 61st Recce Regiment, 1st Dorsets, 288 Anti-Tank Regiment (Northumberland Hussars) and A Company of the Cheshire Regiment. The plan was to achieve a break-out in the direction of Loucelles and St Pierre. The Sherwood Rangers were ordered to carry out a small 'right hook' and capture Point 103 which was the high ground dominating the villages of St Pierre and Fontenay le Pesnel. After running the gauntlet of some anti-tank fire, we duly took up our position on the objective.

On 9th June (D + 3), there was heavy fighting and the enemy seemed to have succeeded in surrounding our position. We sustained a number of casualties including the poet, Keith Douglas, who was killed. It became increasingly obvious that our 75-mm guns would not penetrate the frontal armour of the German Mark VI (Tiger) or the Mark V (Panther) tanks. It was exceedingly difficult to get on their flank and fire at the side armour. We heard that some Shermans armed with the British 17-pounder had arrived in Normandy. This weapon possessed far superior powers of penetration and we sent urgent messages back requesting the new tanks. To help us in our offensive it was therefore necessary to have maximum artillery so that a tremendous 'stonk' could be put down on the enemy armour. It is interesting to note that the British tactical handling of artillery had evolved in a superior way to that of the Germans who were great lovers of little pockets of various arms called Battle Groups, which led to fragmentation. The British concept was that the whole of the fire power, for example a corps' artillery plus that of formations on its flank, could be brought down on a small sector of the front.

*

From Lieutenant-Colonel Peter Sutton, Royal Tank Regiment (Retd)
I was in command of a breaching squadron of eighteen assorted specialised armour, flail tanks for mine destroying, assault vehicles Royal Engineers for destroying concrete pill-boxes, laying mats across mud, and even one tank carrying a 30-foot bridge. We were travelling in three tank landing craft and a similar squadron under the com-

mand of Major Tim Thompstone, Royal Engineers, was in another three.

As dusk approached on the evening of 5th June 1944 we were a group of just six tank landing craft somewhere in mid-Channel, heading south. About a mile away to our right were two warships, going the same way as us. There was nothing else in sight in any direction. Where the hell was everybody else? Wasn't this supposed to be the biggest amphibious landing in history? Was it possible that the Royal Navy were pulling our legs, and that we were making a very gradual right-handed turn which would land us on Studland Beach the next morning for yet another practice?

With these thoughts in my mind I was standing on the side of my landing craft gazing at the nearest of the two warships. A junior Naval rating came up to me and said: 'Do you know what that ship is, Sir?' and I replied 'No' and he said 'She is the *Ajax*, one of the heroes of the Battle of the River Plate, and she's ready to knock hell out of anyone.'

Thus it was that a junior rating of the Senior Service gave a substantial boost to the morale of a major in one of the junior services.

The Royal Navy being the splendid service that it is, the captain of my landing craft had thoughtfully given me his cabin for the night – he being destined to spend the whole night on the bridge – and there I now retired.

The change in the scene the next morning was staggering! For miles and miles in every direction there was nothing but ships and landing craft. What one had overlooked the previous night was that the vast force had sailed from ports along the entire South Coast of England and that they were planned to concentrate slowly during the night.

The sky was overcast and the sea was choppy – indeed it had been rough ever since leaving the Solent. As we were to lead the assault we were among the select few who had sailed from the Solent on 4th June with a view to a D Day on 5th June, only to be recalled when we were well south of the Isle of Wight because General Eisenhower had postponed the operation one day on account of the weather.

During this excursion we had used up all our sea-sickness tablets and the truth is that by the morning of 6th June we had all had enough of ships and the sea. We felt that an enemy who by now had been well and truly softened up by an intense bombardment was really preferable. With these thoughts in mind, except for those who were too sick to care, we went about our normal morning routine – washing, brewing tea, stowing away our bedding – and we were not unduly troubled about what might lie ahead.

But the Royal Navy had a little personal adventure in store for me and my crew. By the time the five tanks in front of us had gone ashore the landing-craft was so reduced in weight that it had floated off from where it was beached. Not only that but a current had swung it sideways so that we landed parallel to the beach. Then I found that we were facing the stern of the landing craft to our right. There was no question of stopping or reversing and the turning circle of the tank was limited so we had to turn out to sea to go round the stern of the neighbouring craft. We were soon in deep water and waves were splashing over the turret. My driver, Corporal Adcock, could see only water through his visor. He was getting his first view of 'Les Fruits de la Mer'!

Happily we got round the stern of the landing craft and were soon heading for dry land.

As we advanced up the beach, looking to the left I could see a house with on its side in enormous letters the words DUBO – DU BON – DUBONNET!

Yes, that settled it. This was certainly not Studland Beach!

*

From Mr R. M. S. Neave, MC, formerly 13/18 Hussars
I remember a very remarkable experience once we touched down at about H minus 6 or 7. The tide was absolutely rock bottom low. Arranged in rows along the beach were various anti-tank obstacles. We had landed amongst a variety of flimsy poles, on top of which were balanced a series of large 7.5 shells, each with an instantaneous fuse sticking out like a pimple on their noses. We edged the tank between these posts, being delighted to discover that there was about two inches to spare on each side of the tank once the canvas screen (our floating equipment) had been deflated, exposing us for what we were – a half squadron of tanks.

Having pulled out of the water's edge, we fired at all before us – partly to revive our confidence, partly to scare the other side, and again to give ourselves time to see our way around. We had landed opposite a huge gun emplacement which pleased me. It gave the impression that it was quite incapable of firing at us, since the gun

embrasures were facing left and right, and were therefore unable to
traverse into the tank. Naturally we had forgotten in the excitement
that other emplacements were enfiladed on to our position! Happily
we had no direct action from any of these emplacements, either due
to the superb work of the Royal Navy before we had arrived, or that
the enemy were even more scared of us than we could have hoped,
since little opposition took place during the half an hour or so whilst
we advanced up the long, sloping beach, and gathered our forces
about us. During this time we fired at likely targets and from various
slip trenches little grey-blue figures in huge tin helmets emerged with
their hands up. Intermittent firing and heavy mortar fire landed
occasionally along the beach now being crowded with assault troops.
On our left a whole battalion of the Lovat Scouts had appeared and
were advancing into Lion-sur-mer from where came continuous and
sporadic firing.

The turret of my tank was hit by heavy rifle fire as we attempted
to find our way into the dunes and cross our first objective – the
lateral road that ran down the length of the beach between the few
houses present. These looked just like any other seaside house one
had ever seen, but were rather sad as they looked the worse for wear
and had long since been in need of a little paint. We saw few positive
targets but heard considerable activity from both ours and the oppos-
ing forces to left and right.

A heavy 'stonk' of mortar arrived at that time which suggested
that we should find our way deeper into enemy territory and try to
stop this activity. We were also involved in a running battle with a
few of the more determined snipers, whose activities were beginning
to make life uncomfortable.

Once the beach had been secured and our routes off it had been
defined, our immediate objectives were the bridge over the river Orne
two or three miles north of Ouistreham. This had been secured by
the Airborne Forces during the night, and it was our task to relieve
them and to secure this bridge from counter-attack. In addition the
squadron was to mount an attack against 'Daimler', a large complex
of coast defences situated behind Lion-sur-mer by some two or three
miles and in the triangle formed by the coast and the river Orne.

The troops who were to capture this Orne Bridge set off across
country in a south-east direction. We could not help feeling rather
sorry for Douglas Coker, the troop commander assigned to this task.
His journey of three to four miles into enemy territory was to be
totally unsupported. He set off apparently unaware of these difficulties.

The 'Daimler' objective was viewed from our maps and after our 'O' group, with the squadron leader, 'Dag' Rugge-Price, we set off in an easterly direction to attack this 'fortress' from the rear, with our infantry company (I cannot remember who). I remember careering over fields in more or less open formation to approach our target from the rear (or from its south side), which was that facing away from the sea. We deposited a smokescreen to the western side of the objective and a troop attacked all guns firing from the rear of this defended area. Almost before we started we saw little dejected figures in grey uniforms appearing from this complex who were quickly taken over by the infantry company, who accompanied us in this attack.

Rather like Singapore 'Daimler' collapsed like a pack of cards almost at once, since it was being fired upon on the very side on which there was no real defence.

By the time this was over it was late in the day. We were recalled by the Regimental HQ to a leaguer point in order to prepare for the counter-attack awaited by the corps, an inevitable response by any enemy of the quality of the Germans. I remember little of that night except that I am sure that I slept well. I remember too we 'stood-to' very early next morning before moving off early to cross the Orne by the bridge now called the Pegasus, and then we spent an uncomfortable and energetic few days defending not only the eastern flank of the British corps, but the Orne bridgehead against constant counter-attack.

CHAPTER FIVE

The Infantry

In earlier wars the infantry had been required – and found – to be brave, cheerful, and enduring to a degree which today seems almost incredible. If the infantryman had qualities of foresight or initiative he was not expected to show them. The result of this philosophy led to the slaughter of a whole generation in the trenches of World War I –a sacrifice that is all too clearly visible in the cemeteries of that period.

By World War II the role of the infantryman was seen very differently. In 1938 General Wavell had said that the modern infantryman would need the ingenuity and ability of a successful cat-burglar. The war then produced a wide variety of roles for the infantryman; he could be dropped from the skies by parachute or glider, he could be landed from the sea as a Commando; he could be required to fight in desert or jungle, on a mountain or in street-battles.

On D Day the infantryman had to struggle ashore while heavily burdened with all the equipment he would need for subsequent fighting, rifle, ammunition, grenades, mortars etc., then to find his way inland through barbed wire, partially cleared minefields, and defensive fire from a resolute enemy. The greatest danger would be to be pinned down on the beach unable to move forward or back.

Gold sector, which included the vital Arromanches area (chosen for Mulberry) was assigned to 50th Division. 231 Brigade under Brigadier Sir Alexander Stanier had the task of capturing Arromanches after landing at nearby Asnelles. (The main areas, Gold, Juno and Sword, were also divided into smaller areas also code-named but to list all these would merely confuse.) A visitor to the Arromanches museum will obtained a clear picture of the entire landing area and find the experience most rewarding.

The attack by the Hampshires, Dorsets and Devons in 231 Brigade went well, though not without cost. The East Yorkshires and Green Howards also distinguished themselves against fierce opposition. Of the landings in the Sword area we shall hear more when we study the Commandos.

The Beach Groups which are referred to in the letters were designed to develop order from the confusion caused by large numbers of men landing on congested beaches. Their task was to clear the beach of wreckage, salvage vehicles which were damaged, unload stores, establish storage dumps, make roads, control and direct traffic, and arrange first-aid facilities. These tasks were undertaken under enemy fire. A beach group was made up of units of the Royal Engineers, Royal Army Service Corps, Royal Army Medical Corps and other specialist units. The beach group for 231 Brigade was partly drawn from the Border Regiment and among its tasks (as we see later) was organising the collection of prisoners. The Royal Air Force Beach Group provided the organisation for the distribution of materials necessary for the construction of airfields; it also provided a defence of the beaches by balloon barrage.

Brigadier Sir Alexander Stanier DSO MC commanded 231 Brigade which landed at Asnelles and liberated Arromanches. The brigadier had served as a lieutenant in the Welsh Guards in World War I and had been awarded a Military Cross. Subsequently he commanded landings in Sicily and Italy. The following notes describe the sector 231 Brigade assaulted. Looking at the areas today it may be easy to forget that such formidable obstacles once existed but an appreciation of the extent and complexity of those defences is necessary if we are to understand the events of those days. His account follows:

*

No 231 Brigade was the right-hand brigade of the Second Army Assault Force landing in France on 6th June 1944. Its tasks were: firstly to assist in establishing a bridgehead through which other formations could pass, and secondly to link up with the American Division landing to the west of 50th (Northumbrian) Division.

There follows now a brief description of the enemy defences on the brigade's sector. The first obstacles to be encountered on the beaches were several rows of hedgehogs, thickened up with Element C, and with poles to which were attached shells and mines which were detonated at the slightest pressure. The beaches themselves, which from Intelligence sources and air photographs were known to be difficult going for transport because of a thick peat surface, proved to be an even greater obstacle than had been expected. The beaches were backed by low sandy grass dunes three to six feet high through which it was impossible for any wheeled vehicle to move, and behind the dunes by a marsh, which extended from five to eight hundred

yards inland. Behind the marsh and behind the villages along the
coast was undulating pasture and with several hills and ridges that
dominated the landing beaches. Formidable-looking cliffs which rose
to a hundred and fifty feet in height began at Cabane and extended
westwards to Port en Bessin.

The defences consisted of numerous mutually supporting strongpoints in concrete emplacements with all-round fields of fire. At
Le Hamel itself were three strongpoints along the sea wall, garrisoned
by approximately one and half companies of infantry, and each
mounting an infantry gun. There was another strongpoint at the
eastern end of Le Hamel that had four guns, three of which were of
75-mm calibre. Surrounding Le Hamel itself was an anti-tank ditch
and a minefield containing eight rows of mines. The coastal minebelt,
five rows deep, extended to the east along the back of the beaches
and encircled another strongpoint in the centre of the beach known
as Les Roquettes. Besides being thickly mined this strongpoint contained two 75-mm Howitzers and five concrete MMG emplacements.

Before the brigade beachhead could be established the following
additional strongpoints had to be overcome. On the coast to the
west of Le Hamel there were the defensive localities of Cabane,
Arromanches as well as more on the high ground on either side of
the last-named village. Between Arromanches and Port en Bessin,
which was the brigade's western objective, and was approximately
seven miles from Le Hamel, there were four additional defensive
localities, one of which contained a four 105-mm battery position.
One thousand yards south of Le Hamel and near the village of
Buhot was the high ground at Point 54. Midway between Le Hamel
and Point 54 was an infantry locality and five hundred yards to the
west of Point 54 was a battery of 105-mm gun Hows. Point 54
itself was held by infantry and was fortified by trench systems and
caves. In all within the brigade sector, there were approximately
eighteen guns of field calibre. Within the sector of the brigade on the
left, and so far inland, and so well supported that it was estimated
that no attack could be put against them until approximately one
and a half hours after the first troops had landed, were some machine-
gun nests on high ground dominating the 231 Infantry Brigade
landing beaches.

No 716 Infantry Division held this portion of the coast, and troops
from 726 Grenadier Regiment manned the actual beach defences.
Further inland was 352 Infantry Division, whose role was that of
immediate counter-attack to prevent any Allied penetration before

the Panzer Divisions had had time to concentrate. The troops of 726 Regiment were wrongly assumed, before the invasion, to be of low category. The troops, in fact, proved to be determined fighters, although many of them were foreigners, coming from Poland, Russia and Czechoslovakia.

1st HAMPSHIRES

The two assault companies A and B, landed at Le Hamel at 0730 hours 6th June 1944. The aerial bombardment and artillery had not proved as effective as had been hoped, and both companies were held up at the head of the beach, instead of being able to penetrate swiftly into the heart of the defences. The two reserve companies, C and D, landed at 0740 hours, and also came under withering MG fire from pillboxes, which the tanks landed at H hour were ineffectively trying to neutralise. 88-mm fire from guns sited well inland, which had followed the invasion craft inland, now concentrated on the troops collecting on the beach. Le Hamel was too strongly held for it to be possible to carve a way through the minefields in that area, and it was not until a gap had eventually been made at about 0900 hours to the east of Le Hamel that C and D Companies were able to get through and approach their objective, Asnelles, from the rear. C Company once through the gap, found itself in swampy ground and under fire, but managed to press on, clearing up odd opposition in pillboxes and woods. In this last task the AVREs were able to play an invaluable part. On arrival at Asnelles at about 1200 hours C Company came into reserve in the neighbourhood of Battalion HQ, which had established itself at the school. D Company, which had sustained less casualties than the other companies, cleared to south of Asnelles and continued to Arromanches, arriving there at about 1830 hours. While the battle was raging in Asnelles, the civilian population continued to walk up and down the street, with as little concern as if an exercise was taking place.

1st DORSETSHIRES

The task given to 1st Dorsetshires was the capture of the beach defences on their front and the capture of the Point 54 feature with the infantry locality at Puits d'Hérode 858858 and the battery position at 848858. Finally, the battalion was to reorganise in the area Ryes 8483, continue to hold the high ground north of the village, and cover the approaches to the Le Hamel beaches from the south and south-east. This amounted to the battalion holding the eastern part of the brigade sector of the beachhead; 2nd Devonshires holding the western part, with 1st Hampshires in reserve.

By the end of the day, 1st Dorsetshires had captured all their objectives, almost exactly according to plan and were established in the area of Ryes. This had not been done without considerable fighting, not so much on the beaches themselves, but further inland.

2nd DEVONSHIRES

The 2nd Battalion of the Devonshire Regiment Assault Group was brought over on HMS *Glenroy*, a ship with a truly excellent company who spared no pains to provide for the comfort of all ranks. A very close liaison had been established for some time before the assault between the ship and the regiment. At 0515 hours on 6th June after postponement of one day the HMS *Glenroy* dropped anchor approximately ten miles north of Le Hamel. Two hours later the battalion group headed for the shore in LCAs. The sea was extremely rough and there were many cases of sea-sickness on the run in. The battalion, which was the reserve battalion of 231 Infantry Brigade Assault Group, was timed to start landing at H plus 40 minutes, and touched down almost exactly on time well to the east of Le Hamel. Landing was extremely difficult and hazardous due to the rough sea. The general plan was that the battalion should land in two waves. A and B Companies with the commanding officer's recce group followed by C and D Companies with Battalion HQ. The battalion would then rendezvous in an assembly area in Asnelles-sur-mer due south of Le Hamel and push on to the first objective which was Ryes. The situation for a short while after landing was rather obscure but it soon became apparent that A and B Companies had landed about 800 yards too far to the east and C and D Companies landed on their right almost on the correct beach. Le Hamel was still strongly held and enfiladed the whole brigade on the beach. The battalion was thus unable to reach its assembly area as planned. C Company attempted to push through to Le Hamel which was then being attacked by the 1st Hampshires. They, however, came under heavy fire and were unable either to advance or to withdraw. D Company immediately behind them was not committed. A gap had now been cleared in the minefield in front of the rest of the brigade and A and B moved inland from the beach on which they had been held up for two and a half hours.

Casualties on landing had on the whole been fairly slight. They included however one company commander and two CSMs. At

0955 the CO decided to by-pass Le Hamel which was then being attacked by 1st Hampshires with A and B Companies with the object of pushing inland from Les Roquettes to Ryes. Communications with the companies were extremely bad, owing to the damage caused to wireless sets by sea water, and the CO had great difficulty in getting the orders of the change of plan to the companies concerned. It was not until about 11 a.m. that the new plan was successfully under way. D Company was withdrawn from Le Hamel area but C Company reported that they were unable to extricate themselves. Their company commander in his efforts to improve the situation had been killed by a sniper.

The welcome our troops received in Manvieux on D Day was genuinely enthusiastic. Four years of German occupation had sobered the staunchest admirers of the Wehrmacht. Hatred of the Germans was deep-rooted and expressed itself actively on the enemy's departure. On the other hand there were few complaints from the coastal districts of the behaviour of the Germans, who appear to have received strict orders as to their conduct to the civilian population, although further inland the Boche acted with characteristic brutality.

A number of Russians manning coastal defences were taken prisoner. When asked why they wore German uniform and fought in the German Army they almost uniformly replied that they had been taken prisoner previously in the East, and, confronted with the choice of service in the German Army or death, with reprisals against their families, they had taken the obvious course. Their eagerness to ingratiate themselves with us considerably reduced the value of their statements, since they would sooner invent than be found wanting in information. Most of the Germans, too, were so afraid of being shot by us, having been warned by their leaders that this would undoubtedly be their fate on capture, that they told us what they knew without being asked. In several cases they corrected possible mistakes we might have made on the map by pin-pointing headquarters, company dispositions, etc. Very few of them appeared to have any illusions about winning the war.

The two days just described were the prelude to over six months continuous contact with the enemy.

*

It is unfortunately impossible to provide accounts from every unit concerned on that day because some regiments have produced more than one contributor to this account while others have produced none. It is emphasised that the actions described are but a sample of a day when skill, courage and motivation reached limits beyond all possible expectation.

*

From Mr J. W. Triggs
Background of writer at time of D Day: Captain J. W. Triggs. Aged 31. Formerly adjutant of 6th Battalion The Border Regiment, now staff captain of No 4 Beach Sub Area, landing at approximately 9.30 a.m. on D Day with his old battalion now forming the nucleus of No 10 Beach Group.

I think few people realise how early the first troops went aboard ship. I, with a few specialist personnel, known as the Staff Captain's Increment (inevitably called Excrement over the ship's Tannoy) went aboard the *Empire Arquebus* on 31st May.

On the evening of 5th June we sailed out past the Needles at the head of the Solent contingent, to meet the Americans coming up from the west and the rest of the British and the Canadians coming from London and the south-east ports. When I and a brother officer turned in about 9.30 p.m. the Channel, as far as the eye could see, was filled with craft of every description. Thirty yards on our right the destroyer *Quorn* was cruising gently along, and at a similar distance on our left a Thames barge was rolling heavily. We agreed that this was a unique moment in history and there would never be another like it. We both felt that it would be impossible for the Germans to prevent the invasion.

Early on the morning of D Day I was standing on deck, waiting for an assault craft to take on, among others, my 'Increment', when there was a terrific explosion and I was thrown flat on my face, in company with everyone else and got a nasty cut on my nose. It was the worst wound I got on D Day and was caused by the *Ajax* firing a broadside from about 200 yards directly behind us!

Except for fools and liars I believe that everyone is afraid when going into action. I certainly was, although it is pretty easy to conceal it when you are sharing the experience with a mass of other people. As our LCA approached the beach at Le Hamel it was clear that the beach had not been completely taken by any means and when our craft blew up on a mine a few yards out those of us who were lucky enough to be thrown into the sea felt – and I am sure that I speak for others – that death or capture was to be our fate. The understatement of D Day came from my Cumbrian batman, Lewis, from

Shap Fell, whom I retained for the rest of the war and who, being small, was up to his shoulders in water.

'This is a rum go, sir,' he said.

We managed to get ashore without loss and took cover until the fighting soldiers cleared enough space for us to start our beach activities. Two incidents are, I think, worth quoting. Firstly, as darkness fell on 5th June, several Border officers, myself among them, drank a bottle of champagne and then, with a great effort, got a piece of paper with our names on it into the bottle, together with a polite request that the finder would send it to the Border Regiment Depot at Carlisle Castle. Seven weeks later it was picked up on the beach on the Isle of Wight and faithfully despatched. It is now in the Regimental Museum at Carlisle. Secondly, in the late afternoon of D Day I went into a nursing home and found the officers' mess table with unfinished breakfast, including two exceedingly ugly but ornate sauce bottles. I 'liberated' them and they survived the rest of the war. They are also in the Castle museum!

POW: At the last pre-D Day briefing of 231 Brigade (I think) of 50 Division which we were responsible for maintaining from Gold beach for the first twenty-four hours – the brigade was composed of Hampshires, Devons and Dorsets – someone asked the brigadier (Sir Alexander Stanier) who would be responsible for POWs for the period until the first POW cages arrived on D plus two. His eyes roved around and finally alighted on me.

'The staff captain of the beach group will be responsible for sending them back to the UK on boats for the forty-eight hours,' he said. There didn't seem much to it at the time so I didn't worry.

However, it turned out that the coast division where we landed was largely made up of Russians, captured on the Eastern Front and drafted into the German Army. Naturally they began, as D Day wore on, to give themselves up in shoals, their German officers and NCOs having been largely killed. Everyone was coming to me with a crowd and leaving them on my hands. By darkness I thought I had got them all off on empty boats (the Navy protesting loudly but being assured that they would give no trouble [true] and would be met by military escorts back at the UK. [I hope they were, but it was only my hope!])

At about 11 p.m., just as I thought that that problem had been resolved, a distant beach commander sent a message to say he had about 500 POWs still with him and was too busy to look after them all night. I told him to send them up the coast road and I would think of something. I gathered together about ten clerks with rifles, headed by a corporal with thick spectacles, and found a house with a wire fence round the garden. When the prisoners arrived one came to me and said he spoke English because he had been a waiter at Kettner's before the war. Thus it was easy to get the sergeant majors to herd them into the garden, with a promise of a hot meal at midnight. In the morning I went to the house and found the garden crammed with POWs and my personal clerk, Harper, on sentry duty.

'Very paying thing, this prisoner business, sir,' he said. 'When we counted them last night there were 522, but this morning there are over 700.' Becoming a POW was a popular idea!

A very different type of prisoner were the first SS men the POW cages sent us to send off to England about D plus 5. Arrogantly they marched on to the beach and sat where ordered, apparently confident that their stay in England would be a short one. The beach battalion colonel said that any man feeding them, or giving them cigarettes, would be court-martialled and that they were to have nothing all day. The signals officer hit on the happy idea of rigging up a loudspeaker and relaying to them the German news. Throughout the day they heard that the Allies were being forced back to the beaches, that ships were being sunk, etc. As they watched the busy peaceful scene in front of them, with troops and equipment of every type coming off ships, without an aircraft in the sky, they must have realised for the first time they had for years been fed with lies. When they went on board ship their attitude had markedly changed!

My most frightening experience on D Day certainly does not show me up in a very good light. From time to time the beach group colonel told me to go up the beach to where the fighting still continued to see if we could begin our supply dump operations. This task entailed scuttling up a dry ditch along the coast road towards the firing. On my way I came upon a lance corporal and six men of the Hampshires, sitting in a ditch by the side of their dead platoon commander. I realised that though it was a good time since I had been a trained infantry soldier I bore on my shoulder flashes the name of an infantry regiment and so there was nothing for it but to lead them on their way. Just when the sound of bullets started I met a young Hampshires' captain with a group of men and thankfully said 'I think these are yours,' afterwards nipping back to say we could not get moving yet. My contribution to the fighting on the beaches!

I think the following must rank high among the funniest stories of the beaches. The commanding officer of 6th Border had a batman well above the age for overseas service but who succeeded in getting to Normandy. On about D Day plus 4, when sailors from American LSTs were swarming ashore for souvenirs I found 'Mr Murphy' as everyone from corporal down called him because of his superior age and position, had discovered a pillbox with a hole in the side rather like a theatre box. He was installed inside the pillbox with an assortment of pieces of cement, selling them at half a crown a time to a queue of eager American buyers as 'genuine pieces of Hitler's western wall'. It was a pity to have to stop him but anyway by that time he had made a small fortune.

My strangest experience occurred on the evening of D Day when I was approached by the village gendarme. He held out his warrant card and made me understand that he wanted me to sign that he could continue his duties. In addition to French signatures there were ones from a British unit in 1940, obviously when it was fighting its way back to Cherbourg, and German occupation ones. Now he wanted a signature from the new arrivals. At that moment a Frenchman whose sash proclaimed him to be the local mayor also approached and I got him to identify the gendarme before I signed. Many years later I had the pleasure of hearing Howard Marshall doing a commentary from Normandy about D Day in which the mayor gave his version. He referred to a 'young English officer' and added that I asked him for his identity as well. Perhaps I did but I have no recollection of doing so.

We had buried British soldiers who had been killed in our area during the D Day fighting where they had fallen, the padre giving them a Christian burial. About D plus 14 the war graves men arrived and negotiated a proper cemetery site towards Bayeux. I was instructed to have the dead disinterred at night and taken to the cemetery. Obviously I could not detail another officer in my place, so I took along the padre, a medical officer, and a squad of volunteers. It was the nastiest experience of my life and I will never forget it and strongly advise anyone from being in the position of having to do it in the future.

One warm evening about D plus seven I went with an engineer officer and a couple of Sappers to see if some German Schuh mines could be located and lifted from a small and, as yet, unused beach exit. As work began I noticed a distinct pattern in rabbit droppings in the exit. Suddenly it was clear that, while these mines could blow off a man's foot, rabbits could sit on them with impunity and did so

because the heat from the day's sun made them comfortable latrines!
The Sappers lifted the mines with ease and this novel method of
finding Schuh mines in rabbit country was subsequently published in
a war office leaflet.

*

*From Mr Arthur G. Sindall (former Major, The Hertfordshire
   Regiment)*
After three or four days' close confinement in the cramped quarters
of a tank landing craft half-way down the Solent, our main reaction
was one of relief when at last the signal came – 'It's on!' The years
of training and months of specialised preparation for what was described as 'An opposed wet landing' had made us, with no feeling of
arrogance, supremely confident in our ability to tackle the task which
lay ahead, and in the excitement of the moment the official forecast
of more than twenty per cent casualties was providentially forgotten.
Our morale was even higher as a result of orders from the upper
echelons that all ranks were to wear best battledress, with brand new
shoulder flashes, divisional signs, etc., and that beach groups, of which
our battalion was one, should carry platoon headquarters' flags;
company HQs were to be distinguished by large Union Jacks, and all
this was done to demonstrate that aerial opposition, if nothing else
would be minimal if not non-existent.

So as No 8 Platoon of A Company, the Hertfordshire Regiment
put to sea the mood was almost one of elation, heightened by the sight
of the myriad of other craft which stretched as – and further – than
the eye could reach –

> . . . behold
> A city on the inconstant billows dancing,
> For so appears this fleet majestical.

Shakespeare, as usual, had it right, and *Henry V* could have been
written specially for D Day; indeed, I had a copy tucked away somewhat self-consciously in my haversack, though there was little time to
read it in the months that lay ahead.

Every officer carried sealed orders, with the somewhat melodramatic
instruction that they were not to be opened until the craft was clear
of the Needles; for no one knew our destination until that envelope
was opened. So each unit ran its own sweepstake, with the choice of

venues wide open – from the North Cape round to Mentone, with the Calais area as hot favourite. In the event, the ticket marked rather vaguely as 'near Bayeux' was judged the winner, and he cleaned up nicely.

The mood of exhilaration continued well into that gorgeous though gusty summer evening, for soon our vast flotilla joined up with an equally gargantuan fleet from the Portsmouth area, and with every craft flying its own protective silver barrage balloon, golden tinted by the setting sun, there was almost a fairground atmosphere. A Free French destroyer, tricolour flapping madly at the masthead, scurried joyously in and around the plodding landing craft like a terrier un-expectedly let out for a run. After four years they were on their way home.

Well before dusk I settled down and checked all my gear, for the umpteenth time, though there was little I could have done about it had there in fact been any last-minute discrepancies. But one chore remained, which I had not had time to complete before embarking. All ranks had received a brand new kit, from battle dress to socks, including two pairs of 'drawers, cellular, short', voluminous monstrosi-ties which buttoned up the front and were fitted with tapes at either side through which one's braces were to be threaded to hold them up. As no one wore braces the problem of support sometimes became acute. But my sewing kit contained the balance of the elastic I had used on previous occasions of this nature, and I spent the last half hour of daylight modernising my undies. As I related in a later diary entry :

> I contemplate the shores of France
> And sew elastic in my pants.

As darkness gathered we became aware of a rising swell, and our ungainly landing craft rolled and pitched, and her steel plates winced, as she took the impact of the heavy sea; and for once the mood was tinged with something of anxiety, not for what might happen on the morrow but for what could happen – there and now. With her deck jam-packed with tanks and self-propelled guns we seemed to be alarmingly low in the sea, in fact, we shipped a torrent of water every time she rolled. 'One more like that,' I thought, 'and we'll be in the Drink.' Our Mae Wests could not have done much in the way of supporting the average infantryman, together with his 70 lbs of equipment.

Our neighbours had disappeared into the darkness, for there could be no give-away navigation lights. I made my way forward as far as I could go, and standing by the top of the ramp could just make out the black stern of the landing craft we were following. Our forrard look-out, and his oppo on the stern ahead kept up a whispered altercation – 'Get off my bloody arse' – 'Where've yer got to?' etc. as we played out our game of blind follow-my-leader across the Channel.

I'd fixed up a stretcher on the open deck, and as I lay down and listened to the unending roar of the stream of invasion aircraft overhead I tried, self-consciously, to remember the words of famous men on such a night as this – Henry before Agincourt, Wellington before Waterloo, and so on. What interested me, in distant retrospect, is that I recall no feelings of fearful anticipation, nor even of resignation; only one of complete, almost bored detachment, as if I were watching a not very good play or film, and to the sound of the incessant throbbing overhead I must have stumbled into sleep.

A tug on my shoulder and it was early daylight, and there was my splendid imperturbable batman, Wheeler, with, just as if we'd been within the ordered confines of Aldershot, my morning tea. Wheeler was just the kind of servant you read about in books, and dream about if you haven't got one like him. A miner in civvy street, he'd modelled himself on his idea of the perfect gentleman's gentleman – he always addressed me as 'We' – 'We'll be Orderly Officer tomorrow, sir,' 'We really must do something about our boots' and on on. Each morning when he brought my tea it was the same – 'Good morning, sir, your tea.' 'Good morning, Wheeler, what day is it?' 'Tuesday, sir.' But this was 6th June, and when I asked 'What day is it?' he replied, 'D Day, sir.' Good old Wheeler.

The fair land of France was well ahead, just a slightly greyer smudge than the sky above, but even from our viewpoint the scene was fantastic, a scene which has been described so many times that there is little to add except that I still had that feeling that I was watching a pretty realistic newsreel. We were due to land at H hour plus 30 minutes, and as we watched the first assault craft touch down, the stutter of machine-gun fire, the first falling figures, my feelings changed to those one had before a vital race on sports day – the wet palms (you kept your hands in your pockets in case it showed), a chalk-dry throat and that overwhelming desire to yawn. And as we first came under fire I saw a shaking hand, and found it was my own. I cravenly gave my cigarettes to Wheeler, with instructions to pass them round to the lads – it wouldn't matter quite so much if they noticed that his hand was shaking too.

I heard myself give the order to load, to load for the first time with live ammunition to be used against other human beings. I loaded my revolver, feeling like an actor in a minor Western, and swung my walking stick (a 'stout ash plant' in all the better novels) in what I thought might appear a jaunty manner as we took our place behind the ramp. What should I say? What on earth could I say? All I could think of, absurdly, was 'God for Harry, England and St George!' But the problem was solved, and not by me but by the opposition, for with an almighty crash the bows of our landing craft hit a mined underwater obstacle, and the ramp fell open at a drunken angle a good fifty yards before we were scheduled to hear the order 'Ramp down'. It jammed fast on the sand, and we had no option but to get going there and then. No words of martial exhortation came to my lips, no 'Charge' or 'Berlin or bust!' only a somewhat mild, conversational (as I was later told) 'I think we'll go in now' and at a slithering trot I led my gallant few down the slippery ramp and leapt into six feet of water.

But, until our first casualty, it *still* seemed just like a film.

*

From Mr M. Gordon
At the time of the D Day landings I was a private in the 2nd Battalion Hertfordshire Regiment, which was part of a beach group attached to the 50th Tees and Tyneside division.

Our boat was towing a Hippopotamus raft; the object was to anchor about three miles off the Normandy coast and load the tanks and trucks etc. from the ship to raft: therefore if the raft was destroyed by the enemy on landing, the Landing Ship Tank would be safe to return for more equipment. The sea, as you know, was very rough, and our Hippo broke loose. We hove to, and the crew lowered a boat to recover the raft. As our ship was flat-bottomed we began to roll terribly, and everybody without exception became sea-sick. The overcrowded boat was a mess. It took an hour to recover our raft and get under way, by which time we were alone on an empty sea, which made me feel nervous and vulnerable.

I remember that during the whole crossing, not a single aircraft was seen or heard. While I stayed on the top deck I wasn't feeling too bad, but whenever I tried to get down below, to my bunk, I felt bad and had to run back on deck again. It was beginning to get dark and I remember thinking that if I didn't get any sleep I wouldn't be in a fit state for fighting. Eventually I succeeded in reaching my bunk without vomiting, and more than anything I wanted to get off the boat no matter what I had to face on the other side.

At our briefing we were told that we were scheduled to land at 0900 hours on King Red beach, which I think was about ten miles east of Arromanches. At about 0600 hours we anchored about three miles off the Normandy coast. We could see puffs of gunfire ashore, but it wasn't until 1700 hours that orders came through to load the raft and make for the shore. The raft loaded with tanks, trucks, and troops, powered by two Chrysler engines, headed for the shore. It was a shambles.

There was now no gunfire. As we neared the beach our main concern was to have a dry landing, so we clambered on to tanks and trucks in order to keep our feet dry. We landed on King Green beach. We made our way past stretcher-bearers carrying men with black faces who had probably been pulled out of burned-out tanks, and reached our planned positions on King Red beach.

That night, at intervals, a single German plane would come over to strafe the beach. Every anti-aircraft weapon – 20-mm and 40-mm Bofors etc. – would open up in an attempt to prevent the plane from coming in low. The whole sky was alight with tracer shells; a sight never to be forgotten. The finest firework display is puny by comparison.

*

From Major C. L. Crauford, MC, 2nd East Yorkshire Regiment
Perhaps I should start by confessing that I am not in the least proud of the part which I played in the initial assault on the beaches. At that time I was a captain, second-in-command of C Company of the 2nd Battalion, and it had been decreed from a great height that all seconds-in-command of all formations should not land with their own men, but should go ashore in the comparative safety of a later 'wave'. It was an order and there was no escaping it, but I was unable to avoid an uncomfortable guilty feeling at dawn on D Day when I was still several miles off-shore but my friends were storming the beaches.

However my twinges of conscience were overwhelmed by the altogether more powerful sensation of sea-sickness, which rendered me temporarily insensitive to questions of personal safety and made me long to set foot on shore –any shore whether friendly or swept by fire –

I just didn't care!

In a sand dune at the far side of the beach I met the padre who was nursing a wounded arm and had been using his other arm to attend to the men wounded in the initial assault as best he could in the circumstances. He told me the immediate beachhead had been successfully established, but our Battalion HQ boat had been caught in automatic fire. The CO had also been wounded and our medical officer, a particular friend of mine, had been killed.

I gathered my little party together, consisting of the second-in-command of each of the nine sections, the three platoon sergeants, my batman and myself. Our job was to catch up with the company as quickly as possible so that we could assist with the assault on the 'hedgehog' positions inland which contained the artillery providing defensive fire on the beaches. 'Hedgehog' was a damned good name for these positions which consisted of massive concrete emplacements surrounded by barbed wire and minefields. It had been planned that in order to soften up our particular 'hedgehog' the RAF would first bomb it, churning up the minefields, and then we were to be permitted to call on naval guns to cover our assault. Unfortunately the RAF's bombs fell harmlessly in the next field, and to add to our difficulties the FOB (who was the equivalent of an FOO* only working with the naval guns) failed to put in an appearance. No doubt he was a casualty, but I never knew definitely what happened to him.

When I caught up with the company one of the sergeants found that he was immediately required to take command of his platoon whose officer had been killed on the beaches. The company commander, who was mortally wounded a few days later, was contemplating the problem of how to attack without the assistance of artillery, but fortunately the situation was relieved by the timely arrival of our FOO from the 76th Field Regiment, who informed us that he already had a troop of self-propelled guns ashore, and ready to go into action in our support.

As the extensive minefields were still intact, the company commander decided to launch his attack down the main track approaching the position between the minefields, relying upon our covering fire to silence the inevitable fixed line† covering this route until our men could fan out at the far edge of the minefields. It was a gamble, but

*Forward Observation Officer.

†Enemy guns trained on to that route.

it worked. We took the position, and I learned my first military lesson of the campaign – that the weight of fire you bring to bear in an attack is far less important than its timing and accuracy. We suffered minimal casualties in this action, but unfortunately one of the platoon commanders was among them, and he died soon after he was evacuated. We now had two platoons commanded by sergeants.

Victory is sweet, and we all thoroughly enjoyed capturing the terrified defenders. I walked into the main gun emplacement just as my batman, with misplaced initiative, dropped a grenade through a ventilator in the roof, but I was saved from injury by the gun shield which was fortunately between me and the explosion. I shot outside like a startled rabbit, and everyone thought it a good joke! Nobody cared – our tails were up – we were winning, and to complete our triumph we liberated several crates of beer from Nazi oppression.

*

From Mr N. Mason, 2nd Battalion East Yorkshire Regiment
Our D Day preparations began when we were moved into our concentration area which was a makeshift tented camp in some woods at Cowplain, Hampshire, just outside Portsmouth.

It was a higgledy-piggledy sort of affair, the discipline was pretty strict and we were garrisoned in small square tents like sardines. When it rained the place was a quagmire but we were still expected to keep things spick and span. Recreation was practically non-existent and we were confined around the camp doing various time-consuming things such as limited training, lectures, etc., and as you can imagine the lads got bored and rather fed-up with things.

All mail was censored and a letter of mine which in one phrase described the place as a 'Whirlpool of insanity' summed up the feelings of most. The letter, after a lot of argy-bargy, went the rounds from company office to Battalion HQ and from thence to the higher-ups. The result was an eventual easing off of discipline and a more relaxed way of life which was quite welcome.

The letter was a talking point for some time afterwards but I didn't mind as it achieved its purpose as a few mornings afterwards I went on parade with a rifle which the inspecting officer claimed had a speck or two of rust down the barrel but nothing untoward happened about it.

One day to relieve the monotony the late King came along and we were assembled down a tree-covered lane near the camp whilst he inspected us. He seemed a quiet and serene sort of individual. Another day Eisenhower came and gave us the once over. He was a bright and breezy person but loaded with bull.

When we heard that we were going to be moved closer to the boats that were to take us over to France things began to move quickly around the camp and prior to moving on all surplus gear was gathered together, piled up and burnt. All sorts of stuff went up in the flames including good food, clothing etc., interspersed with quite a lot of live ammo which the blokes chucked on the fire to liven things up.

Just before this some of the lads had skinhead haircuts, one or two having it slashed off to make them look like Mohican Indians and at least one had his hair cut leaving three dots and a dash on his head to denote the victory sign.

Came the day when we moved to our loading up areas and we marched out of camp. The people of Cowplain who hadn't taken too much notice of us turned out at the roadside with jugs of tea and cakes, some shedding tears and wishing us well.

We were split up, some going to Portsmouth to be stowed out of sight but my party finished up some distance away at another camp behind barbed wire at Lord Gage's estate at Firle in Sussex, not far from Newhaven, which was to be our embarkation point. We were only supposed to be here for a day or so, one of which being bright and sunny, I took a stroll with a pal of mine and, noticing a gap in the barbed wire with a cornfield on the other side, we made a move to walk through. As we got a pace or two out two other soldiers jumped out of nowhere and told us to get back inside the barrier and that they had orders to shoot us if we made a break for it. The thought was never in our minds but we turned back nevertheless. Time in this camp was pretty easy going and we were issued with invasion money which the lads promptly christened 'soap coupons'. A fair amount of this money changed hands for ordinary cash which was used mainly for gambling, and small fortunes were won and lost in quick time by various individuals, tossing coins up into the air for hours on end.

This being the month of June we knew that invasion time was imminent and sure enough that day came and we were assembled and marched in the direction of Newhaven. We hadn't gone far when we were turned back and were told that the weather in the Channel was too bad for shipping and that the plan had been put back for I think twenty-four or forty-eight hours to enable things to clear up. The news evoked cheers from the boys who returned to Firle for another night's respite. Nobody took much notice of days and dates at this time but on the late afternoon of 5th June we were on our way again to Newhaven harbour.

When we arrived there were scenes of hasty preparations for a quick getaway. A number of ladder craft, used in the Salerno landings, having a 3-foot draft at the fore end going to nothing aft, were lined up at the harbour wall and we were shunted on like cattle going for slaughter.

On completion of loading we saw on the harbour side a naval officer of fairly high rank and a big burly redcap. Out in the harbour all done up as if there were to be a naval review was a flotilla of navy MTBs all spick and span, ropes looking as if they had just come out of store and neatly scrubbed, everything in fact looking sparkling, including the matelots.

Suddenly the order was given and we moved off towards the Channel and as we did so, from the safe distance on the boat, knowing that nothing could be done about it the lads blew resounding raspberries and in a good-humoured sort of way shouted insults and profanities at the redcap but he never batted an eyelid. The officer came up to the salute and I swear I saw a smile on his face.

On the way out of harbour the skipper of our boat, a big handsome American, told us they were taking us for a run up the coast but we knew that this was the beginning of the real thing. Out in the Channel we cruised along slowly with the Navy for protection and we congregated in a small room affair below decks which was as usual packed tight with bodies. Here the lads were supplied with a liberal supply of seasick tablets but I refused them as I had never been seasick in my life. After a time being chucked about on the water one or two of the lads turned grey and began to throw up and after putting up with the stink of blokes being sick and their sweaty bodies I decided to go out on deck where I stayed for the rest of the trip across.

My companion on deck was a big grizzly unshaven US seaman who told me he was Alaskan and in between being sick over the side of the boat, kept cursing these goddam krauts and saying what we were going to do to them. The sea was still fairly rough and with the decks awash I sat all night long wondering what the outcome was going to be and watching the shipping which seemed to be quite numerous.

The night seemed never ending but as we neared the French coast everything appeared to come alive with boats of every different shape and size dashing about hither and thither. Quite close to us the minesweepers were cruising backwards and forwards carrying out their good work. Here and there flashes of signal lamps flung out their messages and instructions from one ship to another.

Suddenly we were racing for the shore and the skipper told us to hang on tight as he was going to give us a good landing and added that we would hit the beach with a bump and it was a pity the boat didn't have wheels on as then he could have taken us on to Paris.

There was plenty of noise and confusion as we went over the side to wade ashore and just before I did so the Scots-American sparks* on board pressed a number of packs of Lucky Strike cigarettes into my hands and wished us the best of luck. I stuffed what I could into the top of my battledress blouse and loaded down with the rest of the paraphernalia of war slid over the side into the chilly sea. We waded chest deep up the beach which had been cleared of obstacles and a small section taped which denoted that it was safe to traverse and free from mines.

My thoughts were like the rest, well this is it and biting my teeth together I moved off quickly up the incline of sand which was backed by a metalled road with a few ordinary style houses lying on the far side. Our section was led by a Sergeant Webb, a North Countryman and one of the coolest customers I ever met. He led us forward over the road which seemed to be lined with wounded, one or two dead and some who seemed too exhausted to move, over a field to a hedge bottom and this is where we stopped for our first breather.

Our instructions were to dig in while he went to have a look to see if he could make contact with the rest of our outfit which had moved out from Pompey† and landed on another part of the beach. We didn't need any encouragement to dig and we were out with shovels and got cracking. After a while he came back saying he couldn't see anyone of ours and that we were to have a hot drink from a can of self-heating stuff which we all carried as he didn't know when we would get anything else. He nipped off into the undergrowth to relieve himself and came back hoisting his slacks as though we were out on an exercise. Off again we moved to try to make contact.

After roaming around for some time we eventually contacted someone from our battalion and later that day were taking cover in another

*Radio operator.
†Portsmouth

hedge bottom trying to dodge parachutes from which dangled large containers which looked for all the world like bombs as they plummeted down and which we later discovered contained nothing but spare ammunition which was supposed to be for the Airborne troops dropped on the Orne bridges at midnight of 5th and 6th June.

We were told previously that our objective was the outskirts of Caen by the late afternoon of D Day but that was out of the question as the Germans had so depleted the ranks before and after the landings, causing such confusion that this proved to be an impossibility.

However, back to our temporary haven in the hedgebottom. A signal sergeant who was now in our company ordered me to go out and see what was in the containers which were dropping but I deemed it was too dangerous to sally forth as these things were coming down too close and with too much frequency to be comfortable, and the fact that Jerry was sending over his visiting cards also made me tell the sergeant in no uncertain terms, in front of two HQ officers, just what he could do with the containers and himself.

After a while I sneaked out and opened several of the containers but found only boxes of .303 ammunition. I was more interested in finding food as we were getting very hungry by now having eaten nothing all day. I grabbed a couple of these heavy boxes and dumped them at the feet of the sergeant and left him with them.

We moved off once again traversing miles of lush farming country, back and forth, on to nightfall trying to make contact with our own outfit. At long last in the middle of the night I recognised a voice as one of my platoon mates and asked him where Reggie (our platoon officer) was.

Immediately another strident voice piped up with 'Here's F - - - - ing Reggie. Where the bloody hell have you been? We have been fighting and dying and having a terrible time . . . '

I replied in a like manner and stated we had not exactly been on a picnic ourselves.

After digging in once again, so ended our first day in Normandy.

The mood of the men prior to D Day was of frustration and everything that goes with it. On the word go it was elation and buoyancy of spirit, wanting to get the job over with as quickly as possible. During the initial stages everyone lived on their nerves and it was a case of hunting and being hunted.

To me it was all like a bad dream.

In my writing I forgot to mention the fact that the regiment suffered severe casualties in dead and wounded.

From Mr J. Garner

I was a member of the 1st Battalion, the South Lancashire Regiment, an assault battalion of the 3rd (British) Division. The battalion was allotted Sword (white) beach in the vicinity of Colleville-sur-Orne to carry out its assault. I was not part of the initial assault troops, my role was as a driver in the Carrier Platoon and was to come ashore on the third wave.

The ship which brought us to the battle area was the SS *Olav* (Norwegian), launched about 1890; it must have been a coaler on the Newcastle–Norway run as most of its past cargo was still in the hold where I was to bed down. My patch was slap bang under the anchor chute. The noise when the anchor was lowered was pretty frightening I may add.

We arrived off the Normandy coast early on the morning of the 7th. Very soon landing craft were buzzing around us and an LCM manned by Royal Marines came alongside. Once the jib was set up to offload the Bren carriers a small problem arose : should the carrier crews be lifted with their vehicles or should they scramble down after? To save time, the former was decided; we were expendable!

I was to be the first off so once the jib had been hooked up we climbed aboard the carrier, the lift took place and we were swung out over the LCM which was at the bottom of the trough at this moment, up she came and the ramp support thudded into the metal plates of the carrier hull. The noise was ear splitting. I imagined at the time that one of the shells from Le Havre had hit us, we were not aware of the problems of transferring cargo in rough seas at that time. However, after much lifting and lowering which must have taken at least thirty minutes we were installed or should I say dumped in the LCM with our vehicle's rear facing the ramp. Though its load was generally three carriers the LCM was only going to take this one, after the fiasco of loading us, operations were suspended. My unit would have to make do with one carrier for a little while.

With my vehicle's rear facing the ramp I could see another small problem arising. I would have to reverse off the craft; there was no room to turn. I would probably be the only one to advance towards the enemy with my backside. Whilst all this was happening the intensity of the enemy gunfire increased and no doubt we were the target for observed fire, as the shells were landing very close indeed.

The LCM left the side of the *Olav* and steered for the beachhead. When it came to a halt I risked a look over the ramp. Good grief, I thought, or words to that effect! There were, at least, one hundred and fifty yards of water between us and the exposed beach and it was evident the beach boys hadn't cleared the obstacles yet. There they were in smart array; some, I suspect, still had mines attached. I had to reverse my carrier that distance relying on instructions from my crew, a skid turn in the water would be too risky, might shed a track, that would be fatal. The ramp was lowered and down I reversed, into about four foot of water. I was conscious at the time of the fact that the tidal surge might increase this depth; however according to the flotation instructions a carrier should float with at least six inches of free board when flotation panels are fitted. I had never yet put this to test and I think it referred to still water. My fears of being drowned were groundless and after much 'left hand down, right hand down, steady', we dodged around the obstacles and hit the beach proper. I was now aware of my heavy breathing and pounding heart, a sort of delayed reaction of the tense moments we had just gone through. All that remained now was to get off this shooting range beach as soon as possible.

Then it happened, so quickly it was very difficult to take in, out of the clouds to the east, came thundering at least seven Ju88s. In a flash every AA gun, machine-gun and probably rifle on the beach and in the ships was directed at them. I estimate that a minimum of five of these planes were hit and were hurtling at the beach with their tails or wings on fire and one of them was on line to crash on to, or very near, us. This must be the end, my past short but not uneventful life panicked through my mind; it was not to be, I was being prepared prepared to suffer more horrors yet to come.

The blazing plane ploughed into the beach about thirty or so yards away to my left, it was a mass of flames. Suddenly there was a huge explosion, the carrier lifted and rocked violently, the plane's bomb load had gone up. There was a loud clanging from bomb splinters, hitting the armour plating of the carrier, some of them piercing the lighter flotation panels; dirt, sand and smaller debris rained down upon us. After a minute or so of comparative quiet, I ventured to look over the panels, what remained of the plane was burning. Green, red and white Very lights were shooting from it, and small arms ammunition was going off like Chinese crackers at a funeral. An unusual fireworks display. I could see no air crew, either living or dead.

I got behind the steering wheel once more and carefully manoeuvred the carrier on the sand so that the front was facing a set of tracks leading from the beach. I then tore the front flotation panel off the carrier, so that my vision was restricted as little as possible. I had a nagging fear that there would still be mines around. There was no marking tape in this area. I drove towards the track cautiously. Suddenly there was another huge bang and I felt something hot hit me in the eye, and on the right side of my face. The pain in my eye was unbearable. I've been hit in the face by shrapnel was my immediate thought. Stark fear of being blinded gripped me, anything but that, please. I could feel the matter oozing down my face. Fearful of what I might discover, I put my fingers slowly to the face and felt the damage, no cuts or gash were apparent. I brought my hand down and looked at it with my good eye. I was astonished, no blood or gore, just good old seagull's - - - -

Though the pain in my eye was excruciating, I was overjoyed and laughing aloud. I shouted : 'Muck for luck.' My wild outburst alarmed the crew and for a moment they thought the past ordeal had sent me in shock. The explosion must have been another of the aircraft's bombs going off.

After a difficult drive we eventually arrived at the first staging area, called 'Finger' (code word) where the first de-proofing had to take place. I gave my eye a good wash out, though much inflamed and painful at least I could open it and see a little. There were large deposits of the 'goo' on my helmet and carrier steering column; there it will remain and be my talisman, I said to myself. What is more, I sincerely believed in its powers.

From 'Finger' the next staging area was called 'Thumb' where we would carry out further de-waterproofing and be directed to our unit. However, it appeared that a few enemy snipers were disputing the tenancy of this piece of estate. Fortunately one of the crew had spotted our unit route sign; it was decided to ignore Thumb and follow the sign, which we did and in due course arrived at Hermanville and our unit. Once settled we enjoyed a mug of the finest compo tea.

I didn't bother the RAP with my eye, they were far too busy with real casualties, though it was rumoured that some chaps were being evacuated after cutting themselves shaving.

During the atrocious landing I do not remember being afraid. Real fear, however, came after the incessant shelling we received later in the wooded area of Le Landel – day in, day out, it was constant. Jerry seemed only to know this target; it had, of course, been their officers' mess. Thoughts of self-inflicted wounds or even complete suicide passed through the mind, how much more could one take. I know of men holding their arm above the slit trench parapet in the hope that a piece of shrapnel would hit it; whether anyone was successful I don't know.

Each day the shelling went on and comrades whom I knew well were killed, wounded and smashed in the mind. Strong men who'd boxed or played soccer or rugger for the unit and had suffered the horror of Dunkirk were led or carried away shaking and blubbering like small children. WOs and sergeants and even the odd officer, my heroes, disgusted themselves in my sight reduced to crying babies. I was barely twenty at the time and was deeply affected by this behaviour. If anything it made me more resolute to keep going no matter what. One may refer to the heavy shelling in the Great War; at least they had a good trench system to protect them and could move around. We had only a scrape in the ground and no material for overhead cover. The trees made ninety per cent of the shells air bursts; the most vicious sight I've ever seen is a cluster of air bursts going off above you. Moving from one area to another was most hazardous to say the least.

After a while one could read the shell fire (providing it was not a very flat projectory weapon the missile of which arrived before the bang) and could pinpoint their landing. Mortar bombs were very different; the pop of the weapon could be heard and sometimes the swish as they landed close to you. Nasty, but in the main they were all 'wind and p - - - '.

What I really feared were mines and aimed small arms fire, the latter meant that the enemy could see you, the former could be anywhere.

During this period I remember that everyone seemed to be under the influence of drugs, the way they spoke and acted was so deliberate. I felt somewhat dazed myself, and as I have been given morphine since, I realise that the feelings are not unlike.

Pity, if that is what it was, came to me when we were consolidating after the bloody attack on La Londe. I saw in a ditch an MG42 behind which two dead Germans lay face downwards, obviously Nos 1 and 2 on the gun. They were young, blonde and well built. The No 2 had across his back the spare barrel and his arm was around the shoulders of the No 1. It saddened me even though moments before they had been trying to kill us. Funny how I have remembered the picture though I've witnessed far more horrific sights since. I can still visualise it in every detail.

I managed to survive throughout the whole campaign and except for bullet splash on the wrists and being struck by spent shrapnel was completely unscathed in body, the mind was a different matter. The crew were all KiA* on various operations, Caen, Troarn and the Vire Road.

The carrier was blown up on the Vire Road, in an ambush. Incidentally that very morning a replacement carrier commander had unwittingly cleaned the seagull's goo off the steering column; he was badly wounded in the affray.

My steel helmet carried the stains throughout, despite many requests from various platoon sergeants to remove it – the wrath of mortals could not compensate for the revenge of the unknown. I could never understand how or why that seagull was in that area of the beach, when all the noise and chaos was going on. If I had the powers of flight I know where I would have been. I do understand why he s - - - himself. A lot of us were doing the same.

*

From Mr Richard Harris, formerly Private R. Harris, B Company, 1st Battalion Suffolk Regiment, 8th Brigade, 3rd British Infantry Division

Trembling, my rifle tightly clenched, I crouched awaiting the dreaded shout of 'Ramps down'. We seemed to inch in, in between craft already beached, some of which were burning. The diesels went into reverse, the bows ground into the sand and pebbles and we came to a standstill. 'Ramps down.' This was it – I was determined to present myself for the minimum time as a target at the top of the ramp and being one of the first off I had a clear run. On the order to go, I leapt up, bounded down the ramp, jumped and landed in about four feet of cold sea-water. Though it came up chest high I managed to retain my balance and holding my rifle clear of the water waded as quickly as I was able to the shallows and the beach. My impression of the scene there was of a complete shambles. Had the whole thing failed, was it a gigantic cock-up? Against a backcloth of smoke, gutted blazing buildings were several burning knocked-out DD tanks and strewn about from the water's edge up to the sea wall were sodden khaki bundles staining red the sand where they lay. The thought that for them the day was already done appalled me. But there was no time to be staring at my first experience of corpses, a

*Killed in Action.

mad dash up the beach to gain what I hoped was the shelter of the sea wall. Find some sort of hole. Keep your head well down and try to locate a beach exit.

For how long I was on the beach I do not know. It was all very confused. Between the crunch of mortar bombs and the whizzing sounds of shells and chunks of metal flying about I remember hearing cries of 'Stretcher bearer' and one plaintive youthful voice repeatedly calling, 'Help me, boys' and then breaking off into shuddering sobs. I never saw this lad nor do I know what happened to him, but his plea for aid was one of my most poignant memories of the beaches.

Suddenly a welcome voice called from the road above me, 'Get along here about thirty yards, there's a gap in the wire' and a hand indicated the direction. I needed no second bidding, the beaches were a distinctly unhealthy area and the sooner I was off them the better. A mate followed me as I stumbled, running and crouching to the place where the wire had been blasted apart leaving a gap to squeeze through on to the sea front. Nearly opposite was a road which I knew should lead to the second lateral. In a series of dashes we gained the road and then squelched on across rather flat country. To our great relief we found that for the present having got clear of the beaches we were out of the firing-zone. Eventually we met up with a captain and a sergeant of our B Company and most of the other LOBs* I suppose we were about a mile inland, in an orchard somewhere between Colleville-sur-Orne and Hermanville. We were told to dig in and stand-to and await the arrival of the battalion which would assemble and prepare for the assault on its objectives.

Rapidly we dug our slit trench. It was a great relief to sit in the bottom of it and feel three feet of solid earth all round you. After the boat how beautifully motionless it was! All feeling of nausea had left me, but I felt parched rather than hungry, as if all my saliva had dried up.

By mid-morning we left our trenches in the orchard and moved through the devastated village of Colleville without opposition, for it appeared devoid of Germans and civilians, and made our way to the slope of the Periers Ridge where once again we dug in. This slight rise dominated the beach area and from it I could see the vast number of craft disgorging quantities of men and materials on to the chaotically crowded beaches.

*Left out of battle. Troops not engaged in that particular action.

Because of their dominant positions on the ridge it was essential that the German gun batteries be overcome quickly.

The battalion formed up for its attack. If casualties were high the LOBs would be needed for a second assault. Tension began to rise again! Until needed we would guard the line which marked the extent of our penetration inland. The first objective, 'Morris', had suffered severe damage from naval and air bombardment and the defenders must have been pretty shaken. I was relieved and overjoyed to learn that soon after the attack had opened at 1300 hours, sixty-seven Germans emerged with their hands up and decided to call it a day.

The other objective, 'Hillman', half a mile to the south, was not only more strongly fortified, but had not been badly damaged by the bombardment. It also possessed a network of underground fortifications which were not apparent on the aerial photographs. It was going to be a tougher nut to crack than had been expected. Confident after their initial success, the companies of the battalion mounted their attack on the outer defences which were protected by wire and mines.

These were breached but the inner redoubt remained intact. A second attack would have to be mounted, this time with support from a squadron of tanks from the Staffordshire Yeomanry. Whilst this attack was in preparation, for the first and only time that day the Luftwaffe decided to intervene in the shape of four Junkers 88s which, to our great joy, were pounced on by a horde of Spitfires and all were destroyed.

It was, however, a day of rapidly changing emotions. Our elation was short-lived, for we were warned to stand by for a counter-attack by German tanks advancing quickly north of Caen. Even though Harry and I had dug a good protective slit-trench we nevertheless felt, with only a rifle apiece, somewhat inadequately equipped to take on what was later identified as part 21st Panzer Division. Fortunately the tanks were engaged by our anti-tank gunners athwart the Periers Ridge. Eleven were knocked out, but a number by-passed the ridge and actually reached the coast at Lion-sur-Mer between the Canadians and our division.

By 2000 hours the second attack on 'Hillman' was eventually successful, but not until some nasty business had taken place in the basement with some Germans intent upon winning an Iron Cross. Fifty prisoners were taken and our casualties, happily, had been light. The LOBs had not been required. For this I was thankful. To conclude the saga of 'Hillman' I must relate that on the morning of

D + 1, the colonel of 736 Coastal Defence Regiment emerged with his remaining officers and seventy ORs and surrendered. They had been in a part of the underground labyrinth which had been overlooked the previous evening.

By now the other two brigades of the division, the 9th and 186th, had long since passed through our positions and having gained our objectives we made ready to leave the ridge and consolidate outside Colleville for the night. As we prepared to leave at about 2100 hours, the Grand Finale to D Day was enacted. Lit by the evening sun came an armada of 240 gliders and their tugs carrying the Air Landing Division, whilst above circled and weaved a strong force of escorting fighters, possibly 600 aircraft in all. As they flew low over our positions, the gliders cast off from the towing planes, half-banked steeply to land between Colleville and the Orne, whilst the remainder wheeled in a gentler arc to alight at Ranville. A most impressive sight, never to be forgotten by those who beheld it. If we were greatly heartened by this final show of strength, the Panzers on the coast were so dismayed, they retreated whence they had come fearing their escape route might otherwise be cut off.

Shortly after the airborne landing we left our positions on the ridge to consolidate near Colleville for the night. Wearily we set about digging another slit-trench, our third that day. When this task was completed it was dusk and time to stand-to for one hour, after which one of us might, with a little luck, snatch two hours' sleep in the bottom of the trench before it was his turn to keep watch until dawn, when again we would stand-to. This procedure was to set the pattern for each of the next seventy nights, unless we were on patrol.

So ended this long historic day. At its close we had established a firm foothold ashore and the objectives we had been set had been accomplished. Perhaps I was surprised to find myself alive and intact, many were not. I had a great feeling of relief that it was over and like all the participants, however humble their role, it was a day for ever etched on my memory. The very fact that thirty-five years after the event I can pen this account without difficulty of recall is a clear indication of the lasting impression D Day made on one young infantryman.

On D + 1 we moved well forward of the Periers Ridge to Le Mesnil wood astride the main road to Caen. We remained in these positions carrying out patrols and exchanging mortar and artillery fire with the enemy until 28th June when the East Yorks and the Suffolks put in an attack at dawn on the strongly held Château de la Londe. There was great carnage. That morning the Suffolks lost 161 killed, wounded and missing. Of my platoon, which numbered thirty-three on D Day, only five were left.

On 8th July we survivors of the Château attack took part in operation 'Goodwood' and followed up a massive air onslaught which was to herald the great breakout. This did not fully materialise. We occupied the shattered villages of Sannerville and Banneville la Campagne where the bombing had been so intense that the whole area resembled a lunar landscape.

In early August we transferred to the American sector in the vicinity of Vire. On the evening of 13th August, having made a successful advance the night before along the Vire–Tinchebray road, the Suffolks put in a further attack. My company was caught in murderous counter-battery fire as the attack opened and was virtually wiped out. All three platoon commanders were killed as was the CSM and one sergeant.

Of the five survivors of the Château attack on 28th June, three were killed. A corporal and myself were later evacuated after receiving multiple wounds that night. All the D Day platoon had finished their stint in Normandy.

*

From the Reverend P. C. Webber, formerly Lieutenant P. Webber of 2nd Middlesex Regiment

Four officers of the 2nd Middlesex were detached for duties with the beach group, under the command of Major Langley, the battalion second in command, to form traffic control groups at each beach exit, on Queen beach, the landing area of 3 Division in Sword sector, the left of the Allied assault.

My task was to control traffic leaving the beach at the right-hand exit, which was the main exit at La Brêche on the crossroads leading inland to Colleville. With me there was a sergeant, a wireless operator, and after we landed, two military policemen, and it is only fair to say I felt a proper Charlie landing with two large red and green flags, like a railway guard. I was virtually right-marker to the division.

We left the Solent in the *Empire Cutlass*, one of three Liberty ships converted into LSIs (Landing Ship Infantry) and we were very fortunate compared with our comrades in the smaller craft, for the ship's officers gave up their cabins for the unfortunate 'pongoes' who were to make the landing, and I shared a cabin with the infantry platoon commander who was to be responsible for local protection of my exit.

We had been issued with bogus maps at the briefing centre before embarking. These showed the landing area, with code names for the various targets and villages, but we did not know where we were going until we were handed the true maps on the eve of D Day, and then had to mark out our own localities and try to learn the place-names. Needless to say none of us slept that night, but we were buoyed up by the staggering sight of the massive force which all through' the previous day had quietly made its way out from the assembly area off Portsmouth, the smaller and slower ships first, followed in the evening by our own large 7,000-ton vessels, with the infantry LCAs slung from their davits.

Many of us felt a sense of taking part in something far greater than ourselves, and our personal anxieties and fears, though very real, were largely lost in the feeling that here was an event which would rank with the greatest happenings of history, perhaps the greatest amphibian expedition ever mounted, and utterly overwhelming in its remorseless power. The rough weather seemed almost incidental, and I never had any doubt that we would get ashore, although if one were to survive the first day it was quite impossible to project one's thoughts beyond the first twenty-four hours. The thought of facing a whole campaign scarcely occurred to me, and I suspect that most of us could not bear to think beyond the immediate landing. Perhaps our worst fear was of the possibility of German 'secret weapons' and particularly of flame-throwers. An idiot of a colonel, who was not taking part himself, had told us at the briefing that if they did use flame-throwers the best thing was to run right through the flame as it didn't harm you then! We had no intention of putting his theory to the test. In fact, the only thing resembling a secret weapon we came across was a miniature radio-controlled tank, though as it was unarmed, what purpose it served remained a mystery.

Soon after dawn I went on deck, feeling safer there than in the cavernous depths of the hull, which looked too vulnerable to a torpedo. Almost immediately I saw a great flash in the distance on our port quarter. I could just distinguish the bow and stern of a destroyer standing out of the sea after being torpedoed amidships. Soon twinkling lights appeared, from the life-jackets of the crew as they dived overboard. It transpired that she was a Norwegian destroyer, the only victim of a rather abortive E-boat attack, but it was not a very heartening beginning to the 'Longest Day'.

My party was to proceed in the second assault wave, in LCAs landing at H + 20 minutes, after the initial infantry assault which was to clear the beaches. We watched with mixed feelings as the leading platoons embarked from the boat-deck and were lowered into the distinctly choppy sea. We cheered them off, then our turn came, and we too were cheered as we circled the ship to take up formation and then set off in line-abreast, two deep. The sea was rougher than I had thought, and at times we could see only the funnel of the assault ship. This is probably why Major Langley's craft struck the stern of my LCA, and we had to leave him wallowing, and looking decidedly apprehensive, in a leaking craft which fortunately was rescued later on. He walked ashore, nonchalantly carrying a weekend bag in one hand and a rifle in the other.

As always in a large-scale operation there appeared to be confusion, with the larger LCTs threading their way through our struggling ranks, and warships dotted here and there shelling the shore defences. As we drew near the land I was very moved by the sight of a Polish destroyer which had steamed right inshore as though to draw fire from the defenceless landing-craft and was letting the strongpoints have hell. We were also stirred to observe the two-men crew of a miniature submarine standing quite unconcernedly on the deck of their tiny craft as they marked the way to the landing zone. Perhaps the most spectacular sight was the hedgehog of rockets fired by specially adapted LCTs, which rose with a great flash and roar. Whether they did any damage is debatable, but they certainly were good for morale.

The coastline was almost obscured by smoke, but as we approached the underwater obstacles we could see the vague outline of houses on the edge of the beach. Just as we had thought, the RAF had missed! Apparently visibility had been very bad for the bombing attacks which were meant to eliminate the main defences, so the strongpoints were more or less intact, and the houses were alive with snipers, who surfaced after the initial assault had passed through. We were almost among the lines of obstacles when I heard the midshipman in command of our LCA yell, 'For God's sake hard aport.' We just missed an ugly-looking obstacle with a Teller mine attached, and almost immediately we beached.

I was greatly relieved to be first ashore from the bow and thus have a chance to miss the expected machine-gun fire. To my great surprise the beach looked deserted. In fact, we had been landed too far to the left, on Red instead of White beach, and we were right under the guns of a strongpoint, although I didn't realise that at the time. I trod delicately, like Agag, in the tracks of a tank, and took shelter under a groin while I tried to work out our position. Looking up I noticed that there was a very live-looking shell attached to the post of the groin. Time to move on! We met a similar party from 3 Recce, who had been landed too far to the right, so we exchanged greetings and rather unsteadily zig-zagged our way to what was meant to be the right-hand exit on Queen White. Of course, no exit, just barbed wire and the decapitated body of a British officer. Perhaps I should say that it is quite inaccurate to state, as I have read, that the East Yorks on the left were pinned down on the beach for some time. They were certainly not there when we landed, only dead and wounded, among whom was the mortally wounded commander of the East Lancs assault company, on my position, who kept asking to be allowed to join his men.

The reason for the lack of activity at my exit was the sinking of the craft containing the AVRE tanks which were to open up the exit. Our portable radio was out of action because of penetration by sea water, but fortunately another team soon opened up the exit. At first little traffic could pass through because of intense shelling on fixed lines, which naturally were ranged on the crossroads. By this time my party were by the sea wall and we dug-in very rapidly, protected on the one hand by the wall, and on the other by the soft sand, which absorbed most of the impact of the shells and mortar bombs. However, many of those around were killed or wounded, including the assistant beach master. Scarfe, the platoon commander of the local defence platoon, was killed by a surrendering German, who threw a grenade and was rapidly despatched by the enraged platoon sergeant.

Soon after I was able to take up position on the crossroads a strange apparition appeared. A little man in blue dungarees, wearing a brightly-polished fireman's helmet and pushing a bicycle came up to me and announced in French that he was the Mayor of Colleville. He demanded to be taken to the commander as he had information about the enemy positions. We appreciated the nature and content of his welcome to the Allies and he was passed on as speedily as possible. I noticed that in the film *The Longest Day*, this incident has been immortalised in a more glamorous version. Our admiration for his courage in braving both German and British fire was immense.

As the morning wore on I was able to take a more detailed interest in what was happening. The arrival of the follow-up 9th Brigade was rendered more spectacular by the cycle company of the RURs,*

*Royal Ulster Rifles.

pushing their bikes like so many tourists, and also the KOSBs,* led by their piper, duly kilted. Sadly, I believe they had to give up the practice of being led thus into action because of casualties among these gallant men. The day was also enlivened by the passage of the Royal Marine Commandos, sweeping clear the last resistance of the coastal defences, and also by the sight of a paratroop brigadier who had come to the beach, presumably to report to higher authority.

Sniping went on throughout the day, and mostly took toll of officers. One naval officer was shot while sitting down changing his socks. Two officers from a beached landing craft came up to me to remark how quiet it was, only to be greeted by spurts of sand from a Spandau operated from a nearby house. I called up a 25-pounder SP† gun, and there was no more trouble from that quarter.

The so-called quiet was deceptive, for the tide rose to an unusual height, due to the strong wind, and there remained only about twenty-five yards width of beach for the whole invasion force to disembark. Operations almost came to a halt, and we were very anxious that there might be a counter-attack which could push us into the sea. The consequent lack of tanks to support the infantry certainly delayed the capture of their targets and may even have been responsible for their failing to reach Caen, as was laid down by Montgomery.

There was little air activity, but the balloons used to mark the beach exits were a wonderful target for German gunners and the few bombers who dared make a sortie. The rapid boomp boomp boomp of the defending Bofors guns was heard several times, and I was told that six German aircraft were destroyed, either by AA fire or our own fighters. I saw at least one Hurricane ditch offshore, and later a British pilot came up to me, asking to be directed to Beach HQ. He did *not* think it was quiet, and said he would far rather be in the air. Each one to his own taste!

Fortunately it was possible to clear the log-jam of traffic by nightfall, and we settled to a very uneasy night. There was a good deal of enemy air activity, with flares, and a good deal of bombing, either from aircraft or mortars, or both. Also it was rumoured that German tanks were mounting a counter-attack, which was all too true, for they had reached the coast just behind me, and discovered that an infantry patrol had returned, and either did not know the password, or it was not heard, for they were shot up by their own people, and a corporal

*King's Own Scottish Borderers. Mistaken identity. The 7th KOSB now in England as part of the 1st Airborne Division.
†Self-propelled.

was killed. Such things were probably commonplace. I had told the
two military policemen to take cover during the worst of the bombing
and shelling, as there was not much traffic then. I went to see how
they were getting on, but could not find them. I asked my sergeant
if he had seen them. He pointed silently to a heap of clothing in the
centre of the crossroads. A mortar bomb had scored a direct hit on
them. I shall always remember their quiet gallantry, reminding me of
the sentry discovered at his post in the ruins of Pompeii.

The following day was certainly quieter, as the snipers had been
winkled out, and as the enemy had withdrawn the fixed-lines were
no longer laid on the exits, though the beach still faced sporadic
shelling. An occasional explosion came from seaward as old merchant-
men were sunk as blockships to form part of the harbour. There had
not been much enemy activity from the sea during the night, although
E-boat warnings had been sounded. After forty-eight hours the four
exit parties returned to our Battalion HQ at Colleville, where I heard
that my company commander, his second in command and the
company sergeant major and despatch rider had all been killed at an
O-group* on D Day. At last one had to think beyond D Day, and
the thoughts were not optimistic. I felt a deep gloom, not only for
comrades to whom one had become attached, but over one's own
future which seemed likely to be brief and brutish.

However, it is true in a sense that everything after D Day was an
anti-climax, because we were most of us going into action for the
first time, and the type of fighting was quite unlike anything else we
experienced subsequently. We had screwed our emotions up to a
pitch for the assault landing, which was probably as eventful as most
of us had imagined. The remainder of the campaign was more in the
nature of long periods of boredom interspersed by short periods of
feverish activity, which is the more usual idea of war. We had to
adapt to a kind of numbed acceptance that many of us would not
return, and when one has reached this mentality, which is probably
that of the average infantryman, one can take almost anything. It is
significant that most of the 'battle fatigue' cases I came across, at
least in the early stages, were men who had not been deeply involved
in action, but more on the periphery, with time to think about themselves. Later in the advance through Normandy, and in Holland, one
became more aware of the docile acceptance of the ordinary soldier
of his lot, and I have vivid memories of long lines of infantry advanc-

*Small briefing meeting at which orders are given to key personnel.

ing to an attack, faces expressionless, heads often bowed, as they plodded slowly forward to what many of them looked on as an inevitable end. Certainly, every man has a limit to his endurance, and many reached theirs if they survived several attacks in a rifle company. I can only admire those who endured that hell to the end.

In 1977 I returned to La Brêche, to the exact spot where our beach exit had been. There is now a war memorial to the Allies between the crossroads and the beach, and also a lifeboat station right in the path of the route taken by the tanks as they set off on their journey of destruction. I like to think there is some significance in that. The house from which I was sniped still stands, and the window looks out on the lifeboat station. I think that is appropriate too.

*

From Mr J. A. T. McDermott
I served five-and-a-half years with the 2nd Battalion Lincolnshire Regiment (now, Royal, of course) in 9 Brigade, 3 Division, mostly as lance-corporal company clerk. I refused a commission twice and steadfastly refused to be drawn into Battlation Orderly Room, hence no promotion.

My recollection of D Day is crystal clear even after thirty-five years. After all, we had trained for it for three-and-a-half years, and after missing Dieppe by the skin of our teeth (the Canadian 2nd Division were substituted for political reasons at the last minute) and similarly being switched from the Sicily landing (for the same reason) it just had to be the high point of one's military career. Indeed we were led to believe that 3 Division and 50 (TT) Division were to be written off after the landing because of high casualty rate expected. In the event, things were a lot different and my post D Day experience was that we must have been a bit of an embarrassment with no clearly defined role.

But, to return to D Day, or rather just before it. The whole business was postpone twenty-four hours, of course, and for us the postponment came when we were in buses actually heading for Southsea. I had been trained (it's hilarious to recall in retrospect) on the bugle as a last line of communication if all else failed. I had already ditched the bugle, en route, into a bed of nettles and sweated out the long wait in case anyone discovered it was missing. I ditched it, of course, because sunlight on a polished bugle would have made a perfect target. No one ever knew and it was never required.

We did the crossing in an LCI(M) No 248 if I remember correctly, and the boat carried two rifle companies (mine was B) and odds and sods from HQ. For our role on landing we had been supplied with folding bicycles and motor-cycles, and these did the crossing slung, just like the laundry, on wires across the boat.

It was rough, very rough, and nearly all the lads were seasick, once we got on the move. While we were parked in the Solent (one could almost have walked across to the IOW the ships were packed so tight) we played cards, naturally. It was the only time in the Army that I ever won a big amount – and it was my belief that they let me win. After all, what good was a pocket full of copper and silver in France. It weighed very heavily and I was soon giving it away to French kids as souvenirs.

We got our heads down and somewhere about 4 a.m. I was woken by the CSM, who asked me if I would dish out the breakfast – there was no one else to ask. Apparently, the cooks had put the meal on (it was only tinned bacon heated in boiling water!) and then succumbed. In the event a stretcher bearer (Bob Blackburn, who came from Fulham) was there to help me. *No one, not even an officer, came for that breakfast.*

We had all we wanted, and then time began to drag. At some point we realised we were surrounded by 14 man-packs, there must have been two hundred of them and I remember being told at some time that the boat was indeed equipped for fourteen days. We must have rifled a good half of them for the chocolate and cigarettes they contained. We went round most of the ship distributing largesse to the poor devils who were seasick – not that they were very grateful in their state.

Came the time for us to return to the fo'castle where we were allocated sleeping space. It was Bob's idea to take one of the tins of bacon with us, for a laugh on the lads still sprawled in their bunks. Tinned bacon was fatty and rolled in a sort of greasepaper in the tin and you could unroll it and lift it up to hang rather like spaghetti. We started to eat it like that with upturned faces and I shall never forget forty-eight pairs of eyes following us. In the event Bob himself felt sick and rather spoiled the joke.

Now the landing itself – 2 Lincs were the reserve battalion of A Brigade who were themselves reserve brigade in 3 Division. We landed on Sword Green beach at 0835 (the 2nd East Yorks of 8 Brigade had actually assaulted our beach, Lion-sur-Mer, at H Hour which to us was 0725) and the LCI skipper did a marvellous job. He rammed it on the beach so hard that we almost had a dry landing. For some reason the ship was not square on; whereas the port side gangway went on to dry land virtually, the ship was slewed and the starboard gangway was about 10–15 yards from the shore. Even so, the water was no more than knee-deep. Our whole complement was fortunate (all the practice landings had been very deep, 4–5 feet, and often in freezing conditions from January 1944 on) except two.

I have mentioned the folding bicycles and motor-cycles. Well the chap in front of me was a regimental policeman pushing a motor-cycle and a Sten was slung across his back. This gun actually got caught in the chains forming a hand-rail and naturally I, in my new role of Good Samaritan, had to bend down to free him.

And then it happened, whether from a shell-burst or a wave created by HMS *Warspite*'s broadside (we had passed her earlier) I know now, but an enormous wave hit us at that exact moment. So it was that he and I were the only drenched squaddies from our ship. In a couple of minutes we forgot all about that in the chaos on and just off the beach.

But that's another story, ending in the battalion getting no more than 400 yards off the beach instead of the planned ten miles beyond Caen.

I forgot to mention that, with the 14 man-packs, was a large reserve of tins of self-heating soup and cocoa, and several of us had stocks of these slashed in our battledress blouses, so that we finished up looking like the Michelin silhouette.

*

From Major F. D. Goode, formerly Officer Commanding D Company, 2nd Battalion Glosters

We ran in, grounded and the Navy let down the gangways. I took the first one down to port, and wearing my waterproof trousers ran down the gangway to be the first of the regiment to land in Normandy. Alas, I stepped off into five feet of water, tripped over some obstacle and fell flat. Scrambling to my feet, I saw I was about three feet from a very ugly looking sea mine, which I avoided and waded ashore, kicking off the useless trousers. There seemed to be quite a lot of noise and certainly there was still some small arms fire but one did not really have time to notice it and we did not seem to be having any casualties. I was too anxious to clear the beach, in accordance with firm orders, to notice much.

I concentrated on following the taped gap to my left through the dunes, marked by a wrecked Sherman flail tank. Keeping to the middle of this and followed by a mixed bag of troops all anxious to get off the beaches which were a target area, I went through the dunes, hoping to gain control of the situation once we hit the lateral road. I stopped for a while to look at my map but we were off it and my best bet was to find the lateral road and turn right in the direction of Le Hamel. We were now in the area of the main German beach defences which had been heavily plastered by the Navy and RAF. Pillboxes and blockhouses were shattered and I have a clear recollection of one embrasure out of which a German officer had tried to climb; it had descended on top of him and squashed his top half leaving his legs with a pair of well polished boots protruding.

At this point a problem arose. We had cleared the dunes and come to a field. The noise was less intense as we were off the beaches and the Allied shelling had lifted further inland. It seemed quite peaceful for a while. But ahead of us and barring our route was a minefield, protected by barbed wire and signed 'Achtung Minen'. The maps with which we had been provided had, thanks to the French Resistance and our 'I' staff and the RAF, shown the German defences in detail. But we were off our maps. I did not like the idea of walking across a minefield and we certainly did not have the time to clear a way through, so this was a risk that must be taken. My mixed bag of troops were as unenthusiastic as I was. However at that moment a cow wandered across the field unhurt, so we hoped that it was a dummy and ran across it. Whether it was a dummy or not I never knew, but my party was unscathed.

A little further on and we came to the lateral road and began to sort ourselves out. The sun had come out and it promised to be a hot day, which was just as well as we were all soaking wet. We moved along the road, dividing it right and left, and keeping well spaced out and soon arrived at the rest of the battalion lining the road. The road was very flat and no proper ditches, in fact no cover at all, so we lay down flat on the forward edge and hoped for the best. At this moment the enemy started shelling with 88-mm guns and they had the road ranged to a nicety, as was to be expected. There was soon news of our first (known to us) casualties further up the road. My second-in-command 'Butch' Hedley Holgate was lying next to me and consoled me with the thought that here at least he would not get an income tax demand

Shells burst fairly close and one within a few yards, but it made a shallow crater in the road and the fragments went upwards.

We then moved on to our next halt on the road to Ryes. Here, just off the road, there was a stout stone wall surrounding an orchard which gave us good cover and we waited there for further orders. At this moment a gunner major came up riding a bicycle far too small for him, and I recognised John Gaye who had been in my house at Bradfield. He was two years senior to me, the son of the Commissioner of Crown Lands and I had stayed with his family and his cousin Robin Corbett in their house in Windsor Great Forest. John and I chatted for a moment or two and then he cycled on, he was moving up to spot for the guns. He was shot by a sniper a little later. The shelling had ceased and we moved on along the road in the direction of Le Hamel, where we turned inland in the direction of Ryes and Bayeux. By this time the rain had ceased, the sun had come out and it was going to be a warm day.

Our advance was to be supported by rocket-firing Typhoons of the RAF. The enemy were holding the hedge of the opposite side of the field some 150 yards away. At this point, I took the time to change my shirt and vest for dry ones from my pack as I was soaked with sea water and sweat. I am vague as to the time but it must have been after midday, as the sun was high. We heard the roar of the engines of the aircraft as they swept over us at almost ground level. They released their rockets behind our position and we could hear these swish over our heads. The whole line of the hedge opposite burst into flame with a thunderous bang and we clambered through our hedge and advanced through the dead cattle. There did not seem to be any firing from the direction of the enemy and when we arrived at their position it was deserted. The Germans had left some litter behind, spades and one Spandau machine-gun, but no men.

The colonel called an 'O' group to meet in the village of Ryes and we sat in the ditches by the roadside. The village had been heavily shelled and most of the trees were cut down, some across the road, and nearly all of them about ten feet up were bent over. There were a number of dead Germans lying about and there was a sickly smell of death in the air. It was hot, sunny and smelly. Colonel Biddle had a bad cold and could smell nothing, but I for one was glad to get back to my company. Our orders were to continue along the road from Ryes towards the St Sulpice heights. By now we had been joined by the A Echelon Brigade Transport and we had our carriers and Jeeps but these were to march in the rear. I heard that there had been one vehicle lost, the battalion office truck which had reversed on to a Teller mine and was destroyed.

As D Company we brought up the rear of the battalion. We were marching with some fifty yards between companies and the transport was in rear of my company. The roads were bordered with trees and grass verges which we presumed were mined. There was a certain amount of sniping and one who was firing at us turned out to be a Japanese. Every now and then we came across parties of German prisoners being escorted back to the beaches. Our next surprise was a young Frenchman on a bicycle who was wearing an FFI armband. After a brief interrogation we sent him to Battalion HQ. He said that he had been arrested the evening of 4th June and taken to a château, which was the local German HQ, with a number of other men of the Resistance. They had been called before a military court and sentenced to death for sabotage. They were due to die the morning of 6th June but the naval bombardment had hit the château and the blast had broken open their cell doors so they were free.

We continued our advance until we arrived at a fork, there was a military policeman controlling the traffic but no sign of the rest of the battalion. I asked him which way and he pointed to the left. We took this route but after about 400 yards we were blocked by a battery of our self-propelled guns debouching from a field. I looked at my map and realised that we were on the wrong road. It was now about 6.30 and just at that moment three Heinkels flew over us in V formation. They took no notice of us and were heading for the beaches. These were the only enemy aircraft that I saw the whole of D Day. Turning round we regained our route and rejoined the main body. We were detailed to remain in reserve while C Company cleared the farm buildings and church of a hamlet to our right. We rested in a ditch under the trees and kept in touch by wireless.

*

From Major A. R. C. Mott, formerly B Company, 1st Battalion Hampshire Regiment

One of the main snags was the weight the men had to carry. We did not expect carriers ashore until H + 90 minutes so had to be self-contained in ammunition. Every rifleman had fifty rounds of SAA, some Bren magazines, grenades and perhaps some 2-inch mortar bombs, as well as special equipment. In spite of this speed up the beaches was essential. I was lightly loaded but apart from my clothes I carried :

Steel helmet	Small pack with :
Mae West	24 hour ration
Binoculars	Washing & shaving kit
Compass	Socks, PT shoes
Sten with 180 rounds	Mess tin, knife, fork, spoon
2 Bakelite grenades	Emergency ration
2 HE grenades	Flask – medicinal whisky
Map case	Morphia tablets
Entrenching tool	Gas cape

And for landing two packs of 2-inch mortar bombs to dump some way up the beach. We carried no respirators.

We came ashore, the LCAs finally grounding about 100 yards further on. I saw that B Company's assault parties were all correct, as we waded through knee-deep water. My GS watch stopped at 7.48, my map-case had floated away, my binoculars were misty and for all I knew my Sten would not work. It seemed a long way to where we could see flail tanks and others high up the beach. We toiled on, walking rather than running and I found myself in the lead, wading through a large, shallow pool as I could not get any wetter. At last we reached a thin belt of wire. We paused and I joined 11 Platoon and got a man organised with wire cutters, also a tape man. The latter very slowly and crookedly felt his way through a field of reeds while we waited for something to open up on us. Eventually it did and most of us got inland from the shingle. Some of Company HQ sheltered behind a tank and I heard a bang, and a steel helmet flew up into the air and I think that was Dossor who died of his wounds.

As soon as the tape man was well forward we followed in a long snake. Only a direct hit could have done damage in the thick reeds. We safely reached the hedge which should have been La Grande Rivière (some 2 feet wide and 1 foot deep) leading to Asnelles, but clearly wasn't. We had landed in the wrong place. No doubt the incoming tide had edged us to the left, and when the smoke cleared we were perhaps 250 yards east of where we should have been. This was disastrous for A Company who should have landed at the Le Hamel strongpoint, which now had time to come to life and took a long time to subdue.

In our area the grass was burning and the whole company in a long snake. It seemed safe as we were defiladed. I noticed birds singing, perhaps hesitantly, in the hedge. Soon I saw Meuvaines church and looking over the hedge could identify Asnelles spire. Then we came to some ruined and deserted buildings which were Les Roquettes.

I made a little plan to attack Asnelles – 10 Platoon giving covering fire from Les Roquettes, while 12 followed by 11 used what cover they could.

My Company HQ were missing after that mortar bomb, so there was no wireless communication with platoons. 12 Platoon went forward in a savage mood as they had been shelled or mortared. Indeed I had been warned not to go on a path as mines were going off. They went up the lane and turned right over the open, then snipers and a Spandau opened up. Lionel Bawden, the platoon commander, was killed almost at once. Sergeant Smith, the platoon sergeant, was wounded. I told Graham Elliott to get 11 Platoon on as 12 had come to a halt and I went back to 10 Platoon whose covering fire was not needed when 11 reached the orchard wall. Mortar bombs started pitching among the corn. (This was the first time I had been under heavier fire than Pathan riflemen on the NW Frontier.)

By this time D Company were ashore and waiting and the Dorsets behind them, ready to go on when the way was clear. I told them how we were situated and they went on up the lane where 11 and 12 Platoons had gone towards Meuvaines and behind Asnelles. I found Charles Williamson and he said there were mines all over the field ahead of Les Roquettes, but we flagged down a flail tank which went over the field setting off the mines which was fun to watch. I think 10 Platoon eventually went direct when the mines were cleared. Charles Williamson was killed about now and Sergeant Bisson took over 10 Platoon.

I went back to 11 Platoon to find a Sherman near the wall and Graham talking to it and asking it to deal with the enemy, but it knew about the anti-tank gun and was reluctant. But it stood by and fired its cannon and m.g. into the wall, so I told Graham to get on. We could see the Germans in their post, firing at us, but the troops were not clever at firing back. Graham dashed forward into a crater at the corner of the wall and I followed him.

We got to within five yards of the trench and when two enemy appeared, threw a 69 Bakelite grenade which did not explode. They returned a stick grenade and I was nearly killed when Graham hurled his 15 stone on top of me, but the effect of the grenade exploding was minimal. I lay by the wall, hoping no one was in a tree to pick off a sitting duck, while Graham went back for his men. Sergeant

Bisson also came with some of 10 Platoon. I passed round the wall again but no one was in the trench, which was connected by tunnels to other positions.

We went cautiously through the orchard, looking through gaps in the wall for enemy, who fired at us occasionally. Bisson was excellent, fearlessly exposing himself and firing at any enemy. He got a bullet through his helmet which nicked his skull, but went on. At one time I saw two Germans through a gap, so fired my Sten (which worked) at twenty yards range. One fell down, and next day there were two corpses there with bullets through them.

I explored some back yards and came to the village street without seeing anyone, so collected most of my company and was about to tell them to go for the enemy anti-tank post 100 yards away, between us and the sea, when David Warren and some of Battalion HQ came down the lane from inland. He said that the CO was wounded and Charles Martin (second-in-command) killed, so he was Acting CO. He told me to take a patrol into Le Hamel and see if I could find A Company of whom there was no news. I collected Graham and some men and went down the road and some of our tanks came towards us. Suddenly there was a blast and splinters flew into my face. I didn't know immediately what it was until I saw that the tank close to me had been hit. Then another was hit, so that the enemy gun was in action and other enemy between us and Le Hamel, so we came back, intending to find another way to go round to Le Hamel. About now Graham Elliott was mortally wounded by a piece of metal that blew away his jaw. I started off with rather fewer men to get round to Le Hamel, about ten with Bisson, Lance-Sergeant Collins of 12 Platoon. I got to the edge of Le Hamel and found Lieutenant King of C Company mopping up some snipers, so I went towards Le Hamel West. We got there. I left some men in a garden overlooking the strongpoint. There was a cottage with a French family who were happy to see us. There was also a tank cruising along the edge of an anti-tank ditch and another in flames. There was the odd sniping shot as I spoke to the tank commander.

I told Bisson to make for Le Hamel West strongpoint through back gardens and trees. He came back with about fifteen prisoners, but shots still came from the strongpoint. David Warren appeared and along came an AVRE which pumped in shells from its petard. Bisson went in again and collected more prisoners, but the dose had to be repeated before the strongpoint was quiet, producing several dead Germans and one or two wounded.

Le Hamel East was still not quelled. A Company had had a very
bad time having to attack it without support. Dick Baines was
wounded and lay behind a tank which moved and crushed him. C
Company had partly supported A and partly gone into reserve.
D Company had gone virtually unopposed, taken their battery position and were dealing with the Arromanches radar station.

It must have been early afternoon now and my carrier turned up
and replenished us with ammunition. I reorganised, splitting 11
Platoon among 10 and 12. My three platoon commanders were dead
and all the platoon sergeants were wounded that day. Cecil Thomas
(my second-in-command) had joined us and always knew what to do
and coolly walked around with a walking stick and displayed no
concern under fire. He had won a fine DSO at Tebourba. I put him
in charge of 12 Platoon and Bisson commanded 10.

We went inland for a bit and found boards with '*Achtung Minen*'
at each field, but David Warren said they couldn't all be mined, so
we struck across in a long snake and were unscathed. Peter Paul,
second-in-command of D Company, met us by St Côme de Fresne
and showed us a safe way to the battery position and radar station
which his company had occupied. The canteen was undamaged until
the troops arrived, and the ration store the same. D Company had
rounded up many prisoners, some of them sailors, and more came
up from Arromanches, just below, with a large white flag.

David Warren then organised naval support to assist D Company
to their final objective, the battery beyond Arromanches, while I took
some of C Company and some of mine to search Arromanches. We
expected tanks to stand by, but they never came, so we went in and
were met by a dog, which seemed to be German. His masters followed
with a white flag. Arromanches was surprisingly full of French people
as we had heard they would all be evacuated and out came flowers,
tricolors and Union Jacks.

Cecil then took a patrol to clear Tracy, about a mile away, the
battalion's final task, but rifles and a Spandau fired on them. The
only damage to our side was when a bullet blew off a man's water
bottle. We were then told to stay at the radar station for the night,
instead of returning to Asnelles. I organised what men I had into two
posts and sent Bisson, who got an MM, back to the RAP.

Then to Battalion HQ for orders and the brigadier came and said
the Hampshires' name was at the top of the list for doing so well.
I had expected a blast for taking twelve hours for a four-hour task.
We had news of the progress on other beaches. Then a few German

bombers came over when it grew dark, but I doubt if they did any damage.

I went back with Colour Sergeant Eastburn in the carrier and it was midnight when my day's work was done. We issued blankets and I had a bit of chocolate and a biscuit and a drink of water before turning in for two hours' sleep. I doubt if I had eaten anything since breakfast until then.

Casualties had been heavy. A Company were left with Tony Boyd, their second-in-command, and 27 men, B and C about 55 each.

D Company only lost about 25. A high proportion of officers were killed or wounded. I think some 270 casualties out of 700 were sustained on D Day.

*

From Major R. R. Rylands, W Company, 2nd King's Shropshire Light Infantry

The night of D Day passed quietly – more quietly than we had anticipated. In the early morning of 7th June, we heard tracks from the enemy side, and the writer seems to remember calling for help from the gunners, in some panic. Later in the morning W Company had a grandstand view from our forward slope of the 2nd Warwicks' attack going in on Lebisey, just across the valley, and of their subsequent withdrawal, covered by the 1st Norfolks. That left us once again the most forward troops on our front.

Throughout that day, and the succeeding ones in that position, we were bothered by snipers, firing peculiarly silenced weapons, apparently in our very midst. Some were in the trees and scrub that lay in the middle of the triangle formed by W, X and Y Companies, and some, I feel sure, operated from houses in the village. Certainly Privates Bennion and Luscott grew to hate the trip back to Battalion HQ with messages. But though we organised many 'beats', during dull moments, we never wholly eliminated the problem, which remained rather mysterious. The writer found for instance that he was always potted at along a line through a gap in our rear hedge to a small window in a farmhouse – yet this house could be found to contain only a typical peasant family, with a bevy of children eager for our ration of sweets.

We also learnt during these first days how to distinguish between the various kinds of Jerry guns and mortars, and knew just when to duck. We had a slow but steady drain of casualties, because the enemy shelled the edges of our orchard with regularity and accuracy. Some reinforcements were sent up under Corporal Ellis, unfortunately by day, and we were shelled immediately, with fatal casualties. This almost unheralded arrival of reinforcements during daylight happened too often in the early period.

That night, 7th June, Major David Stancombe (OBLI*) arrived to take over the company from Captain Rylands. It was a confused night, with many false alarms, during which Corporal Ball was accidentally wounded. Sergeant Jordan reported enemy AFV movement on our right flank just as it got too dark to see clearly. Our helpful gunners bombarded the area, to make sure, and indeed the movement must have been part of that Panzer counter-attack between 3rd British and 3rd Canadian Divisions which took place on 7th June.

The next night was a grim one; we were shelled with great intensity, and had more casualties than our SBs could deal with. The carrier platoon nobly came to our rear, to assist evacuation, and suffered losses themselves. Fatal casualties included the company commander, who died of wounds, and Privates Richardson and Roberts. Our gunner OP was also completely knocked out. It must be confessed that many of us had the jitters that night, and the arrival of Colonel Maurice, calm but understanding, to see how things were, was a relief; he promised to arrange as much retaliation by our gunners as possible. For the rest of this period the company had only two officers, Captain Rylands and Lieutenant Wright, as Lieutenant Murray had been evacuated earlier.

On the night of the 11th we handed over to a company of the Warwicks. This was done copybook fashion in the position, but the movement down back the road to Beuville was terrifyingly noisy, partly because uncertainty about mines made cross-country travel by night too dangerous. We stayed in a compact position round a farm house in Beuville until 15th June, where we cleaned up, shaved (water had been desperately short in the first position) and wrote letters. We could not relax completely, because much of our position was under observation from Lebisey, still less than two miles away. We were busy almost every night with large-scale mine laying on our open right flank. The writer, Private Luscott and some Pioneers also had to recce and chart an enemy minefield to our right, which was reached by a precarious route through one of our own minefields. In Beuville, Major Brooke Smith took over the company, and Lieutenant Tamplin (DCLI) joined us.

*Oxford and Buckinghamshire Light Infantry.

*

From Major M. J. F. Wilson, King's Shropshire Light Infantry
... We're at the end of the village and there's our road running
straight up a gentle hill between fields of green corn No hedges, no
trees before the top of the hill. X Company is moving up the hill
extended on either side of the road. Shells fall amongst them – whose
shells? Someone says, our shells. We haven't yet learned to tell where
they are coming from and we have never met Boche shells before.
X Company lie down. I go forward and talk to the company commander and learn there are German posts in the corn. X Company
moves on and over the crest of the hill. I reach the crest and see
beyond open rolling country broken by tree-clustered villages. A gun
fires at us at close range from our right flank. The tanks, now coming
up, report an 88-mm anti-tank gun and ask us to deal with it. My
colonel joins me by a hedge where we hope the Boche gunners can't
see us. He decides to to send Z Company to destroy the gun whilst
with the rest of the battalion he pushed on down the road. I am to
stay by the hedge, keep touch with Z Company and brigade headquarters; collect Support Company and send it forward when it's
wanted and it's safe to do so. Everyone moves off. For the first time
since landing I have time to think. I feel for my tobacco, it's sodden,
so are my maps. My field glasses are full of salt water. But what's
that matter, the sun is shining and larks are singing and all is going
well if a little slowly.

Wireless report of snipers in the village at the bottom of the hill,
Beuville. Z Company has located the guns and is fighting hard, they
want help from the tanks. I speak on the wireless and try and arrange
matters. The afternoon is passing. The CO wants the anti-tank guns
up. I tell them they will be shot at coming over the hill, to drive fast
and keep well separated. One, two, three, four, the Hun misses every
time; then the fifth; it's nearly out of the danger zone when the Hun
fires. The carrier drawing the gun bursts into flame, the crew leap
out. Carrier and gun trundle on down the hill burning fiercely. I walk
over to the crew. A little shaken that is all. I get them under cover
and go back to my hedge. All quiet except for ammunition exploding
in the burning carrier. Z Company call for help again. I can't get
the tanks on my wireless. I see a tank, walk over to it, climb up to
the turret and tell the troop commander to pass the situation of Z

Company on his wireless. The battalion reports being in Biéville, the second village on the road. Z Company reports the capture of the guns but many casualties. I tell the MO of the casualties. I decide to move battalion HQ on to Beuville.

Across the road in Beuville lie two of our men, killed by snipers. I see some men by a house, entering I find a room full of wounded, some German. The vehicles of battalion HQ arrive and are parked. The CO reports slow progress. No news from our flanks. I stand in a small garden wondering how the great adventure has really progressed. We have done moderately, have others fared better or worse? Suddenly there is a cry of gliders – what a wonderful encouraging sight! Slowly the aircraft circle loosing their tows away to the east of us, then as they turn for home pass low over our heads. Look! They are jumping. Crash! A roar of flames, just over the garden wall. Well, the crew are safe. The CO calls me up to him and up the village street I go, ready to shoot at any sniper. A man in grey uniform sticks his head out of a window and I am about to shoot my first Boche only to realise, just in time, that he's an Air Force man, one of the crew of the crashed plane. I meet the CO, learn the details of the day's fighting and that we can get no further. I move up battalion HQ. As it gets dark we begin to dig. Will we be counter-attacked? I walk around till dawn.

*

From Mr David Holbrook, former Lieutenant Holbrook in the East Riding Yeomanry

Out of sleep throbbing with the diesel engines to meet the disabling heaving of the sea, the oily stench of the LST. The rolling sleeping bodies and somebody being sick further down the companionway. So hard to believe that it was not just another exercise except for the fear in the bottom of your stomach and the notes about German defences and photographs of our beaches trodden into the greasy floor. Under the bunk a map marked with Queen beach, through the villas on to the first lateral, assemble at Lion-sur-mer, intention to drive south, blue route. D Day morning, the new Christmas morning of the world. Now 7 o'clock and H Hour is at 08.45. The little ships gathering off the coast now and the well-fed occupiers of Normandy seaside towns frightened in their early morning by the terror of phone messages from their headquarters and soon by the black and orange flowers of direct hits about their ears and all our planning of the last two years falling on their backs, bullets to collapse their arrogance. The watery noise of the sea burbles down to the inside of the ship and suggests the world outside, the swept channel fifty miles from the coast of France; I crawl out of the steel net bunk and in an overcoat slither past the sleeping bodies of invaders so that I can put my head through a hole in the upper deck. A line of LSTs following one another like ducks across the Channel with their little toy barrage balloons, with a little smoking escort, no other smoke or shape to show the weight of our armadas. Only the dull endless sea, the hungry heaving sea of early morning. By sea a liquid holiday of peace coming to land with the end of the hopeless boredom of our training and our wait frustrated for food for our guns and liberated soil under our tank-tracks. The sea, the gentle mother of our attack.

There is the hum of planes but they cannot be seen and the dull sea is cold and there is nothing to do in the thick stench of the ship except sleep, for everything is ready in the tank deck, everything is trained and greased and loaded, and we know the plan backwards and it will be different when we land anyhow. From the calm heaving belly of the sea into the heat of an insecure bridgehead about 1 o'clock today, and perhaps this is the last morning alive for me. Such a landing never before in history. The excitement when the secret is known back in England, but some won't care, I suppose. It would be nice to see the coast of France coming out of the mist, but so cold and you get seasick standing up looking over the bows. People swore as I stumbled and rolled back to bed.

Later I dress for the beachhead. These clothes may have to stay on for many days. A string vest to rub the sweat off, a smart shirt for the well-dressed corpse if I am to be one. And gathered up all the personal effects that seem so trivial with my own life in the bigness of events today, compass, pistol, field-dressing, morphia. I roll up my bed and lurch down to the tank deck with it.

The black line of France has grown and grows now as the morning goes on, out of the mist. And a feeling of immediate urgency, of real time, grows with it. The little towns all over those hills and Le Havre over there and the French subjugated and armed, waiting for what has already begun and the news now reaching them passed on with joy. And the men in grey-green rushing about in a new urgency, shouting war-wearied commands to one another and realising their comfortable occupation as brutal landlords in these villages is now to be torn apart. From the cruising capital ships over there the blossoming beginnings of great salvos coming in to blast them. We

are sailing west now along the coast. And the calm slowness of the
size and power of the onslaught breaks to us and the frightening
greatness of it as the ships accumulated back to the circle of the sea.
Gradually all the contents of the harbour we were in yesterday when
the ships began to move out are off these beaches with the contents
of other harbours. Till now we had not really believed in our own plan,
in the theory of D Day which we had helped to put together on the
beaches of Wales and on the bays and headlands of Scotland.

Now we sailed near enough for us to recognise from our photographs and see the line of villas on the shore behind the beaches we
were due for. Lit occasionally by the sun this coast smoked with the
heaviness of the H hour barrage which had fallen on it. The whole
of the assaulted bit of France before us was wreathed and flown with
smoke-tattered flags of the explosion and burning of buildings, and
now and again, as we watched and got nearer, a mushroom of
black or white smoke pillared up. But the noise and rumbling were
lost in the clopping and rolling of the sea. Watching from the sea the
men and steel striving for Ouistreham and striving inland, dying and
shooting under the smoke clouds drifting across the Orne, we were
watching the newsreel of the harsh forefront of world events which
we were making. A fighter fell burning from the grey cloud-base and
slowly dropped the other side of the river. What we had read about
and prepared and trained for and thought about was here, with only
a little strip of the neutrality of the sea between us and our first work
in action. War had come to us and to me.

Then with our heads swimming with diesel fumes we went up
again to gather the full scale of this thing we were watching from the
safe ample grandstand of the sea. The assault landing craft coming
out now tired, with wounded, and holes in their sides. The innumerable large ships with big code names on their hulls audaciously
anchored off. The frightening hugeness of it undisturbed. But two
shells straddled our ship and with cracking pillars of sea spoke to us
closely of death and the enemy.

This was the new thing that showed it was not an exercise. Everything else we had done so much before that it was automatic and
uninteresting, but the violence of the battle on shore and the new
factor of calculated death directed at you produced a dryness of the
mouth and a brightening of the whole scene. Never were there such
vivacious waves and bright glimpses of sun as we fought with the
landing ramp and the pontoon ferry that was to take us inshore, and
the hectic fury of the ship smashing the ramp on to the engines of the

ferry and smashing their covers and the yawning gap between the ship and the ferry over which at a wave of my arm the blundering Sherman would roar at me, perch for a moment over the depth of the generous sea and a plunge to the sands, and fall reckless on to the pontoons on its last stage of the journey to Europe for France and Paris. And over the last stretch of peaceful breakers (why they don't shell and bomb us floundering out there, we can't think), the exciting beginning of the touchdown on the new-won beaches and now soon to drive inland over the uncared-for corpses of defeated Fascists and at last to implement our military politics.

At H plus 5 hours we bellowed ashore through the breakers on to a beach cleared by those who had left their derelicts behind them and their dead mourned by the white beachmarker flags and the windsocks showing the gaps they had made spoke their message – get on and inland through our achievement. And we went on into the nearest battle, into the streams of red tracer and the vicious crack of the anti-tank shell and the hammer-clarion of the screaming shell that arrives for you and the sad pyres of burning tanks blowing up with yesterday's comrades and the rodents lying in the ditches outside their opulent and vulgar billets grinning in the blankness of well-deserved death.

*

From Mr C. J. Potter, South Lancashire Regiment
I remember it being dark at the time we sailed, and as we got nearer to the French coast, it was daylight. The first thing I saw was a battleship firing inland. Then all at once, we seemed to run up the beach. As I went down the front ramp, I saw my first dead. It was a Commando, I think, who had landed in the first wave. Before we landed we were told after the landing craft stopped to get down the ramp and wade through the water, and get across the beach and coast road, as quick as we could. I waded through the water chest high, got on to the beach and passed three German soldiers lying on their backs, dead. I crossed the coast road and as I did, I looked right and left. I saw bodies lying in the gutters, and to the right, saw what seemed to be a Bren gun carrier on fire.

Later I started crawling through the corn and came across a path cut through the same. I did not think anything of it at the time, but doing it nearly finished my life. I crawled about six or seven yards and came across a body lying across the path. I crawled over it, and

I think I passed over about six or seven. I had just crawled over the
last one, when this burst of machine-gun fire came over my head.
It did not make me get out of the path, but I think I put on speed.
Now I know what happened. It must have been a German machine-
gun on fixed lines at the other end of the passage. The boys that were
dead must have been killed as the attack went in, and they were
upright. Anyway, I managed to get back to our lines and what a mess
they were in.

I saw as I was crawling, trenches caved in, with the bodies still in.
These would be the men who had been left behind as what they
called LOBs – Left Out of Battle – the men left to stop a counter-
attack if we had been wiped out. I am only presuming this, for I did
not know much about battle tactics. Anyway, I eventually reached
my dug-out and was just going to jump down, when I saw a large
shell at the bottom. I got down, got the shell in my arms, and rolled
it over the edge of the trench, then I got down on my face, for the
shell fire was still falling very heavily. It was not very long after, we
had a roll call, and I do not think many of my company had come
back. My friend was blinded, but thank goodness, he got his sight
back, and came back to me (five weeks – roundabout) and he was all
right. He went on to the end of the war. I finished in Holland.

*

From Mr R. S. McDowall, then Private, 5th East Yorkshire Regiment
Although I was in the OTC at college and passed 'Certificate A', I
was never at all keen about soldiering and remained a humble private
throughout almost the entire Second World War period, from January
1940 onwards.

I was a private in the 5th Battalion, East Yorkshire Regiment in the
50th Division, alongside battalions of the Green Howards and Durham
Light Infantry. I served with them in the Eighth Army under Montgomery from El Alamein in Egypt to Enfidaville in Tunisia. Then
we were withdrawn and returned to Alexandria. Later I took part
in the invasion of Sicily, landing on the first day at Avola and finishing
up in Messina. Then the 50th Division were withdrawn because there
was talk of starting a 'Second Front' in Europe and we were wanted
to take part in that.

We descended the rope-ladders into the LCAs about 4.45 and set
out in high seas for the French coast. There must have been about
twenty of us in the small rectangular assault craft, all sitting un-

comfortably on the low-raised woodwork which served as seats. We wore gas-capes to protect us from the flying spray and clutched our 'bags, vomiting', which only too soon were having to be put to use as our tiny craft made its way through mountainous seas. Many of those who had had occasion to use these bags attempted to throw them into the sea but the wind merely blew them into the soldiers sitting behind them!

As the light began to dawn it became clear what was going on. To our left and right were the rest of the little landing-craft steering towards the shore, while away behind us lay the ships which had brought us over. Warships were shelling the shore, which was as yet scarcely visible and rocket-ships sent their missiles into the air with terrific roars. Above us flights of bombers droned their way towards the land ahead of us while we ploughed forward below, miserably sick and not feeling the slightest bit like attacking anything or anybody.

Slowly the land showed up clearer and closer, and spouts of water rose from the sea around us as the Germans returned the warships' fire. Suddenly it seemed to be fully light and we could clearly discern the shore in front of us.

'There's the lighthouse,' shouted Lieutenant Lowe, second-in command of our company, 'and it's still standing.'

I remember that I felt just a trifle discouraged that all our bombing and shelling had not managed to destroy it.

As we got closer to the shore and into calmer waters my sickness began to disappear. 'So far, so good,' I thought, and felt my excitement mounting.

Almost before we had fully realised it, the Marines were preparing to let down the 'front door' of the landing craft and we were making final adjustments to our equipment preparatory to disembarkation. At first the Marines, seemingly anxious to get rid of us and 'to hell out of it all', were going to release us farther from the shoreline than was practicable. Lieutenant Lowe persuaded them to take us in just a bit closer in case we found ourselves in water that was too deep for us to wade through. They moved the boat a little further up the beach and a Marine promptly opened the front and jumped into the sea to test its depth. He had barely done so, however, before the first men were out of the craft and ploughing through the water towards the shore. They were quickly out and away up to the land. When my turn came I found myself jumping out of the craft into the water, my only thought being to make sure that I didn't fall in as I had done on the exercise and I remember feeling relieved that on this occasion I had not done so.

Before me was about forty yards of heaving sea reaching almost up to my chest, and ahead a slowly-rising beach covered with round, flat stones. Some posts strung with barbed wire were sticking out of it, but altogether it did not look a very formidable obstacle. Beyond this again were green-tufted sand-dunes, marshy fields and then some stony, higher ground rising towards one or two large houses and the lighthouse building which stood back facing the sea along a road. These buildings would have been about 300 yards inland. Away to my left other landing craft were disgorging their loads, a tank was blazing and exploding, while further to the left there was a sea wall and the village of La Rivière; also some pillboxes. A slight headland obscured the view to my right.

We were making for dry land in a kind of ungainly file. I was now wading through little more than two feet of water and making surprisingly swift progress. In one hand, above the water, I held my rifle, and in my other hand was a case of three-inch mortar bombs, with which at the last minute I had been presented and asked to dump alongside the mortar crew who had landed from our boat just ahead of me.

As I went ashore, being of a musical turn of mind, I resolved that I would keep in mind something worthy of the occasion and chose the Bach chorale 'Was Gott tut, das ist wohlgetan' (What God does, that is well done) and was surprised to find that, when I had a moment to think about it, it had turned into a very much lighter piece of music – Delius's 'La Calinda', which has a similar line to that of the Bach chorale. Still, at least the Delius was British and not German in origin, and in its way may well have reflected my optimistic and confident outlook at the time!

For in fact there seemed to be very light opposition at our particular place of landing, although it was very noisy away to our left. It seemed an age before I reached the shore and could walk without the water dragging at my legs. As I advanced over the round, flat stones I realised that it was improbable that the enemy would have laid mines on such a shoreline. Reaching the top of the shingle, I found the rest of Company HQ laid flat on the ground behind the sand dunes while one of the platoons went forward towards the higher ground ahead of us.

As we laid there I added more of the big stones about me as additional protection. All at once a tank close to my left blew up, and scattered fragments of jagged metal flew over my head. Meanwhile, shells from our warships still screamed over our heads, together with bullets from our own craft just out to sea.

Then we got off from the shore and moved up to a gap in the barbed wire and crouched for a while in a large bomb-crater. Here we remained for a minute or two while the three-inch mortar beside us pounded the buildings in front. Close by us a 'flail' tank (one equipped with ground-beating chains for setting off mines) pushed its way forward until a marshy stream halted its progress; the ditch was just too wide to enable it to cross.

The crater would have been a nice place to stay in, but our duty was to 'push on'. A white tape had been laid down by the engineers who had gone in with the foremost platoon to guide us through the minefield (which in fact may have been a 'dummy'). However, we followed this tape over the marsh stream, across the side of a field and then across another field where we rested behind a slight ridge, on which we were sorry to see that one of our friends in the company lay dead. A few yards ahead there was a stony road which led up from La Rivière to Ver-sur-mer and on to a larger village inland. We had reached our objective and received orders to remain there. This was another large bomb-crater and it was already filling up with German troops who had been taken prisoners, and one or two of them proved to have been wounded. They all looked dazed and shaken. One was Polish, another Russian, while another, who had a Red Cross painted on his helmet, told me he came from Dortmund.

As we had discovered on previous battle occasions, liaison between forces had sometimes been suspect. Our warships had started shelling again and some fell very close to us. Also the offshore landing craft were firing their machine-guns, and bullets were passing uncomfortably close to our heads. Through the smoke we looked back across at the nearby village, where bursts of machine-gun fire and exploding hand-grenades revealed that Jerry was still giving battle there. Meanwhile, fellow-signaller Sid Martindale and myself took the opportunity to remove the waterproofing from our '18-set' and got into radio touch with our Battalion HQ and other important contacts. At the same time, a house close to us was billowing forth smoke, and explosions kept taking place; it must have been an ammunition dump.

After a time it became evident that the village below had been 'liberated' and we saw the first of our tanks coming up the hill from the village. At intervals it was followed by further tanks. Our company commander had himself recced a little way up the road and had warned the leading tank that there were mines laid in the road further up the hill and he indicated an alternative way around them. But for some reason the tankmen ignored him, and later, when we ourselves passed that leading tank, we found it wrecked with its front track ripped right off.

In the wake of the tanks came our own battalion transport and some of our own Bren gun carriers. It was good to see our own trucks had got ashore; for one thing, our rations were aboard them! Then part of two other of our own companies came up the road, but sadly one company had become so diminished in numbers that on the same day it was united with the remains of another to form one new whole.

The day wore on and we continued to march further inland with our vehicles following behind us. Daylight began to fade and quite suddenly things seemed to quieten down. What opposition there was had either been finished off or had run for it; the only noise was the sound of our own steady advance and the crackling of a wildly-burning farmhouse, the flames of which provided a welcome light in the gathering darkness.

At the end of a tree-lined drive we at last halted in the precincts of a large manor house. In the grounds of this building our Battalion HQ, the Bren gun carriers and our own company were to spend the night. We had penetrated several miles into France, but in fact had not quite reached our intended objective, which was a village on the Caen–Bayeux road, called St Leger, only in fact about a mile ahead of us.

We made ourselves some tea and cooked some sort of meal in a barn. With what we had for bedding we settled down to sleep among the farm machinery, first tuning in our wireless set to a BBC programme to hear the historic news we had made that day. Way back on the beaches German planes were bombing our beachhead, some flying low overhead.

Otherwise, all was quiet – oddly quiet after so hectic and noisy a day. From 1 a.m. until 2 a.m. on 7th June I had to do a spell of guard duty. All was peace, and I discussed with a fellow-guard the day which had just passed – how well we had done, the prospects of holding the bridgehead, the number of dead Jerries we had seen, and our own losses, how (because the enemy had then recovered from the bombardment) friends of ours who had come ashore later than we had done had been mown down by machine-guns as they got off the landing craft. It had been an incredible day, but perhaps that quiet night was more incredible still.

From Lieutenant-Colonel G. A. Shepperd, Manchester Regiment
At the time of these events I was on the Headquarters of 3 British
Infantry Division as GSO I (L) the L standing for 'liaison'. In this
capacity I found myself carrying out reconnaissance and contact
duties, usually under the personal orders of the divisional commander.
These recollections cover about fourteen days. They are brief as I was
unconscious during most of this time.

It was already late afternoon. Time was getting short, as the tanks
would be on the move before dawn and there were several forward
routes to be reconnoitred as well as a control-point to be set up.

We were the other side of the Orne, where the ground was more
open, and it was an area that had been fought over ever since the
drop by 6 Airborne Division. The young major from one of the
forward companies was leading and his orderly was behind and to
my left. We were moving parallel to a farm track that itself was
partially screened by a line of trees. The explosion was deafening,
branches of a tree high above seemed to envelop me, but I don't
remember falling.

Struggling against the ear-splitting crash and the blinding light, all
now seemed very quiet. I found myself half sitting in a shallow slit
trench facing the other way from our route forward. The major had
dropped on one knee and seemed to be shouting, but I did not hear
what he said. The orderly was slumped on the ground and looked all
right but had blood on his face. A mist drifted away – momentarily
I could see my wife and children sitting in a garden and I called out
but they did not hear me. Now I looked down. My right foot had
been blown off and I was gripping my thigh in an attempt to stop
the blood flowing. There was no sense of pain at all. The mist came
back, but later I heard voices. Two soldiers were calling to each other.
Each had a bayonet in his hand and was crouched down prodding
the ground. Soon they were very close and the darkness closed in.

How many hours or days I was held in the forward area by 223
Field Ambulance I don't know; my only recollection is of being lifted
on a stretcher high up on to a frame above a Jeep. It was cold and
I felt very vulnerable, but a soldier stood beside me with a bottle
and a long tube.

The journey to 32 CCS didn't take very long. Much of the tent
where I found myself in bed was below ground, and one of the MOs
was speaking to me. Evidently a lot of my other leg had been blown
away and it would have to be amputated to save what was left – he
seemed to be asking my permission, and I thought it was very nice of

him to put it that way. The operating theatre was in a much smaller tent, rather several small tents. Everyone was very friendly – but I did not realise that they were far more worried about gangrene having set in.

I seemed to sleep a lot, but one day I was shaved by an orderly and felt a good deal better if only for a short time, as the pain was getting bad. Another day I remember a nurse feeding me as my wrists and hands were heavily bandaged. She was wearing battle dress and I could not understand as I thought all nurses wore starched white dresses. Then the gunfire reminded me that we were still in the all too narrow bridgehead, where I had earlier nearly driven into the German lines looking for one of the units on our flank. But where was the division now? How long had I been lying there unable to move, but with a growing awareness of the gunfire and the aircraft overhead?

What I did know was that I was very lucky to be alive. Judging by the bits of metal casing dug out of me, the mine that I had stepped on should have killed me instantly and must have been buried very deeply indeed. Lucky too that I had been picked up so quickly. Now with the wonderful medical attention and nursing that I was getting, and in spite of the problems ahead I felt that at least I had a fair fighting chance.

Note – I was evacuated by air to the UK and in a little over a year of my being wounded, which was spent in hospital and getting fitted with artificial legs, I was fortunate to be able to return to duty as a DS at the Staff College, the first of several staff appointments before I joined the Civilian staff of the RMA Sandhurst early in 1947.

CHAPTER SIX

Marines and Commandos

The part played by Marines and Commandos is not given full justice here, as they undertook a very wide variety of tasks. However, these samples give some idea of their participation and a fuller description may be obtained from some of the accounts listed at the end of this book.

*

From Brigadier Peter Young, DSO, MC (This excerpt was originally published in his 'Storm from the Sea')

It was now about ten o'clock. We were in touch with 45 Commando in the brigade's first forming-up place, but progress was delayed by minefields, confining the brigade to one track which had to be followed in single file. No 6 Commando was ahead, but the advance was still maddeningly slow; and so leaving John Pooley and Donald Hopson to bring on the main body of the Commando, I pushed on with Sergeant Leyland, Corporal Christopher and a few others to get through to the Benouville Bridge and find out what was going on. Our rear-link wireless set had broken down.

We passed through 45 Commando in Colleville, where, except for a little small-arms fire, all was quiet. Along the road to St Aubin d'Arquenay we met no resistance, though there was desultory sniping at the far end of the village where we met some of 6 Commando escorting prisoners.

Beyond St Aubin the road was clear of troops. It led down hill to Benouville; we covered the distance at the double. Entering the village, my party passed a post manned by airborne troops, obviously delighted that they were no longer isolated.

The bridge over the Orne was under rifle fire from a château on the west bank of the canal, about eight hundred yards to the south. A number of dead Germans lay sprawling around an abandoned glider within thirty yards of the road, while the bridges, still intact, bore witness to the success of the airborne *coup de main*.

217

Here I saw half a dozen men of 3 Troop, who had dismounted from their bicycles and were taking cover under the low bank to the left of the road.

'What are you waiting for?'

'They're sniping the bridge, sir.'

'Well, get on your bikes and go flat out; you'll probably get away with it!'

They leapt to their feet. One man fell shot clean through the head. The rest reached the other side. Now it was our turn. We ran across the bridge as fast as we could. On the other bank in a ditch beside the road sat a row of German prisoners. Almost at once Lord Lovat appeared and told me that our advance on Cabourg was off. The airborne troops had dropped over a far wider area than had been intended. The Commando was to move into Le Bas de Ranville, so as to protect the Headquarters of the 6th Airborne Division, and to block any enemy advance from the south.

By 3.30 p.m. most of the Commando had crossed the bridge and was taking up defensive positions. Ten minutes later the Transport Officer got through with the first of our Jeeps, piled high with reserve ammunition – a good effort.

When we had been in position for less than two hours four German tanks were reported on the rising ground to our south. They were engaged by 3-inch mortars belonging to the Airborne Division, and withdrew. At the same time HMS *Serapis* fired twenty rounds into some German infantry who had been seen digging in the forward edge of a wood.

No 3 Troop, carrying their parachute bicycles, with cases of 3-inch mortar bombs strapped to the handlebars, had toiled across the swamp, with some loss. But when they came to the road leading to the Orne the cyclist troop came into its own. Ordered to press on with all speed, they did so, running through a fair amount of sniping before they reached the bridges. According to Keith Ponsford, when they arrived there they were the leading troop of the brigade. However this may be, Lord Lovat, who had no other troops available, sent them to support Lieutenant-Colonel Otway of the 9th Parachute Battalion, who with eighty men had captured the Château d'Amfreville, after clearing the Merville Battery.

The village of Amfreville stands on a low ridge east of the Orne and overlooks a great part of the lodgement area. It was essential that this ground should be firmly in our hands on D Day. If not, the

German artillery would have observation posts there and life in the beachhead round Ouistreham, and, indeed, much farther west, would be intolerable.

Otway suggested that he, Westley and Ponsford, the surviving officers of 3 Troop, should go forward and reconnoitre the village. This they did from the area of the château – later to be my head-quarters.* It was arranged that the parachutists in position south of the building would give our men covering fire. Lovat now arrived on a bicycle and ordered Westley to attack the village without delay. In consequence 3 Troop went straight up the road leading into the village from the west, and came under heavy fire at a place where the road ran between high stone walls.

At once Westley was hit in the arm; Abbott, who had been my Bren-gunner at Dieppe and Agnone, and two other men were wounded. Sergeant Hill, Troopers Osborne, Barnes and Jennings returned the fire and the casualties got away. As they withdrew a bullet made a neat parting down the sergeant's scalp!

While Westley was having his wound dressed Ponsford took command. He ordered the sergeant-major to reorganise the troop, while he made a quick reconnaissance round the right flank and found a covered approach. After clearing some houses which overlooked the village square, Ponsford put one of his sections in position to give covering fire. Here the 2-inch mortar proved invaluable, for its high-explosive bombs, fired at a low angle, did much to demoralise the German garrison.

When he judged that his men had got the better of the fire-fight Ponsford charged across the open to capture the school, the main centre of resistance. Seizing this, the troop then swept through the village, killing six or eight of the enemy and capturing more than twenty others besides several horse-drawn vehicles. In this dashing assault the troop lost not one man. They then took up a position in the hedges east of the village, where Roy Westley, his wound band-aged, rejoined them.

No 6 Commando had now arrived in the southern end of the village, and Ponsford, who did not know where 3 Commando was, went off to place his men under the orders of Derek Mills-Roberts.

While Ponsford was talking to Mills-Roberts the latter ordered his bombardment officer to bring down naval gunfire on Bréville Wood.

*The Château of Monsieur Leboucher. This had been a German battalion HQ until that morning.

The first 15-inch shell landed between them and the wood so the gunner gave a correction. The next shell arrived with a deafening crash about fifteen yards from the group, making a massive crater and tearing branches from the trees above their heads. The air was blue with Derek's language : the shoot was over.

Once the village was in our hands the Germans began to shell it.

*

From Mr Rex Bateman
I was a captain in the Royal Marines and commanded 543 Flotilla of assault craft in HMS *Glenearn*, leader of a squadron of LSIs in Force S which landed the 3rd British Infantry Division. The units aboard *Glenearn* were two battalions, one of South Lancs and one of East Yorks. I had the privilege of landing the East Yorks.

H hour was 0720 hours on Sword beach, dead low water, We were second wave on the beach about 0750 hours and the tide had risen, covering some of the beach obstacles. We succeeded in landing the soldiers but some of my craft were damaged, only five out of twelve returning to *Glenearn*, also the opposition had warmed up a bit since the first wave landed but the casualties were surprisingly light. We were stuck on the beach for about five weeks and assisted the Senior Naval Officer in the task of beach clearance.

My feelings were mixed, one of elation during the run-in but angry and frustrated when unable to return to *Glenearn*. The weather was rough and some of the soldiers were seasick, but for all that there was a touch of humour, the officer commanding one of the MLs escorting had connected a gramophone to his loud hailer and was playing 'Roll out the Barrel' as we bucketed through the seas, a bugler on board one of the craft responded by sounding 'Cookhouse door'. We eventually passed the first wave returning to *Glenearn* and they hailed us with 'It's a piece of cake !'

*

From Mr S. V. Peskett, formerly Lieutenant-Colonel, RM
My regiment was allocated to Force G, and was given the task of supporting the landing of 50 Northumbrian Division. The beaches were at Ver-sur-mer east of Arromanches, and I had thirty-two Centaur tanks and eight Sherman tanks divided into two batteries and eight troops, with a small Regimental HQ (myself, Major B. J.

Mabbott my second-in-command, a signaller, Sergeant Harris, and a batman-driver, Marine Collis) in a waterproofed Jeep. Our brief was to stay in Normandy for a maximum of seven days; in the event we lasted three weeks, until ammunition was expended and tank maintenance exhausted.

If I were to single out a few memories, these would be they :

(1) My own landing was an extremely wet one. The LCT in which we were being transported beached a good way from the edge of the sea, and the depth into which we drove (about four feet) put paid to our 'careful' waterproofing. We managed to clamber aboard a passing LCA after our Jeep overturned. Mabbott was wounded (and had to be returned to UK) and the other three of us got to the beach extremely wet and without transport. First choice was a RN pedal-cycle, but second thoughts rejected this. A lift to the Meuvaines area, where we spent the first night, was on a US Army half-track. I eventually secured an ex-German Army staff car (a Ford V8) which served me for the rest of our time in Normandy – once strafed by the RAF, who didn't recognise me !

(2) I spent the first night in a field on a farm near Meuvaines with the forward HQ of the leading infantry units. Mortar fire had killed or wounded a number of cows, which added a surrealistic (and odorous) air to the proceedings. With us was a US Army major, whose job it was to liaise with the Americans immediately to our right, in the Arromanches area. I clearly recall the air of nonchalance with which he approached this task. He selected a spot by a hedge, opened his haversack, brought out his writing-pad and pen, and then arranged the photographs of his wife and children on the bank before starting to pen a letter home.

(3) Several of my landing craft, being heavily armoured, did not weather the crossing, and either sank or turned back to land on the Isle of Wight. Others were beached in the wrong place, and the troop commanders had somehow to get themselves back into the battle as planned.

I recall one such (a SAUDF subaltern, one of several posted to our outfit) arriving in the farmyard some four miles inland where I had my HQ. It must have been D + 2 or thereabouts.

'Where have you been ?'

'I've been in Bayeux.'

'That's impossible. We haven't taken it yet.'

'Yes, that's what I discovered.'

From Mr John Godwin, then Lieutenant, RM

As we approached Sword beach we could hear and see the effect of the naval bombardment from the larger ships further out to sea. This bothered me because having been on a naval gunnery course I knew that shells could be faulty and fall short, a numbered drill was practised to correct this. I assumed that the German shells coming towards us would be aimed at larger ships behind us and that the notorious German efficiency would never allow theirs to be faulty, but now the enemy mortar and machine-gun fire grew, and there was a fair amount of enemy and friendly shrapnel about. I moved about three feet to my left for some reason and shortly after a three-inch ragged piece hit a steel plate about chest high in my old position; then it fell to the deck receiving a brief glance from others standing nearby. On our port side we could see a sinking destroyer belonging to one of the Allied navies, Polish or Norwegian, its back broken by a torpedo. Ahead, flying low over the villas on the sea front at Ouistreham, was a RAF Mosquito harrying the German defences.

We grounded on the beach at H hour, the ramp was lowered and the AVRE tanks went off and up the beach under the close covering fire of our oerlikon guns, then there was a loud explosion and a lot of black smoke from the flotilla leader's LCT on our starboard side caused by a German 88-mm shell hitting the tank containing the colonel of the Engineers who was killed instantly; the hatch of this tank was thrown open and the sergeant driver climbed out and ran around the deck of the landing craft screaming and holding his head. I thought that the flotilla leader might have drawn this fire by flying an outsize White Ensign which others had suggested he should not do; some also thought it unwise to have the senior officers of the Navy, Marines, Army and Naval Engineers in our group together in the one LCT.

We raised our ramp with a hand winch whilst going astern off the beach at the same time rolls of chestnut paling tied to the port and starboard catwalks were released, dropped into the sea to be washed ashore to fill in ditch obstacles. As we did so I noticed a Marine firing a .38 revolver at the houses and I suggested that they were out of range but he said that it gave him satisfaction and continued to do so. As the LCT went seawards we passed rocket-firing LCTs of the next wave pounding the defences completely covered in smoke and fire as the rockets were released; further out we saw destroyers, battleships and cruisers firing their large guns, we could see the gun crews of the battleship *Warspite* wearing anti-flash gear standing on the turrets to watch the landings and the bombardment.

We then steered towards the west, moving along the coast watching later craft carrying the infantry ashore and seeing black columns of smoke coming up from the land. At 0800 hours we heard on the BBC news that the Allied forces had landed on the coast of Normandy which caused crew comments of 'fancy that' or 'what a surprise' and someone suggested that 'we should give the skipper the news'.

*

From Captain L. W. Bridger RM
At the time I was a lieutenant Royal Marines with the appointment of Assistant Brigade Signal Officer, 1st Special Service Brigade under the command of the Lord Lovat. As you will know, the title of the brigade was later changed to that of the 1st Commando Brigade.

I was the first man to disembark down the port side ramp and had the misfortune to slip on one of the wooden cross-members, finishing the descent to the water in a crouching position and having thoroughly wetted not only much of myself but also the whole of my rucksack. As the rucksack dry weighed nearly 90 lbs its new wet weight can perhaps be imagined. I ought perhaps to explain that it wasn't my habit to slip down landing ramps and I think the reason on this occasion was that I had had to wear a pair of brand new ammunition boots due to my usual pair having 'holed' in the camp at Southampton. Naturally our first task was to get off the beach fast, especially having in mind what we had been told as to the number of enemy guns trained to bear on our section of the beachhead. A powerful inducement so to do was also to be seen around us in the number of casualties from the assault battalion of the East Yorks whose tasks it had been to go in first and clear the beach for us to go through and capture Caen by the end of D Day.

So I tried to see that everybody for whom I was responsible doubled across the beach until we took a short rest some eighty yards inland under a sort of bluff. Never before and certainly not since, have I ever been so physically extended and temporarily exhausted. The sodden rucksack plus the new boots plus the yielding sand really exceeded all previous demands imposed in training.

However, with minimum delay, we pressed on in single file with 6 Commando in the lead. The whole brigade was in single file, so the more certainty to penetrate the coastal defences – 4 Commando detaching leftwards so to take and clear all strongpoints in the town of

Ouistreham. As we traversed the straight road approaching Hermanville we passed a small cluster of cottages on the left of the road. At
the doorway of one of these cottages stood an old lady dressed wholly
in black, gazing at us as we passed. She stood absolutely still and said
no word but she was weeping all the time, making no attempt to hide
or wipe away her tears. She was the only one to be seen, which wasn't
at all surprising.

Soon after this, we linked up with the 6th Airborne troops who had
dropped on the Orne bridges in the early hours of the morning. As
is well-known the recognition signal agreed by Lord Lovat with them
was the music of his personal piper Bill Millin. The linking-up should
have taken place at 1200 hours and actually occurred at 1203 hours
and provided me with another permanent memory of the day. I was,
I think, the person nearest to Lord Lovat as we crossed the bridge
afterwards to become famous as Pegasus Bridge. There was, I remember, not only mortar fire but lots of small-arms fire at the time of our
approach and crossing. Lord Lovat, who was in the middle of the
road, had his rifle resting comfortably and easily on his left shoulder
and looked entirely at ease. I remember thinking at the time, 'Well,
you are a cool customer.' It was with great interest therefore that
many years later I saw the incident re-created in the film *The Longest
Day*, wherein the actor taking the part of Lord Lovat affected a
poacher's crouch with his rifle held in both hands in front of him.
It wasn't like that.

At the end of D Day Brigade HQ laagered for the night in a field
with rough stone wall boundaries adjacent to farm buildings to the
right of the road linking Haute Longueville and Sallenelles. Next
morning brought the experience of aimed small-arms fire direct into
this HQ area. The fire was coming from snipers in the trees some half
mile or less to the east where there was a heavily wooded patch of
country.

Just to end the story I should perhaps add that 1st Commando
Brigade were under command 6th Airborne Division for D Day and
the period immediately following of, I think, eighty-three days, during
which it was continuously 'in the line'. At the end of that time having
reached Pont l'Eveque we were withdrawn to UK, eventually, against
both intention and expectation, to return to the Continent in January
1945.

*

From Mr R. H. McKinlay CGM

I think that my first feeling of personal contact and the realism of it came a couple of days before D Day. I was a PO in a Royal Naval Commando (P) and we were under canvas on Lord Beaulieu's estate near Southampton waiting to embark. It was the early part of the morning when a Dornier twin engine 88, I think, came over the camp very low pursued by Typhoons. I was up early because I was duty PO. As it passed overhead it was hit and crashed just a couple of hundred yards away on the edge of a pond, and just disintegrated. I was about first on the scene but there were no survivors just a mass of flesh of the eight bodies. We found out later that it was a very large crew because it was on a high reconnaissance mission. Later that day, with the help of a couple of my men, we gathered all the remains in their parachutes and took them to a local aerodrome. This was the last I saw of the bodies. I met the pilot of the Typhoon who was credited with the kill. The Dornier, I believe, came from a squadron whose insignia was a flying stork carrying a baby. The airmen were buried in a small cemetery in Fawley. For all I know parts of this aircraft could still be there. It may sound rather callous, but I had no feeling at all towards these men, or hate.

I think we all know the run up to D Day, how it was delayed and the bad weather that was encountered. My job was as a PO in charge of a small bunch of RN Commandos who were to be landed before H hour to set up signs and indicators for the assault force to land. In overall charge was a lieutenant called a beachmaster and his bodyguards. He had a bodyguard because like all of us after taking over our bit of the beach most of our time was working with our backs exposed to the enemy.

Our method of landing was not a great spectacular. All of our equipment was lashed on top of a DD tank; these were special floating type tanks which were to land and go to designated positions at the back area of the beach to give covering fire to the landing and also to help secure vital positions. We were to land sitting on top of the tanks and as they left the water and proceeded up the beach we were to cut our equipment off and abandon the tank the best way we could. This was the plan, but as of all mice and men on the approach to the beach the LCT landing craft tank we were in was hit up forward and the ramp which was partly lowered just dropped and hung underneath the bows of the craft, thus making the only way to get under way astern.

This, I think, was when I can first remember any feelings. I was bloody mad, to think that after all my training day and night, weeks on windswept beaches from Scotland to the south coast, Berwick to Land's End, I was suddenly going to be denied my finest hour. Frustration was the greatest feeling. Here we were a sitting target, just wallowing around like a sick elephant. We were slowly taken by the tide and it must have been an hour or so later – I cannot say how long – when we finally managed to hail an LCV (P) and persuade the coxswain to take our party ashore, which he did, straight into the beach. By this time we had drifted out of the landing area and our landing was our own little invasion with all odds and sods. We were under fire as we hit the beach and we all made for cover at the top of the beach and sort of consolidated our positions.

When we had sorted ourselves out the best we could there seemed to be quite a number of soldiers in this area with their officers. My boss was a lieutenant RNVR. I remember a major and a number of junior officers; our only other personnel on this beach were dead. I vividly remember their bodies on the shoreline being washed in and out with the waves – they just rolled in and out, in and out. I still at this time had no feelings of fear or regret; I seemed to feel guilty that I had not landed where I should have done and not made my contribution at the right time.

I knew that my destination was the Courseulles area and I was nearer Cabourg. The only thing was to start walking. I don't remember anyone giving any orders, but off we started to amble. Although enemy fire was still coming from inland and along the beach, I never felt it was aimed at me. Before we could start our country walk we were blocked by two large gun emplacements with some of the other side still inside. I was near the senior army officer and asked if I could go ahead and lob three grenades in each and on their detonation the rest advance and take the emplacements.

I remember him saying, 'How many grenades have you in your pouches?' I think my reply was the most out of this world answer he could ever have.

'Sir,' I said, 'in one pouch I have my boot cleaning gear and in the other my soap and towel.'

It was then he first discovered I was a sailor and not a soldier. Anyway, I obtained the necessary grenades and, with these distributed about my person in pockets and down my jacket, I went over the top for glory. Honestly, I still cannot remember seeing any danger in this at any time and at no time did it seem other than what I had to do. I suppose it was about fifty to one hundred yards across the beach to get there. I started weaving in and out of sand dunes; my first face-to-face encounter then came with the enemy. As I rounded one dune there was this large German pointing his rifle at me. At the time he looked ten feet tall. He lowered his rifle and I lifted mine, I was not afraid of him nor did I have any feeling to kill. I took his rifle, searched him and directed him to carry on around the dune and back to our lines.

Then something happened that I will never be able to account for which made me feel very ashamed. As he continued to walk around the dune, a single shot rang out and he fell clutching his hands to his stomach, he half turned and came to rest in a sitting position up against the dune. As I got to him the blood was coming through his fingers which were still clutched to his belly. He looked up at me, and I can assure you I will never forget that look as long as I live, it was as if to say, 'You bastard.'

I found myself saying to him, 'I'm bloody sorry, it wasn't me.'

But inside at that time I was really angry, there was this man surrendering with his hands in the air just shot. My anger then doubled when I realised that if he had been missed I could have been shot in the back from our own lines. Anyway I propped him up and carried on.

When I got as close as possible to the first gun I lobbed three grenades in one, then three in the other. I then up and charged like the gallant Six Hundred, but became aware that there was only me leading the charge and only me in it – God knows what happened I suddenly felt, is there no one else here to help? Anyway this lot was sorted out. I don't remember how or the rest of this period. My next recollection is of being the other side of the gun emplacements and finding that further up the beach were machine-gun pits. I don't think these were manned (and it wasn't till later I found out why). We were still under spasmodic fire from inland at the time . . .

*

From Major P. H. B. Pritchard, AM, JP, then Trooper, No 6 Commando

The ramps were dropped and down we went into waist-deep sea water about thirty yards from the water's edge. I can remember getting out of the water by a DD tank (Sherman) and pausing behind it. However, in the rather grey and overcast weather I noticed that sparks appeared on the turret of the tank caused, I imagine, by bullet strikes. I then went up to the beach some two to three hundred yards to the shells of some houses which had been demolished and cleared, leaving only open cellars lined with concrete. Here my troop gathered and I bound up a slight hand wound occasioned by Trooper Jim Carrigan (R Scots Greys) who was our sniper. He had been hit by a shell splinter which had hit the rear of our large LCI. No 3 Troop was now the leading troop, and we moved out over a road with a parallel tramline alongside it.

We then moved over about 500 yards of open marsh land with several dykes which had evil smelling muddy banks until we reached a three-strand wire fence over which we climbed. We noticed little yellow pennants with black skull and crossbones hanging from this fence and presumed this indicated a minefield. As nobody was to my knowledge injured during the crossing I imagine this may have been one of those phoney minefields laid to deceive us (and perhaps Rommel himself?). Here was a small wooded copse where we assembled for an attack on some pillboxes. I was in a ditch which lined the edge of a cornfield (wheat I think) firing at the pillboxes and from here I was ordered forward through the corn after dumping my heavy Bergen rucksack.

I seemed to spend most of this attack crawling through the waist-high corn until a light tank (Honey) appeared and we returned to our assembly area in the copse. Here we picked up our kit and moved on through a small village where some of the local people came out into the street. I was handed a bottle by a middle-aged Frenchman and having taken a drink found it to be a strong rawish spirit which I later discovered was distilled cider (Calvados). We soon went through this village, and into open country until we came to the bridges. Here we doubled across the best we could with our heavy loads. I can remember the bullets striking the ironwork of both bridges which were not too far apart. As I ran across one of the bridges I stopped near a dead British officer who had a Colt automatic .45 pistol attached to his neck with a lanyard. I broke the lanyard by putting my boots on it and secured the pistol in an inner pocket of my BD blouse. This pistol came in very handy later on. This officer was one of the glider party that had landed during the night and did such good work in capturing the bridges intact.

We moved very rapidly, and by about 1400 hours were in Bréville occupying a house on the outskirts on the other side of the village and we passed through it to get there. Here we dug in and I, with several others, Gunner Puttick, Gunner Smith were two I could remember, looked through the large home which was set in its own grounds enclosed by a high brick wall. In one of the rooms we found a German army leather pistol holster (empty) lying on a bedside table and in a wardrobe in the same room a uniform coat. The evidence seemed to point to a hasty departure. In the drawers of a chest we found a couple of pairs of neatly rolled socks made of some heather-coloured coarse mixture. I believe Gunner Smith put a pair on in exchange for his own.

We had started to dig in when my sub-section was ordered to accompany Captain A. H. Pyman MC, our troop leader, together with one or two others including Lieutenant Colquhoun, on a recce to find the enemy. We moved out from the rear of the house, and went into the garden of another quite large house. Captain Pyman was on the other side of a hedge with Lieutenant Colquhoun, and the rest of us were in the garden behind the hedge and I was actually behind a large marrow heap next to Craftsman Layton and Sapper Pealing.

Captain Pyman said, 'I can see someone waving a yellow air identification slip. I will wave back with one of ours, who has one?' One was passed to him, and he put it on the barrel of his rifle, stood up and waved it.

There was a sudden burst of fire (20-mm cannon shell) followed by a pause when Lieutenant Colquhoun said, 'Captain Pyman has been hit.' Another pause. 'Captain Pyman is dead.'

The enemy then fired mortar bombs (60 mm) into the garden, wounding several, including Craftsman Layton. As things were getting hot we moved out of the garden to the front of the house. I managed to carry Lofty Layton, plus his weapon, and mine. After a very short pause to re-group we headed back to the main house via the back gardens of various houses. In going back, still carrying Layton I stopped in a laneway and laid him on the ground. Two old French people (husband and wife) came out of a house adjoining the lane. They became very concerned about Layton, and asked us to put him into the house which we did. His face was a grey colour and his eyes appeared to roll up into his head. We gained the impression that he was dying.

The enemy started to press us and we moved back into the main house as quickly as we could firing Bren to slow them up. Once back at the house we restarted to dig in. This time I was asked to help Trooper Carrigan who was hit in the hand, and could not dig. As we were digging in several shells (105 mm) fell into the garden, and hit the house, causing many casualties including my chum Gunner

Puttick who was very badly wounded. About 1900 hours a Jeep arrived and took some wounded, and we moved back to Amfreville (Le Plein) where the main commando was carrying the remainder. I helped to carry Gunner Puttick. We placed him on a folded deck chair used as a stretcher, and carried him that way. He must have been in great pain as a shell had virtually exploded alongside of him shattering his right leg and arm. He made light of these injuries and cracked jokes when he could.

Because we couldn't carry him any other way than along the road we were forced to keep in the open and under constant enemy fire. Corporal 'Taffy' John or Trooper 'Pluto' Friend fired a few 2-inch mortar smoke bombs to cover the worst area which was just after we left the house. On arrival at Le Plein we put the wounded into the RAP which was located in a large cider press, and which was part of a fine farm called, I think, La Grande Ferme. It was typical of the old Norman farms consisting of a single large building surrounding a courtyard of about an acre in size. The building had no outer doors except for one large double door on to the road and another entrance/ exit gateway which led to the fields. It had the look of a fortified building which it probably was. We had lost twenty-two killed and wounded out of the sixty-four present at the landing.

*

From Mr J. W. Berry
The 4th (Franco-British) Commando was commanded by Captain Phillipe Kieffer, and was part of the 1st Special Service Brigade commanded by Brigadier Lord Lovat. It was landed by Lieutenant J. W. Berry, commanding LCIS 523. Lieutenant Berry emphasised that contrary to general belief both *the artificial harbours were British built, as were most of the landing craft.*

I was merely a lieutenant at the time (I joined the Navy originally as an ordinary seaman) but I was one of those briefed at HMS *Vernon* some time before D Day – I surmise I was there because I had a specialised job to do. We were told about Pluto; Gooseberrys; artificial harbours; etc. and given the date and place of the intended assault and the twenty-four hours tolerance allowed to the Supreme Commander. Quite a secret! Later I was invited to confer with the French to whom I had been assigned. The French were required to land on the extreme left flank of Sword, to capture Riva Bella/

Ouistreham, secure the canal bank and work along it to link up with the Airborne at Pegasus Bridge. Then, with No 4 (British) Commando, to cross the bridges over the canal and river, circle left and take and hold the higher ground at Amfreville/Bréville/Hauger to prevent enemy gunners from firing into the Sword beach area. Quite a job. They were going to be first ashore and deserved all I could give. I therefore undertook to land them as far to the left as I could without running on the rocks, to land them dry and land them well fed. I picked myself out a visual marker (transit) by planning to keep in line the gable of a boarding house on the seafront and the slated spire on a château a quarter mile inshore. (The château was still there in 1979 and there is a monument there to Phillipe Kieffer. The boarding house has disappeared.)

The Airborne (General Gale) were to drop on Pegasus Bridge and hold it at, I think, 0300. It was vital that the French and No 4 Commando (who had similar orders) and landed at Bella Riva, should link up with the Airborne on time, cross and then capture the high ground beyond.

There was much noise. The bombardment from the sea had begun. A Norwegian destroyer (*Stavanger*) was torpedoed to my left by an E-boat and sank by the stern.

I looked through the binoculars and picked out the château I was looking for. Sword beach was small, with rocks on both sides and I knew I had to cut it fine; keep to the left to oblige the French; and still miss the rocks. I saw about six rows of stakes and tripods in the water, some with converted captured French shells on top as impromptu mines. There were bits of wire rope and chain hung between. Fortunately, since it was shortly after low water, I got a good view of some of the obstacles, and could make a good guess where the beach minefield would be. The plans were that a way through would have been made the night before. Something had gone wrong for it had not been done. LCIS 527 hailed me and suggested we try further along. I refused; for I was committed to keeping to the left and had every intention of carrying out my task to the letter and right on time. We were getting within range, so I told 527 we were going straight in, as fast as possible, and signalled the LCAs astern that where I ended up was the place.

I did the rest of the run at emergency full ahead. The coxswain, Ken Dawson, a powerful steadfast man, steered, and I worked the engine telegraphs myself. Everyone else was advised to crouch low. We smashed straight through the obstacles, weaving from side to side and hit the beach so hard that we were dry as far back as the bridge. The idea was that since I could see no chance of ever getting the ship off again I would use her to bridge the minefield so that the French could land in good shape (as promised), and I would sweep up the beach devices with my lovely vessel instead of with French feet. As we grounded, the ramps were run out in a flash, the French moved off like lightning, led by Francis Vourch, André Bagot and Alex Lofi. One of these must have been the first armed man to land from the sea, but as I used four ramps maybe it was a deadheat between them. *None* of them dropped on the beach. We got the ramps in again, fast.

I had worked out the tidal harmonics at least a dozen times before leaving the UK. The tidal rise I could expect was a few inches, but to my surprise 523 floated off directly she knew I needed it. This was impossible on paper but since she clearly wanted to leave I started to wriggle out stern first – and found that, contrary to expectations, the propellers had not been ripped off. There was a slight set from starboard to port which set the ship down on one of the obstacles, but it did not go off. I got out without human casualties, which was a minor miracle considering the shelling and mortar fire we had ploughed through.

*

From Mr Frank Wright
Mr Wright was in the leading troop of 47 RM Commando. Their objective was the village of Port-en-Bessin – –through seven miles of enemy territory.

. . . Suddenly the journey was transformed by the loud cracking of machine-gun bullets immediately overhead from mere observation to participation in the battle itself. The bursts of firing seemed to split the air above our boat. Heads tucked in noticeably lower and no one stood up unnecessarily after that so that we lost track of the distance still to go. I found now though, as we drew nearer, that one caught glimpses of the shore as the boat's stern lifted on the swell.

I saw the sloping yellowish coloured beach quite clearly, black-looking tanks crawled along it like squat stag beetles. One tank was standing still and burning with a hot transparent red flame. There were a few dark brown, scurrying figures on the open beach too, running backwards and forwards with some equipment. These images branded themselves on my brain and I shall never be free of them.

BOO-O-O-OOM – there came a terrible roaring explosion on the starboard side and I felt the shock of it through my boots. A great pillar of smoke and debris shot high into the air on our starboard bow until it became a great, spreading tree over a hundred feet high. Two irregular black shapes rocketed straight upwards through the smoke, they turned slowly over and over, slowed, hung stationary for a moment and began to plummet downwards.

I wrenched my gaze away, feeling sick and cold. That must have been one of our LCAs, it was only fifty yards away . . .

I stepped down from the bow of the LCA, into only a couple of inches of water, some of it entered my boot through the lace-holes and felt luke-warm. By the third step I was on dry land and running, Bangalore Torpedo* in my left hand and rifle in my right, after the rest of the troop. Everyone seemed to be heading up the beach towards the shelter of the sea wall, the machine-gun was still firing long bursts though no one seemed to be hit, I derived no comfort from that thought but ran on, looking neither to right nor left. I was mortally afraid and fear clogs the brain, destroying reason. For a few yards I ran through an imaginary tunnel of safety which shut out all the terrors, but then, as I ran, I saw that my way lay close to a burning tank. The beach sloped upwards at this point and the sand was drier. The tank leaned towards me, menacing. I felt the heat of the flames on my face and made a wide detour to the right in order to gain the safety of the sea wall.

A khaki-clad figure lay almost across my path, curled up on the sands on his left side in an attitude of sleep. His knees were drawn up and his arms folded across his chest. His head was bent forward so that his face was turned towards me but where his face should have been was a featureless, red mask. As I stared down in horror a medical orderly with a white armband came up without fuss and quietly dropped on one knee by the soldier. I plunged on, scattering sand, my legs mechanically propelling me towards the safety of the bank.

*Weapon for demolishing walls etc.

CHAPTER SEVEN

Intelligence and Signals

The D Day operation was a triumph of successful planning, deception, and interpretation of enemy intelligence. However that story has been frequently told in accounts by senior officers and others. Here we have an account by an IO in the field, and personal accounts by members of the Royal Signals. Unfortunately none of these gives much idea of the type of work the writers were engaged on. Without an efficient signalling system any co-ordination command of operation would be impossible, but the signaller – who may be in an exposed position – is required to send and receive as if he were nowhere near a battlefield.

*

From Mr Ian R. Bell, then Captain RA, IO, 3rd Division
During the night of 5th/6th June we crossed over to the Normandy coast in a destroyer. I was Intelligence officer of the British 3rd Division and one of the advance party of Divisional HQ. No accommodation could be spared for us on board of course, but the naval officers were friendly and helpful. I spent the night in a hammock slung across the fireplace in their mess. The Navy didn't call it a mess, and a good deal of cheerful banter was exchanged about naval terms and army terms, naval ways and army ways.

We assembled at our rendezvous in a field behind the village of Ouistreham – or what was left of it – about eight of us. The ground rose up steeply just ahead, so our view was very restricted. Ahead lay Caen, our objective, but some miles away, and it seemed that the Germans hadn't been driven back far in this sector. Bullets from their rifles and machine-guns were ripping through the leaves of the trees above our heads.

Our small party included one draughtsman, Private W., a sort of Cockney sparrow, but with rather flat feet. He was older than I was, and I'd wondered why he'd been put into the advance party. The noises and smells of the fighting going on around affected his nerves badly. He was shaking. I encouraged him to get on with digging a slit trench, but the guts had been knocked out of him already. He looked as if he was going to scream or cry. It was sickening.

The trouble was we had very little to do once we had reached the rendezvous, until the main part of Divisional HQ arrived, and it was not due for some hours. We had to put together reports about our advance and the enemy's reactions, but this gave W. nothing to do. He just went on cracking up. I think this had some effect on the morale of the rest of us. I remember thinking then for the first time : the Germans seem to be pretty well established just here– perhaps we're not going to make it after all.

I remembered the Dieppe raid, with which I had had a slight connection.

Cedric Rowntree and I did the night shift alternately. It meant writing the intelligence summary at the end of the day's fighting, seeing it off the duplicator and sending it out to the battalions. The pauses in this work gave me a chance to make a few notes in a diary. This was the first entry :

'Three days here now. Just beginning to realise the new form of things. At first too busy dodging bombs and bullets; then too busy trying to sort out a confused battle situation. Rumours fly round. Le Havre captured, say the villagers. Of course, not within thirty miles of it. Tiger tanks penetrated two miles away. Also nonsense. Anything on tracks is a Tiger. Troops a bit rattled. Heavy casualties in some battalions. Several friends killed. Seems curiously natural in these surroundings. Anyway the fighting goes on and we forget.

'Prisoners a mixed crowd. Colonel Krug, a haughty old-timer, surrendered with his staff in an easy manner. A medical orderly on his staff, who had been tending wounded in a half burnt house, burst into tears when I told him Krug had surrendered – not because he felt sorry for Krug, but because he had gone on trying and suddenly felt the futility of it all. An Austrian. Sensible bloke.

'Been a bit quieter today. Situation looked bleak last night.

'Most of the French people round here very helpful, some terrifically enthusiastic, although the general mood is not exuberant. But met an exuberant little man this evening. One of our sergeants came to me with a very small-calibre pistol and said he had seen this Frenchman taking it out of a little hole in a wall. I anticipated an awkward scene, having to tell him that, even though the Boches had gone, it was still illegal to carry arms. But not a bit. He gave it up gladly, he offered it to me. Three years ago, he said, he hid it in that hole in the wall because the Boches had ordered all arms to be handed in.

' "*Pour les Boches – rien,*" he said with a throat-splitting gesture. Then he had left this area. Two hours ago he came back to his village – and to the hole in the wall. It was still there. He gave it to us, his liberators. He would give us milk and eggs – his wife was even now milking the cow, his daughter out looking for eggs. He would give us cider. He had given a soldier some money to buy a fountain pen. I protested that we had our own rations and that they themselves were short of food. But no, he shook my hand over and over again, tears came to his eyes. Nothing was too much.

'Had a lucky escape last night. 25-foot crater a few yards from me. They are shelling us again now.

'Later. They did. Hit a store. Two stores burnt out. Cedric's kit in one of them. Telephone and cipher office gone One killed, I think.'

Next morning I had my first trip to the front line. The battalion there had reported German troops in front of them with different uniforms; thought they were German parachute troops.

My official vehicle was the motor-cycle. I wasn't very good on motor-cycles, and felt rather exposed driving along the chewed-up lanes with shells exploding in the fields on either side. But I got there all right.

This was our leading assault battalion on D Day and they'd taken a lot of punishment. Now they had dug in on a narrow sector with the Germans dug in fifty yards away. From Battalion HQ in the cellar of a battered country house, I went forward to the leading company. The battalion IO showed me the way. I didn't know him as he had just replaced their original IO who had been killed two days earlier.

Mortar bombs were bursting in the garden as we made our way to the look-out post. He was so used to them he took no notice. Just before we reached the look-out post I was taken aback to have to step over the body of one of their own men. He had obviously been dead for some time, because under the rim of his steel helmet, which had been knocked forward when he fell, his face had turned green. I was surprised nobody had moved him.

From the look-out I saw the German standing quite upright, quite openly, in their post about fifty yards away. His uniform, with yellow tabs on the lapels, was that of the German equivalent of the RAF

Regiment, not paratroopers.

What struck me was the quiet of the front line. He stood up over there, visible to the waist; we stood here. All easy targets, but neither side was attacking, so no harm came from standing peacefully there.

Leaving the look-out post, I had to step over the rotting corpse again. He was only a young lad. Perhaps a lad nobody had liked, so nobody was going to carry his body away.

General Montgomery – I don't think he was a Field-Marshal then – paid us a visit about noon one day. He was standing in a scout-car in front of the house where we had our mess, an ADC on each side of him. He gave us a morale-boosting talk and said it had been 'a jolly good show'. Then, with the help of his ADCs, he started distributing presents like a fairy-god-father. They were magazines, packets of cigarettes, that kind of thing, and were still in their civilian wrappers, which said 'From Lady X' and 'The Hon Mrs Y.'

There was an element of farce in the performance.

*

From Mr M. W. Carter, then Signalman R. Signals with B13 Beach Signal Section

At last the great day has come; we can see the white-looking buildings on the French coast. Will France be as I have imagined it? Shall we find anything standing when we land or will it have been flattened by the barrage of bombs which were supposed to have rained on the landing beaches during the night, from the RAF, and the bombardment from the Royal Navy. I wonder how close the LCT will be able to get to the shore? If the beach was right, it was possible to land almost without getting your feet wet. I suppose it will mean another pair of boots in a few weeks' time (for some reason or another, our boots seemed to rot a few weeks after being submerged in salt water).

My goodness, the landing craft has stopped. Surely they could come in a bit further. We shall be in up to our necks, and I don't think my Mae West will keep me up with all the rubbish that I am carrying including the extra tins of self-heating soup and cocoa. Oh, how ridiculous, they have changed the order for disembarking. Tanks off first. Doesn't he (the captain) realise that every time a tank goes off it lightens the craft, and so it rises in the water making it deeper for us on foot. Oh well, the nine tanks have gone now, our turn with the barrow. It is heavy enough on its own, I don't know how we shall move it through the water . . . Oh no, it's out of control, hitting the water, and has gone into that iron post. And now the shaft has broken, we shall have to leave it until the tide goes down. I hope those tins of cocoa will be all right. What are those things popping up in the water? Is it shrapnel or are we being fired upon? Now my rifle has fallen into the water. Oh well, I expect that I can find another somewhere. What an effort this is, I'm tired already, it's taking ages to get ashore.

Thank goodness, it is getting shallower now, steps are easier – I'm glad the sun is shining, I shall soon dry in it. At last, Sword beach. Which sector I wonder? There's the beach major. Why does he always shout to get off the beach, no one in their right minds wants to stay on it, let us find some cover at the back of these houses. I wonder what the corporal expects us to do now, now that we have no equipment. He will be in his element. He doesn't look very heroic now. Oh, he has decided we should have a rest. I will have a drink of cocoa. Matches are all right. The personal waterproofing worked. I think I will leave my watch in the bag, in case I get any sand in it.

Did I see those dead bodies on the beach? Yes, Corporal, I did. The sight will haunt me for a long time. They didn't look mutilated, it could have been us . . .

I wonder whether these houses will ever be lived in again They look a bit damaged. I wonder what we do now? Bob looks better now. He had a nasty attack of seasickness, which must have reduced his effectiveness. I wonder how the rest of the section are, and how we meet up with them. Now the corporal is going on a recce. What does he mean 'keep him covered', how can I when I haven't got a rifle? I suppose he thinks he is in films again.

(Later)

Nice sand this. I wonder how far it is before we can dig in. The entrenching tool is very useful. I would like one at home for digging after the war. I suppose there will be big sales of army surplus. There's the signal flag. Most of the others. We can dig there. There's the officer, still with the portable radio set. We shall be able to hear the news.

(And at one o'clock we did.)

. . . Mother always listens to this. She will know where I am. There is not much in the way of communications on this beach. It seems the brigadier has moved on, not using us. He never liked us much. He seemed very annoyed when the King inspecting us last week said, 'So these are the Beach Signals,' as though he knew all about us.

What an incredible sight – an old woman in black and a young girl both wearing Red Cross armbands walking across the beach to see if they can do anything for the casualties.

*

From Mr Eric Warburg, formerly Major E. Warburg (from a letter to his mother, 10th June 1944)

Well, on the 6th – D Day – we drew in to shore about 11 a.m. We were due to land at about two in the afternoon but in point of fact we only got off at 10.30 in the evening just as it was getting dark. During the waiting period our planes were overhead continuously (as they have been ever since) and we only once saw some Jerries when two Messerschmitts shot out of the clouds to drop four bombs and shot back again before anything could open up at them. When our forward parties landed at about 11 a.m. there was still some sniping going on in the houses along the front though these were a very sorry spectacle, having suffered severely during our naval bombardment. Desultory shells were fired by the Germans on to the beaches from away inland, but when we got ashore everything was more or less established. From the next morning I was on my feet continuously for the following thirty hours. Fortunately I did get some sleep that night which helped, but I finally got some relief and some rest and some food. I find one can go without sleep if one has enough food – but going without both makes one almost sick. The situation improved on D + 2 when my relief signalmaster arrived and the situation was restored.

Now we have been in this place some time we are settling down. Of course it's great to be able to speak French again and find out the country's views. We usually wander along to a little café in the evening, owned by a Frenchman and wife with a sweet little girl. He was captured at Dunkirk and taken to Germany whence he escaped and finally got back over 600 miles to France without any food etc. There he acquired false papers, which he has been living on since then. He has only recently come here from Paris, which town, he says, is just waiting for us! We set up here in a wood adjoining a German strongpoint which had been overrun by the Commandos only a very little time before we arrived – in fact there were still some German dead lying about, so the padres got busy burying – they have done a good deal of that especially on the beaches where we inevitably suffered casualties, though I understand these are far below what we expected.

Yesterday I saw our Commandos take a German strongpoint which had held out for over a week. It was made of a series of concrete blockhouses deeply embedded in the earth and we had made several attempts to secure it. This was to be the final onslaught. I arrived just as the Commandos were setting off – going over the top – and we watched from a barn through glasses. There had been a colossal bombardment aided by 15-inch guns from the Navy and shells had been whistling overhead for half an hour, when the tanks rumbled forward into action along a sunken road on the left. They formed up in a circle round the blockhouse and shelled it. I was sitting by a wireless over which the report of the battle was coming and as we saw the infantry start to approach we heard coming over the air reports that white flags were starting to appear and so many prisoners were being taken by such and such a platoon. Soon I was able to approach myself up the sunken road (for two pins I'd have gone along with the Commandos) and soon we saw the prisoners being marched back with their hands above their heads. As there were only a couple of soldiers with them I lined them up along the hedge and we made them take off their equipment and we searched them for any hidden weapons etc. We then let them sit down. They were a sorry-looking lot and had not had a shave for a week or more. Then one of them said that he had some food in his gas mask, so one by one I let them get whatever they wanted from their cast off equipment. The fellow who had started this movement seemed to be no German, or anyway I couldn't make out a thing he was saying – he was probably a conscript from somewhere. Anyway they all seemed somewhat sullen and very silent. I don't think their morale was absolutely cracked despite the colossal bombardment. I'd run out of cigarettes to give them, but some of the lads produced some and I gave them some matches. The non-German fellow then unrolled a couple of filthy cigars and was so pleased at my giving him a match that he offered me a cigar – I told him to keep it as he would probably need it some time or other !

CHAPTER EIGHT

The Medical Services

The fact that many of those wounded on D Day survived was due to the courage and ingenuity of the medical staff. Courage was needed to remain steady in conditions of extreme danger; ingenuity was necessary to operate on and repair bodies whose injuries presented problems well outside normal medical experience.

*

From Dr Peter Johnson
As we came closer, we saw that we should have a long wade – indeed, it was nearly five hundred yards to the top of the beach. We couldn't come far in because the ship had lost her anchor and so couldn't winch herself off again. We saw the wrecked craft, drowned tanks, the obstacles and mines – all so suddenly brought into focus and held there even more firmly as the door clanged down into three foot of water. No one was shooting at us, there were just a few shells dropping haphazardly and quite a number of mines going off. Although we heard bullets crack and whizz no one knew where they were coming from or going to. I got my crowd off the LCT and we waved goodbye and set off. Just like any other water – cold, and wet, and having an unpleasant tendency to get deeper in odd places. It did, and we got wet to just below the armpits – which wasn't too bad, I suppose. We had our packs hoisted high and were soon after it. As we trudged up the broad beach I realised that I would meet all my BG friends who must now have been in some time, unless they were delayed as I was. I passed a war correspondent wading in and said good morning to him – he looked at me as if I was stark mad.

Not much organisation on the beach that I could find, and nowhere to set up my show. Dotted everywhere were sodden bundles – men of the Hampshires, Devons and Dorsets that had led the infantry spearhead. Tanks still burning, LCTs blown up by mines, houses afire, craters, smells, *Achtung Minen* and skulls and crossbones. And crowds of French civilians rushing down to the LCTs and getting taken back to England. And a few prisoners – and so many, many wounded and nowhere to put them. So we moved gingerly through a minefield to the first lateral road – just a track, and we set up on the grass verge, which was three feet wide and bounded by traffic one side and a minefield the other.

Here we looked after our first wounded, my HAA MO carrying on while I went to find out what was happening. I soon ran into friends, including my Jeep, and a lot of FDS. I heard that the armour was due to come over Item Red that night and as Dobson had pinched my site, I had better take his, the other side of Asnelles, in Le Havre on Item Red. So I went along and found a likely lot of buildings, getting them cleared of booby traps and while I was away, after I had been over them, a dozen Hun who were hiding in the roof – 'what the eye doesn't see' – !

Back a mile along the beach again, a race against the tide, passing the now so familiar corpses and dead tanks, to collect the lads and move them in. Time had ceased to matter now, and it was getting dark by the time we had settled in our new quarters . . .

So many things happened in the next ten days that combined to make them perhaps the most enjoyable of my Army career. Of course, I was soon dead tired, as I was singlehanded and we had quite a few bomb casualties at night for the Luftwaffe came most of the time – nothing like the London blitz, thank goodness, but unpleasant enough. The AA was most colourful and dangerous too, and fell down like rain. *Warspite* and, I believe, *Rodney* came and anchored ten miles out and took the slates off my roof in handfuls, as they fired salvo after salvo continuously day and night for four or five days at a time, then a pause, and begin again.

Mine casualties by day were very common and some were most frightful to see. My most vivid recollection was being called suddenly to see a man, or what was left of a man, lying on a door in the back of a truck. All was covered with a blanket save for his head. He had no face that was not raw and torn, and his eyes were dull and opaque, wrinkled like those of a dead fish. He was conscious and moaning. I put my hand under the blanket and felt for his wrist. To my horror all I could find was a bloody stump – and it was the same on the other side too. He had a gash in his stomach, and a large wound in his thigh – and was still conscious. I gave him a large dose of morphia, bound up his stumps and sent him away to the ASC. Later, I heard that he was 'doing well'. But who are we to judge whether a man lives or dies?

But we had our lighter moments. Patrick landed on D + 4 and came to visit me. Pure luck as he had no idea where I was, but just asked an RE at the jetty. He was in good form but could not stay long. A lieutenant-commander Fleet Air Arm came in with a sprained ankle. He had been spotting for the *Rodney*, who immediately shot him down. His escape hatch was pinned and so he fell, trapped, hundreds of feet. In desperation he shoved some of his parachute through the trap and was pulled out just above the ground. He nearly landed on his Seafire, which blew up on the beach. As he was making his way up the beach his parachute caught in a mine and sent that off. And so he came to me with a sprained ankle and the naïve explanation that he had fallen out of his aeroplane; such are some of the truly silent service !

As a postscript to the above, I remember too that I had an Income Tax demand given to me on the beach, by a triumphant post corporal, on D Day.

*

From Brigadier E. H. P. Lassen, CBE, DSO
As we steadily approached the distant beaches we were gradually able to make out detail, the outline of houses on the skyline, and later the drowned or burnt-out tanks on the foreshore, and the line of under-water obstacles, rapidly being totally submerged by the rising tide. The beach itself was littered with not readily identified objects, abandoned equipment, casualties – a sombre and chilling sight.

Activity there was, of course, but it all seemed rather remote and strangely quiet, no roar of guns, or aircraft overhead. However this impression was rudely shattered by an enormous explosion at the rear of the ship, followed a little later by another and it took just that amount of time for it to dawn on us that we were being shelled. By now the ramps had grounded and a number of men were already wading ashore; the requirements of duty and the instincts of self-preservation fortunately coincided and I clambered forward and down the ramp as quickly as I could. As the water closed about my neck there was a moment of sheer panic until with flailing arms and scrambled steps I made the shore, soaked and shaken to the core.

I turned to see the LSI now several yards from the shore, and moving out to sea with most of her troops still aboard.

I must have been the last to get off the ship, and while one cannot and would not criticise the decision of the ship's captain for a moment, that decision seriously prejudiced the prompt collection of casualties lying on the beach.

As I tried to gather my wits and get my bearings, a further explosion behind me threw me off my feet and I required no further reminded that this part of the Red Queen beach at least, was distinctly unhealthy.

It was not a dryshod landing.

I made my uncertain way off the beach, checking and doing what I could for any of the casualties I came across, and eventually found a beach exit helpfully marked, and therefore presumably cleared of mines. After a few wrong turns I came on to our duly allocated medical area, which turned out to be a good flat grassy field abutting Hermanville churchyard.

My recce party had barely finished marking out the unit circuit and the departmental locations, and the signs to the beach, before the first of the unit 3-tonners loaded with equipment and tentage arrived. With no delay the men got down to the business of offloading the vehicles and setting up the field dressing station in the way it had been practised so often before in rehearsal, and shortly after the arrival of one of our two surgical teams, the unit was ready not only for the reception of casualties but also to act as an Advanced Surgical Centre.

The conditions in the medical site only a few hundred yards away from the beaches could not have been more different from those on the beaches themselves. While the beaches continued to be an enemy target, we were not; no shells or mortars came near us, and at least by day enemy air activity was nil, having been chased out of the skies by the RAF.

There were the untowards events, of course, and we were late in becoming fully operational because our second field surgical team which crossed on a Rhino ferry failed to make its correct landfall. In the event they nearly sailed up the Orne Canal, before they touched down a long way to the east of their proper landfall. The vehicles could not be landed, and so the surgeon and his team, carrying as much of their equipment as they could, slogged it out on a very hard, unscheduled march along the beaches to our location. On reflection it was a minor miracle that they made that march without mishap, and their contribution was of course vital to our operating efficiency, doubling the speed with which major casualties could be dealt.

The second major unplanned event was caused by the brave and protracted resistance of the enemy facing 6 Beach Group. A concrete gun emplacement with a field of fire which commanded the whole of the 6 Beach Group Area had resisted the combined efforts of the RN guns afloat, the bombing and strafing of the RAF and the closer attention of the Army's DD tanks, to silence it. Their presence made the unloading of the stores impossibly hazardous, and eventually it was decided to abandon 6 Beach Group altogether, and superimpose its stores, units and supplies on to the already crowded 5 Beach Group. With ground at this time very much at a premium, the resulting congestion on 5 Beach Group Area was, as subsequent events were to prove, highly dangerous.

As may well be imagined, doing surgical work under field conditions is far from ideal. However meticulous you may be the risk of infection and the absence of fully trained and experienced SRNs (State Registered Nurses) must be prejudicial to the uncomplicated recovery of the patient. It was axiomatic that only the minimum essential life saving surgery was performed under such conditions, and equally the object of all treatment in such a forward unit was to do the necessary minimum only to fit the patient for his onward transmission back to the hospitals in the UK.

A further disadvantage in such work in a forward area is the ever-present danger of enemy action, with injury to the operating staff as well as possible further injury to the casualty himself. In a battle area, when duties do not require you to be above ground, the prudent man will be in his slit trench, certainly when a bout of shelling is in progress, or an air raid. Every man is expected to dig his own slit trench and does so: the men in the medical unit will also dig slit trenches for casualties, and larger ones to take stretchers, but it is quite impossible to dig down a whole operating area, and treatment area; and it is totally understandable that surgical teams standing up on ground level are liable to work something less than their best when so exposed to enemy action for any length of time. Repeated requests to HQ Sub-Area for bulldozers to help dig in the medical units were unavailing, and while no casualties did occur when in our medical area, the threat, which was disconcerting to say the least, was always present.

However the third unforeseen event very rapidly changed all this. Two days after the landing, a lone and intrepid German bomber eluded the RAF in broad daylight and, despite intense anti-aircraft fire, pressed home a low level attack on the overcrowded beach. His bombs hit the petrol dump which had been built up over the past forty-eight hours, and the enormous explosion and fire that resulted also set off the adjacent ammunition dump.

The result was devastating, and no less than fifty-five casualties were brought into the medical units resulting from that incident, including a number from HQ 101 Sub-Area itself.

All at once the plight of casualties lying immobilised on stretchers above ground was fully appreciated and within a very short space of time two bulldozers reported to us with orders to dig us in. We struck the tents in turn and the bulldozers got to work. Very soon each tent and marquee had a high surround of sandy soil, and the floor had been dug down to a depth of some four feet. The surgical teams worked with a much greater sense of security, and there is no doubt that the casualties appreciated this protection equally.

Over the first forty-eight hours we were overwhelmed with casualties and there was no rest for anyone; I remember that on the first night, some time towards midnight, I counted sixty priority II casualties awaiting or receiving plasma transfusion both inside the department set aside for this purpose, and also outside, lying stretcher to stretcher around the main medical centre vehicle circuit, and in not inconsiderable danger of being run over by the DUKW amphibious vehicles collecting casualties. These numbers, of course, were dwarfed by the far larger numbers of walking wounded and less seriously injured. The reason for the large initial influx of casualties was due to the release of the backlog, which had been held in divisional Field Ambulance, advanced dressing stations, against the time of our surgical centre opening up to receive them. Those who were fit enough to make the sea crossing by DUKW and LCT were not held back, but were evacuated over the beaches via the Beach Group Dressing Station formed by a section of 21 FDS which had been set up very early in the landings, and had operated continuously, under the most trying and dangerous conditions from the first; the section officer, whose name sadly escapes me after all these years, winning a most worthy immediate award of the Military Cross.

*

From Mr Alan Holliday
I went on the D Day landings as quartermaster of No 20 Field Dressing Station RAMC which was to land over Queen Red beach and set up as a Beach Dressing Station as part of a Beach Group.

The flail tanks had cleared paths through the minefields and these had already been marked with white tape. One impression I shall never forget is that of a solitary military policeman standing on the beach exhorting everyone to snap out of it and to get moving. This, despite the mortar bombs and shells that were bursting all around. That lad deserved a medal and I hope he lived to get one. He was magnificent and might have been directing traffic at the Aldershot Tattoo.

I found about a dozen lads from my unit and we went on to locate our allotted site. One the way we came across a number of wounded but could not stop to attend to them. It was the Pioneers' job to collect wounded – ours to rendezvous and set up the FDS without delay. We did, however, find a poor chap who had stepped on a landmine and had his foot blown off. We put shell dressings on his wounds, gave him a shot of morphia and left him for the Pioneers.

On arriving at our location we found it to be an uncleared minefield but I soon came across our CO and we selected an alternative site in a nearby orchard. Already wounded were arriving but the surgeon and anaesthetist and a number of ORs who had come over with me were missing. I dumped my pack, went back to the beach and eventually found them. On my return, stragglers from other craft had turned up and the unit was practically complete.

Mitting, the young surgeon, had been violently seasick but did a wonderful job. He started operating immediately under a tarpaulin stretched over a lorry and kept at it till he was completely exhausted late at night. He should have been relieved by a Field Surgical Unit coming in on the evening tide but they did not arrive so he worked on. Another who deserved a medal.

How we stayed on our feet and the medical officers and nursing orderlies dealt with the many casualties I have never fathomed. We got up in England at 0500 on Monday morning and stayed awake and working under extremely arduous conditions until orders came that 20 FDS could stand down (i.e. stop admitting casualties) at 2400 on Thursday. We were then holding forty or fifty wounded awaiting evacuation so not everyone could get his head down. I found that when I stretched out under a truck I could not sleep and I suppose we were all the same. There were no meals and we nibbled army biscuits and drank tea (laced with whisky if we had any). Our cook made gallons of tea for us and the wounded. Hot, sweet tea was the prescription for badly wounded and shocked troops in those days. We had large quantities of cigarettes (free issue) to give to the casualties. The tea and cigarettes worked wonders. We soon realised that the combatant troops whom we were treating were perhaps even more tired than we were and it certainly opened my eyes to what men could stand. Looking back long after the event I am still amazed that after a long day and a storm-tossed and sleepless night our troops could still fight as determinedly as they did to secure the bridgehead and to do this took several days of non-stop slogging.

The morale of everyone in my unit was terrific. No one showed despair or fear. We cursed our luck but all worked with a will. We saw some horrible sights and many dead but no one shirked and the care and tenderness with which those boys carried out their nursing duties was quite beyond praise. I'm sure they all feel as I do – I didn't want to go on D Day but I did and I survived and now I'm proud of it.

*

From Dr N. J. P. Hewlings

It was now just before midnight on 5th/6th June and dark and many heavy bomber aircraft, all loaded with parachutists, were flying alarmingly close together, with no lights, and making rendezvous with ever more aircraft from other airfields. My recollection is of the second pilot and the rear-gunner continually warning our pilot of other aircraft close above, below, in front and behind our own aircraft, and of the pilot taking avoiding action, causing the aircraft to bank and turn and climb and drop rather alarmingly. Then I heard the navigator giving the pilot courses : then he said we ought to be seeing something soon – he hoped we were on course. At las they saw flak ahead and steered for it.

Next the engines were throttled back to reduce speed to the safe minimum, and the pilot, I felt, was trying to keep the aircraft on a straight and steady course, with nose slightly down to lose height, in spite of anti-aircraft shells bursting around us, and all the time watching for and avoiding other aircraft doing the same thing.

Soon the red light came on and we stood to the door. Then the green light and out we tumbled through the hatch in the floor as fast, and as close after each other, as possible.

Floating down in the dark was quiet and relatively peaceful, except for a few desultory bursts of flak in the sky around us, but not too close. More aircraft followed and roared over my head. Gradually all aircraft noise disappeared into the distance, and I was aware of feeling very alone over enemy Europe. Finally I landed in a meadow, got free from my parachute harness, stood up, and found my only living companion was an undisturbed French cow, grazing contentedly. In spite of all the maps and models and photographs, I recognised *nothing*! Then I saw a lot of flak to the north-west, and started walking towards it. Gradually features on the ground began to take on some semblance of the maps and photos we had studied, and I shortly found the Field Ambulance rendezvous in a small wood. Many less than half our personnel had arrived so far. On my way to the rendezvous I picked up one RAMC sergeant, a private of the Parachute Regiment with a mortar and bombs and Mr Leonard Mosley, who was a well-known war correspondent, I believe, for the *Daily Express*. He had dropped with 5th Parachute Brigade, and I well remember he was wearing Army issue steel rimmed spectacles, stuck on at his temples and the bridge of his nose with white sticking plaster to prevent them being blown off during the drop. He looked comical, and a little lost and bewildered.

As we moved off in small groups from our rendezvous to our appointed dressing station in Le Bas de Ranville, all was chaos – men of all units moving in every direction, looking for rendezvous and their own formations. One German staff car carrying two very surprised German officers drove into our midst. The German officers had to walk to the Brigade POW cage: one of our own brigade officers was delighted with the car. There were intermittent bursts of small arms fire and occasional mortar bombs bursting in the darkness – whether these were 'theirs' or 'ours' I do not know.

When we reached the house appointed as our dressing station we found several very frightened TODT organisation personnel with their hands on their heads, only too ready to be put in the bag. They had been building Rommel's Atlantic Wall!

We had dropped at 0030 hours on 6th June. We reached our dressing station at about 0200 hours, set up our equipment, carried in kitbags strapped to one leg, and opened for business about 0400 hours. A steady stream of casualties soon started coming in.

A little after first light – about 0500 hours – I heard a rumble to the north – we were about four miles inland – which soon increased to sound like continuous heavy thunder. This was the Royal Navy bombardment prior to the assault on the beaches.

We were only disturbed in our work with the casualties once or twice during the morning of 6th June by a stray shell dropping near or in the garden of a house, and ultimately a shell went through our cookhouse roof, killing one of the orderlies, very seriously wounding our padre, and greatly surprising our portly Somersetshire cook-sergeant, who smartly exchanged for his red beret a steel helmet which, so far as I know, he did not take off again until the end of the war in Europe!

*

From Mr J. M. Leggate, FRCS
We were put down on Green beach instead of the expected White beach and we first tried to leave the beach by a narrow road which came down to the shore but were turned back as it was still under fire. As the tide was out we came back to firm sand and made our way between the shore obstacles with explosives attached to another exit from the beach, drove through the village of Bernière to our pre-arranged rendezvous with 33rd Field Dressing Station, part of which had already arrived, but with little in the way of equipment. In the field were three knocked-out tanks which had been hit by an 88-mm battery which air and sea bombardment had failed to silence.

A Field Transfusion Unit was already at work putting up plasma drips on the wounded who were lying in rows on stretchers. There was no blood available except what could be taken from the RAMC personnel, all of whom had been previously 'grouped'. Slit trenches had been dug and while my team was putting up the lean-to tent at the side of the lorry as an operating room, starting up the 1 kw generator for the light (if that had failed we still could have used an extension from the lorry's headlights) and boiling up the instruments, I went round the wounded and made a list of priorities for operation. The list consisted mainly of 'abdominals'. The German and British wounded were all lying together. I came to one young, very young, German lying between two British. 'No, don't bother with me,' he said. 'Take these two first.' He died, in fact, before his turn came for operation.

Each abdominal takes about an hour – a long and careful search for holes in the gut or damage to vessels must always be made, even when there are dozens of wounded waiting; and yet you must operate as soon as resuscitation has raised his blood pressure, for, if he goes back into 'shock' it becomes irreversible however much plasma or blood you give him. If casualties are so heavy that they cannot all be dealt with, they must be evacuated *before* operation. We operated continuously until noon on 7th June, when another surgeon and anaesthetist came from a casualty clearing station to relieve us. Some of us billeted down in slit trenches with stretchers at the bottom to

keep us off the water and some in a large house close by. We had a
tent outside this house, not fifteen yards from where we were; it was
full of German wounded and one night a bomb fell on it and killed
all but one. The owner of the house wanted me to ask the BBC in
London to broadcast to her relatives in Paris that she was safe and
had survived the bombardment! The French, of course, greeted us
with mixed feelings. It was all very well being liberated but they
naturally took a dim view of our destruction of their towns and
villages.

Later I was sent to look after the casualty evacuation point, which
was housed in a large school building. Most of the casualties which
arrived there had been treated by other units but at times many were
sent without having been dealt with. I remember a German (SS); he
had been fighting for three days on short rations, had been wounded
by a shell fragment through the sacrum and abdomen, had lain for
twenty-four hours, had been picked up and sent back through a
regimental aid post and casualty clearing station and by the time he
arrived at the CEP he had suppurative peritonitis, osteomyelitis of
the sacrum and severe dehydration; there was gas gangrene of the
abdominal wall and gas-forming pus in the chest. He had five holes
in the intestine and by the time he came to the operation he had
been wounded eighty-four hours.

Going round the ward next day I wondered what some people
at home would have thought if they had seen doctors, nurses and
orderlies trying to save a storm-trooper's life and I remember seeing
on the bed of the next patient a newspaper with large headlines
'Russians annihilate Vilna garrison'. Of course this man would not
have recovered – as he did – without penicillin. What a difference
penicillin made! I understand that in the Middle East, before penicillin became available 69 % of cases arriving at base hospitals had
wounds already contaminated with streptococci. In Normandy, not
69% but 5%. It was a delight to operate on gun-shot wounds even
of the joints. I never saw pus in a wounded Tommy (a) because
apart from our time at the CEP we were well forward and received
casualties soon after wounding, and (b) because of penicillin; whereas
among the many Germans we treated we found their wounds were
heavily contaminated – foul pus, and even gas-gangrene. I remember
one, however, a British guardsman, who did have true gas-gangrene.
There was just a very small clean rifle bullet wound in the buttock
and yet it required an amputation through the hip-joint and removal
of the muscles. When I apologised to the chap for having to take his

leg off he replied, 'That's all right; I'm just thanking God I've come through these scraps alive.' That was the attitude of nearly all the wounded, no resentment or self-pity, just thankfulness to be still alive. It was the same with the French civilians, even women and children whom we also treated.

*

From Mr M. E. C. Balmer
I was medical officer in a CCS. We set up our small hospital just a few hundred yards from the shore. We had literally hundreds of seriously wounded soldiers on stretchers arranged in tiers up and down our makeshift tented wards. One had a dreadful feeling of frustration as all one could do was to try to alleviate their pain with morphia until such time as they had emergency surgery or were evacuated back to UK on LSTs.

*

From Mr E. T. J. Dykes
By 4 p.m. we were open to start treatment. The Field Surgical Unit failed to arrive on second tide as planned and we had to get the reserve team working with our own equipment.

The first German prisoners came past us and one with a Red Cross armband asked if he could come and work for us! I received this request and wasn't sure what to say. I advised him to carry on to POW cage and ask there. He turned up with another next morning, then a German doctor arrived, and we gave them a tent and some instruments and dressings and they attended to enemy wounded for several days.

Of course we had many civilian wounded, as there was no civil hospital and we had the task of telling relatives that their loved ones had either been evacuated to England or were dead. The local priests came around every day and were very helpful, interpreting and attending to their spiritual needs.

The reserve surgeon and anaesthetist worked non-stop all through that night without sleep and existing on self-heating tins of soup and Horlicks.

One interesting case was a Brigadier Cunningham who was wounded in both elbows. He was operated on and plastered up and next morning his fingers were swelling. He had a gold ring which had become very tight and was restricting circulation. As dental officer I had the job of cutting through the ring.

About two or three years ago the surgeon who operated turned up at my surgery after thirty-two years. He told me that the brigadier was the brother of Admiral Sir Alan Cunningham, C-in-C Mediterranean.

*

From Mr J. C. S. Cregan, FRCS

The first dead man I saw was a brigadier, floating face down in the water, I think he must have been an RE man landing very early. LCIs were hit on both sides of us, one badly. We got pinned down by mortar fire on the beach, as the tide receded, and lost many men, and I got hit in the chest by a bullet from a pillbox, which passed out of my back without doing any harm. As you know, during these minutes you were either quick or dead. We were lucky, having got off the beach, to capture an enemy person, who was actually a Russian prisoner from the Eastern front, put on humble duties in the German Army, i.e. laying minefields. We made him lead us through them, towards Luc-sur-Mer and Douvres-la-Delivrande (west of Lion), where we rested a little, but lost many men (about eighty – from a low-flying Messerschmitt group dropping air-burst bombs). It was here that Tim Gray was wounded and he was not replaced for some weeks. We should have returned in a day or so to the UK but, as you know, the weather turned, and we stayed on indefinitely. I returned as a patient in September, having got at the sharp end (roughly) of an 88-mm shell. My replacement, D. M. de R. Winser (a Guy's graduate, poet, and Oxford rowing Blue) was killed in the Scheldt Estuary, but I am glad to say one of my RAMC corporals (Thwaites) survived and is now head waiter in the grill at the Cumberland, and probably earning more than both of us put together.

*

From the Reverend John G. White, then Private White RAMC, 200 Field Ambulance

About 3 a.m. we had our breakfast of bully stew on board our ship before being lowered from the davits in our LCAs into a rough sea at about 4 a.m. The first sensation I remember was the smell of the cordite from the naval guns firing all round us. The second was the

misery of seasickness, which we endured until landing at H plus 15 –
15 minutes after the start. The first thing to come up was our seasick
pills, and when one of the Marines warned us to keep our heads down
as Jerry was firing on the boats, someone groaned : 'And the sooner
he hits the b – – – – thing the better.'

We landed only up to our knees in water and saw a tank ablaze
on the beach, with casualties around it. Coming under small arms fire,
we fell flat, which was my undoing. On my back I carried a col-
lapsible stretcher and four bottles of liquid blood plasma, and the
weight of this flattened my infantry pouches on my front webbing
straps. Among other things, these contained ether croquettes, which
burst under the weight, so I suppose I was the first man anaesthetised
on D Day! Anyway, this was only partial, as my pals saw I was after
a kip and removed my kit. Everything of course was released on
unfastening the webbing belt – a precaution in case we had been sunk.

'This is no time for a kip, Chalky,' said someone. 'Come and help
us carry these chaps off the beach.'

It took several carries on the beach to accomplish the removal of
one casualty, as apart from my anaesthetic, we were all weakened by
seasickness. Unfortunately every man was found to be dead – killed
by blast.

I then lost the gang, as I stayed behind to bandage a second
lieutenant, who had had a shot through the heel, and was lying in
the middle of the road which ran along the side of the beach. There
was a ditch on one side, and when Jerry started to mortar the officer
suggested I took cover in it. However, I had been to Ely on a mine-
lifting course, and had no desire to end my days at the hands of
stick-mines. Much more heroic to be bandaging the wounded, if it
had to be! I remember that, just before this, we had passed a pillbox
where a nineteen-year-old German officer had been the only survivor
and had been loading and firing the 88-mm gun on his own, until
shot from behind by the infantry. The MO tested his pulse, said it had
stopped, 'but his watch hasn't,' and helped himself.

I had had the presence of mind to salvage most of my kit before
leaving the beach, so I sat down and ate two small buns which my
mother had sent in a parcel just before we left sealed camp in Fawley
for embarkation at Southampton. I had kept them to eat on D Day,
should I survive. I thought to myself, 'I guess I'm the first to eat a
home-made bun on D Day.' Anyway, those buns tasted jolly good,
and I then entered with more strength into a cloud of smoke, only
to be blown over on my back by an explosion. In the midst of the

smoke was a flail tank knocking out mines, and one of these had
bowled me over.

The chap looking out of the tank wanted to know what I was doing
there, so I told him I was looking for the RAP of the Dorsets. 'There's
nobody in front of me but b – – – – Jerries,' he replied.

Further on I found a Bren gun team in a ditch, and they did not
take kindly to my enquiries, preferring to be unobserved in their position. But help was at hand! The colonel of the Devons came down
the road, so I asked him.

'RAP of the Dorsets,' he exclaimed. 'I can't even find my own
b – – – – regiment.'

It seemed we had all landed on the wrong beaches, but I don't
know much about that, and the Hampshires had the Dorsets' objectives and vice versa. However, I can't be sure of this, being but a
private soldier.

I then came across a chap named Flint from our unit, who was
examining a bullet which had penetrated a pack of compressed gauze
in his pouch. 'You want to keep that for a souvenir,' I said, and we
both recognised in the same moment that another bullet could come
our way, and dropped to the ground.

When all was quiet, we made our way to our unit, where I met up
again with my second lieutenant friend, who recommended me to my
CO for gallantry under fire! I made my explanation of how it all
happened, and we had a good laugh all round about my mixed
motives. We were then kept busy with casualties until the evening,
when I climbed up the small hill in the lee of which we had our camp,
and saw what I thought to be RAF personnel in the field above.

'I didn't know the RAF were coming ashore today,' I remarked on
my return.

'They don't come till D plus three,' said the MO.

'Well, there's a crowd of them at the top of the hill,' I replied.

On having been up to view, our corporal came back in about two
jumps. 'There's a field full of b – – – – Jerries up there,' he shouted.

'We'd better keep quiet about it then,' replied the MO. 'We've
nothing to throw at them but Thomas splints.'

So ended a long day, and by daybreak our Teutonic friends had all
gone.

*

From Surgeon Captain A. W. Hagger VRD, RNR, then Temporary
Surgeon Lieutenant RNVR

. . . About this time and either just before or after the great gale we
did a trip carrying Americans to Omaha beach, in company with a
few American LSTs. During the night the American LST next astern
(we were leading the group) kept coming up to our quarter and
eventually signalled to us that he should lead because he was senior
to our captain. The latter told him he was welcome to do just that
and he did so. Unfortunately for him, an hour or so later, he was
badly damaged by running over one of the new acoustic mines which
otherwise would have got us. I was standing by the gangway the next
morning as the Americans disembarked and could not understand why
they were throwing tins of chicken, peaches and other luxuries overboard as they went over the side. On polite questioning they said that
they were too bulky to take with them, so, very quickly, we persuaded
them to leave the tins with us and that we would be able to make
use of them.

Shortly after this episode, when one of the three of us medical
officers had left the ship to return to barracks (I lost the toss as to
whom it should be), I had to send our captain ashore to hospital
because of a stomach ulcer, which he had been nobly putting up with.
As I have said before, he was a character (and a great one at that)
and on the last night he sent for me and proceeded to read to me the
'Flimsy' (a short report about an officer) that he had written about me.
With great glee and humour he read out that I had 'served under his
command entirely to my own satisfaction' (normally entirely to his
satisfaction) : that only ten of my patients had died and that they were
the lucky ones : that I had been known to tell the truth at Liar Dice
on no less than two occasions and they still send missionaries abroad.
He asked me if he should send it to the Admiralty and when I agreed
(I heard later that it was nearly framed) said 'Hear what I have said
about the navigation officer.' He had written that he considered the
latter incapable of navigating a paper boat in a jerry.

*

From Dr E. P. Hargreaves

I was OC of the 26 Field Hygiene Section, a small unit, one officer
and some thirty other ranks, all tradesmen and including four staff
sergeants who in civil life had been sanitary inspectors. My ADMS
Colonel R. D. Cameron had decided that for the assault I should be

attached as a supernumerary medical officer to the 9th Field Ambulance for general medical duties and to supervise the purity of water
supplies for the division, one of my staff sergeants being attached to
each of the 8th and 185th Field Ambulances to supervise hygiene in
the brigades; the remainder of my unit, together with our transport,
was to follow on D + 3.

As we approached Sword beach our LCT hit a sandbank some
100 yards from the shore. A lifeline was soon carried to the beach
and troops started to disembark. As soon as they realised they were
out of their depth they dropped their bicycles, and non-combatant
troops being the last to leave the LCT had to struggle through a sea
of abandoned cycles.

We made our way across the beach and through the sand hills
along a track cleared of mines by flail tanks and the REs and set up
a dressing station on the outskirts of Lion-sur-mer. The day that followed was long and noisy in the extreme but we were kept fully
occupied by the continuous stream of casualties. The cycle ride to
Caen was off; most of the bicycles were buried in the sand. Moreover
our salient was not more than 1,000 yards in depth and contained in
it a German strongpoint at Douvre la Délivande which was causing
trouble. This underground garrison continued to hold out for some
ten days despite aerial attack and broadsides from HMS *Warspite* and
Ramillies.

CHAPTER NINE

The Royal Army Service Corps
(now Royal Corps of Transport)

In previous centuries the transport services had a fairly easy time of it, although raids on the 'wagon train' were not infrequent and involved heavy casualties. In the present century the task of the transport services has become one of the most dangerous, as well as one of the most vital. Travelling with little or no protection over open roads, they are an easy target for shelling or aerial attack. As much of their cargo consists of petrol or ammunition a single bomb or shell can cause appalling repercussions. The RCT (RASC) is cheerfully cynical about praise or criticism.

*

From Mr R. E. Fawcett
... Once aboard the ferry we expected landing in a matter of minutes but it was not to be. We in fact spent several hours due first to a landing craft wreck becoming wedged under our ramp preventing the vehicles from landing because of the depth of water. Despite great efforts by the beach personnel it was a long agonising time, made worse by the explosion of a mine in the centre casing of the ferry (I had been leaning on it a few moments before) and a despatch rider, his motor cycle and a 3-ton lorry were badly damaged. The despatch rider was given morphine and taken back to the ship.

However after taking many soundings with a dip-stick we went ashore in the early afternoon and set up a small supply depot of Compo Packs (boxes of rations and cigarettes for fourteen men for one day) which were being brought ashore by DKWS and off-loaded in our area. I well remember an infantry officer from a forward area asking where he could get cigarettes for his men. Officially they should have had rations for D Day and D+1 but we made sure that he didn't go back empty-handed.

*

From Mr G. S. Squires, formerly Driver G. S. Squires, 172 Company,
   9th Brigade, British 3rd Division

I had prepared myself for anything going wrong on the landing, I had
all old clothes on and my boots unlaced. I had a sten gun at my side
and under my seat I had three grenades. In my cab I had my six
weeks' old baby daughter Gloria's first knitted bootee hanging up
for luck.

We made our run to the beach, down went the ramp, my turn
came. As we drove through the sea I thought this is great fun and
very exciting. We cleared the water and on to the beach and suddenly
it was not so funny. I saw the dead and wounded, the smashed vehicles,
but had no time to dwell on this, we were busy stripping off the waterproofing. I spotted the vehicle containing our officer coming on to
the beach and slowed down so he was in front of me. All the vehicles
followed crocodile fashion along the beach, then turned behind some
houses across a field, keeping between white tapes laid down by the
mine clearers.

I was in bottom gear, travelling very slowly in a jerking motion
when . . .

A black fog was swirling, my whole body felt numb, I was all sort
of peculiar, my right leg appeared to be twisted in near my left
shoulder, my boot blown off. My mind cleared rapidly, the corporal
was climbing out of the cab shouting that he would see if the man in
the back was OK. I suddenly thought of fire and screamed out to him
to get me out, that I couldn't move. I was pulled from the cab and
laid on a stretcher alongside about ten others, wounded by the mine
which I had run over.

My officer came back and wished me luck and put packets of
cigarettes under my blanket. I lay there about an hour. I looked at
my vehicle, the front tyres in strips. The road was soon cleared and
all the wounded were carried back to the beach. A medical officer,
his own arm in a sling, examined my foot and put my field dressing
on my foot, my sock back on and then a rifle was bandaged to my leg
as a splint.

The wounded were given lots of sweet tea and smokes. I was
moved into the garden of a house. A wounded German was sitting on
the ground and I threw him a cigarette. About 6 p.m. we were
put on a Jeep and taken inland and our stretchers were laid in rows
on the floor of a wooden church. There was lots of activity going on
outside. When darkness came this increased and panic showed among
the wounded lying in the dark unable to do anything but hope. Rifles

were being fired from the windows inside the church and I began to feel nervous, having thought that the war was over for me.

Next move is out of the church into the back garden of a house (I think), lots of noise and movement of troops. After about an hour I was loaded back on a Jeep and finished up back on the beach, after a frightening and painful journey. On the Jeep an Army padre talked to me and said we had no hope of getting on a ship that night. I was taken off the Jeep and laid on the sand – on my stretcher, of course. Planes came over and we heard shrapnel whingeing through the air as bombs were dropped. I looked around and spotted a body with a helmet on. I decided it would be of more use to me and rolled off my stretcher. Then I saw it was a dead German and there was a gaping hole in the side of the helmet, so decided to leave it on him. I managed to get back on to the stretcher. Most of the other wounded appeared to be leaving their stretchers and disappearing down a trench, and I decided to follow. I managed to get off the stretcher again and to roll about twenty feet and then to fall down into the trench. I was feeling rough and exhausted and fell asleep . . .

I arrived back in England about mid-day 8th June, and my right leg was amputated in Haslar Hospital. I was, of course, critically ill for some time but eventually recovered and was fitted with an artificial leg. My mildewed wallet was sent back to me about six months later; it enclosed my baby daughter's woollen bootee, which I still have.

*

From Major L. Robert Shepherd (Retd), then Captain, RASC
On the principle of 'set a thief to catch a thief' I was detailed for D Day to contact all Assault and Beach DIDS (detail issue depots) in 21st Army Group sector, to locate and report to 2nd Army, all specially marked supplies intended for civilian use and prevent, if possible, their improper use. It was presumed (correctly) that numbers of civilians would be parted from their usual sources of supply or, worse still (correctly) would become war victims.

Accordingly, after being cooped up in a dank, dark coppice on the South Downs for a week, I embarked from a Southampton 'hard' and joined LST 361 as part of a fleet that appeared to overflow the Solent. Naval officers exuded 'Senior Service'; obviously we were an infliction to be endured. The RC chaplain was aboard and a sight in the dusk of 4th June was the shoals of DUKWs heading towards us with loads of RCs bound for a last shriving, Mass and HC. The scene in the gloom of the huge hold amongst the tanks, with soldiers perched upon guns and every point of vantage, was memorable. There was a group of reporters aboard who missed the whole thing through incompetence and preoccupation and whose remonstrance received curt response; we didn't like them anyway! Incidentally, the returning DWKS disappearing into the bowels of their mother ship was really something.

Complete with 'pills-seasick' and 'bags-vomit', not to mention sealed orders to be opened at sea, the fleet successfully accomplished a double inward turn (shades of Victoria and Camperdown) and we were on our way late on 5th June. A somewhat fitful sleep in the scuppers was terminated by the explosion of a shell close by – the prelude to another unforgettable sight, the sea packed with vessels of all classes from battleships to DWKS as far as the eye could see.

There was a heavy exchange of fire with the Germans holed up in fortified beach houses and dugouts. The beach turned out to be that of Hermanville. Our landing was timed for 1000 hours when, I presume, it was expected that LST would be beached. It appears that this idea was disapproved by the Navy at the eleventh hour, and Rhinos were used for disembarkation – with ghastly results. Our tanks (East Riding Yeomanry) were not completely discharged until midnight and were, I understand, badly cut up shortly afterwards. It is obvious how the plan to capture Caen on D Day went awry!

My personal experience of a Rhino was infuriating! A corporal RE was in charge and he had only one idea in his head and that was to retrieve the propeller of his outboard motor at the earliest possible moment to save it from damage in shallow water. The procedure was to drive painfully against the tide (two knots maximum) to a position above the cleared gap in the beach mines and then to return at full speed to the gap, starboard your helm and on to the beach. By raising the screw too soon the gap was missed twice and the painful crawl back was repeated each time. On the third attempt, although there were very senior officers aboard who did nothing, I posted myself beside the corporal and assured him that if he raised the screw before I gave him leave, I would personally fell him. That time we made it – just before midnight!

The remainder of that night was spent in a haystack amidst the noise of planes, shootings, explosions and the rest; one explosion really lifted the stack; afterwards I found the largest crater I was ever to see – rather like the Kensington Round Pond; it must have been an ammo dump or something. In the early light I saw my first Frenchman, an old farmer with a bloody bandage around his head, counting his dead cattle. I now tried to comply with my sealed orders which were to leave by the road to Douvre, turn right on a road running parallel to the beach and thence to a further road down to the Canadian beach. In attempting to do this, I unwittingly crossed what I later saw to be the front line and was heading straight for an intact German strongpoint and an undignified retreat. I learned afterwards to 'feel' when I was in no-man's land; there is something undefinable about it! Later the same day, I was virtually accused of cowardice by a colonel who knew where I ought to have been but who, obviously, preferred dead to live captains.

I saw the first dead that day: the fair heads of two young soldiers protruding from the back of a field ambulance. The village priest, who was passing at the time, also saw them as they halted in a traffic jam; he knelt down in the mud touching them gently in prayer. That night, being somewhat unnerved by the first night, I took refuge in a dry ditch by the side of a field dressing station, under the impression that its illuminated red cross would be respected. How wrong I was! That cross was the target for anything that could be flung at it. Years afterwards, I went to find that ditch. It was still there but it formed the boundary of one of the largest collections of war graves I have seen – all stemming, I suppose, from that one much battered field dressing station.

The next day, I made it! I joined a DID allotted to the Canadians at Bernières-sur-mer, who seemed a wild and jumpy lot. One wondered what they were firing at all night! I know one unhappy stray was shot by the sentry because he couldn't pronounce the countersign quickly enough. Then there was that flap in the DID because the cigarette and chocolate section of the field rations was being constantly pilfered and complaints came back from the fighting men. Orders were given to shoot on sight and, sure enough, a soldier was killed the first night – the defaulting sentry of a neighbouring unit. When I left that sector, means were being sought to post him as 'killed in action' to save his wife and family.

About this time I had to speak with the OC of a DID encamped in an orchard off the beach. On arrival I noticed the acrid smell of a shell burst and the smoke still shrouding the trees. I enquired for the captain and was told, 'We are looking for him too!' They never found him. In another two minutes I would have been with him, but by this time I was beyond rational surmise. I wonder if people who think about these things realise that RASC lost virtually 10,000 men *killed* in this war, not to mention other casualties of three times that figure.

CHAPTER TEN

The Canadians

Unfortunately there are very few contributions from Canadians. Canadian units made a successful landing on Juno beach and fought their way inland with great dash and tenacity. In addition there were 700 Canadians serving in the British Army, of whom details follow.

*

From Mr Frank Helden
I was in the 46th Royal Marines Commando but I transferred to the 601 Flotilla on a landing craft. I was a corporal coxswain and we left Southampton on 5th June and on 6th June I landed the landing craft at Arromanches. I had a crew of four and one sailor with a Jeep. There was also a RN engineer officer and the only two who were not sick over the rough crossing were the sailor and me. The RN officer had sucked back on a blocked diesel line and became quite sick.

We were disabled when we landed between the American and Canadian troops but we stayed with the craft. We got fired on by two French girls and the Canadian troops shot them for that.

During the next few weeks I used to ferry different troops in till the Mulberry was built. There was a violent storm and most of it went west, my landing craft which had been laid up on the beach was an American one, so I got an English petrol one.

*

From Mr H. D. Foster
Re the 700 Canadians that served with the British Army (Can-Loan). You no doubt know of this group, but in the event not, I would like to say something about them. In March/April 1944, the British Army was short of experienced officers – what with African casualties and other commitments etc. around the world. The Canadian Army was

just the opposite, having some 1,700 officers (mostly lieutenants – but some captains and majors) 'backed up' with no place at the time in the Canadian Army in England to take them. A call was put out to 'see immediate action' and thus the 700 strong Can-Loan group was born. Many took a reduction in rank to join the group. We were assembled in Sussex New-Brunswick and proceeded to UK in several ships, arriving for the most part in April and early May 1944. Many of these officers had been overseas before (in my case since 1940) and had been returned home to Canada to take officer's training. Many were Dieppe veterans of the Canadian 2nd Division, who were promoted from corporal and sergeants to attend school in Canada for their commissions. The group won thirty-three MCs, and received 75% casualties – killed and wounded.

On thinking about those days now – I might add that in my case I felt like the 'pinpoint' of a giant needle, that extended back through all of the forces. You had the feeling of 'what am I doing here?'. Of all of the thousands in uniform, how come I'm right at the front of what we knew was the biggest assault in history? The other thing that seemed more or less general was a feeling that we would not return. I know that I felt like this, result being a deep calm – and I noted that in others. It just seemed impossible that we would make it – and we were more or less resigned. About the only other thing that I noted was the expression of pent-up feelings that one noted. You could talk to someone that looked pretty cool, and he would just burst out when replying to you. The other was the restlessness of all ranks when sleeping D night and D + 1. They were very restless and the expressions on their faces as they lay in bunkers or behind hedgerows reflected their inner thoughts and fears as they slept – or tried to sleep.

About the only other thing that I can remember was a great 'awareness' to everything that was going on. Of course we were alert, but this awareness encompassed everything – how a flower looked, the tilt of a vehicle that had been mined, the expression on faces – everything was like technicolor. In great detail.

The coolness of other ranks and officers in this division was remarkable. They had seen action before and if it had not been for this remarkable quality I feel sure that I would never have gotten far.

A Can-Loan officer with the Dorsets

... We ran into first machine-gun fire and casualties right at the water's edge. Right after that we ran into 'Deballikers' on the shore line (mechanisms set below ground that when wire strung above is tripped, rifle shot size pellets shot upwards, time for man to be half-way over it and thus pierced between legs). These were expected and everyone had to move very quickly over the area so that speed was such that when the thing was triggered man above would be over the area or at least end up with one in the fleshy bum.

The first casualties were very difficult to understand and accept. Most of us had seen men shot before but nothing like the damage done by Spandau fire and 88s. Men were blown apart and in the case of machine-gun fire, men were hit a dozen times at once – not a chance for them to live. We had been trained in most all aspects and actually pretty well knew what to expect. However, it was not enough to bolster you for this kind of carnage. It took a few minutes on the beach to comprehend, adjust and more forward. Some did not.

Beaches crossed, we reached the relative safety of some shrubs and other growth, enabling us to set up machine-guns and take on likely targets. Most main installations had been severely hit, and our fire was directed at nearby houses and in some cases ditches that posed a fire threat to us. The advance was rapid, and by noon we had passed through their first line of defence and were in 'Bocage country' that afforded us an equal chance to fight. We lost many good men in the assault, and while I had met these men only two weeks prior, was very saddened by the number that were lost in the first day's action. Most companies were weakened considerably, and in my own case the colonel came up that night and told me I was to act as company commander. I knew that we had lost our company commander Major Allen but thought that someone else would be given command of the company. I mentioned this to the colonel, to which he said that I was the only one left (Leo Heaps had been immediately taken into Intelligence after first day's assault) and by process of elimination I was 'it'. My first inclination was to refuse, for what ever that would mean, as I simply felt that I was too green and responsibility for over one hundred men was a serious business. I was told by the colonel 'not to worry' as this was his first action too . . . He had been in Africa on a staff job and had never commanded troops in action. The way that this was said was sufficient for me to say, 'OK, if you can do it so can I – let's go.' Colonel Norris lasted only a very few days and in that time gained a respect from everyone that would normally take several years to attain under different conditions.

On the first occasion after assuming command of the company (promoted to captain) I gathered sergeants now in charge of platoons and the sergeant major, to arrive at orders for the next step. As we were getting into it, and I was giving some sort of order of attack, I noted the sergeant major looking at me and with his eyes saying, 'Let's cool it.' I guess I was pretty excited and here I was working with troops most of whom had fought for some time in Africa and Malta. They were a cool bunch and I guess the sight of this Canadian giving rapid orders that were probably not too reflective of the real situation caused the sergeant major's look.

I called him aside and asked him something like, 'Do you see anything wrong in plans as I was giving them?'

To this he replied, 'No, sir, but maybe you should have a cup of char (tea) – let's take our time and then look at it and maybe then we can come up with something.'

I just couldn't believe it, as this was taking place under the most dire of circumstances – lots of guns firing and we were really not under that much protective cover. However, I took him up on it and must say that the soon brewed hot tea tasted excellent, giving me a chance to think and I believe that I did reconsider earlier orders given, to some positive effect.

CHAPTER ELEVEN

The Royal Artillery

The Royal Artillery has a wide variety of roles on the battlefield but unfortunately we have only a small selection from which to depict its activities on D Day. Although the Artillery is designated the Royal Regiment of Artillery it consists of a very large number of regiments, each trained for a special task, perhaps as airborne, perhaps an anti-tank, or for static or mobile warfare. Artillery barrages are, for many soldiers, the most memorable and fearsome symbols of battle.

*

From Mr W. V. S. Fletcher
. . . It took an hour to reach the shore and the nearer in we got the rougher it appeared, and one could see the terrible battering the houses lining the beach had received; the beach seemed a chaotic mess. We landed through four feet of water, the engine for one tenth second nearly stalling and at last I was on the soil of France, four hours late, feeling sick, depressed and my first urgent requirement some quiet spot I could use as a lavatory!

I went in search of the CO, whom I found at the planned spot, sitting in a hole in the sand, and looking wan and tired. Peter Tiarks was there too, his hand bandaged where he had stopped a bit of mortar and obviously in pain. He told me things had been pretty bad and he had lost an officer and some men, but they were improving now. The CO said that the Germans had a strongpoint still holding out where my BHQ was to be established and my F Troop deploy but my three troops and HQ due to land that evening would certainly not do so as, owing to the two or three German strongpoints still in existence, there was no lateral communication with the two beaches (all my battery were due to land on the next beach to myself).

There was a Boche strongpoint within 700 yards of where we were sitting, being engaged at point blank range by two 4-inch LCGs. There was a certain amount of shelling, mortaring and small arms fire going on, a depressing vista!

I decided to leave the beach and find another BHQ. My vehicle stuck in the sand but was pushed out by the willing hands of a squad of Boche prisoners passing at the moment, looking very unlike *Herrenvolk*.

I went off on the lightweight motor cycle to do a recce of the area where our BHQ should have been established. This involved reconnoitring the area near the German strongpoint, and it became very obvious that to establish an HQ and deploy a troop in that part of the world was unwise. Quite heavy mortar fire was coming down on the road and Commandos were forming up for the attack. Having decided that a redeployment would be necessary, I carried out a fresh recce, both for this troop and the other two, all without incident. By this time it was getting late, and I was very tired and hungry, besides being still worried with diarrhoea. On getting back to RHQ I found Alan and the others ensconced in a ditch, having tea of the powdered variety but none the less delicious. I had two cups, some concentrated cheese and chocolate, and felt much better. We were further cheered by the unforgettable sight of hundreds of gliders and their tugs coming over to reinforce the Airborne Division; the gliders coming down in turn followed by hundreds of different coloured parachutes dropped by the tugs.

It was then getting late and as there was nothing more we could do, we decided to turn in, and slept the sleep of the just in the ditch, occasionally disturbed by rather alarmingly close rifle shots. This phenomenon continued for some days and nights after D Day but though there were snipers about (I was shot at and felt the wind of the bullet on at least four occasions), I am sure most of the noise was caused by the itching trigger fingers of our own soldiery.

The next day (D + 1) I decided that I must try and find out if the battery had yet landed on the other beach. The Germans still had two strongpoints holding out on the coast road, so it was useless to attempt that, and no one knew for sure if the next road inland was clear.

There was no sign of the battery and after scouting for a couple of hours I gave it up as a bad job. We were stopped in a small town (La Delivrande) on our way back by a very excited old Frenchman who said he knew of four Boche who wanted to surrender. Amid the cheers of the populace we started off with the old man as a guide. I was terrified, feeling that we might be led straight into a trap. After twisting and turning through some very narrow streets, we came to a farm; the old man told us to wait, and left us fingering our guns nervously not knowing what to expect. In a very short time the old man returned with four seedy looking Boche, one of them slightly wounded, and all cringing and anxious to please. The farmer now appeared with his large family and a bottle of Calvados which we, including the prisoners, drank. The farmer said they were *'sympathetique'* to *'Victoire'* and *'La France.'*

Our guide now said that he knew of a German doctor in a nearby house whom we should take in. We crammed the four prisoners in the back of the truck, nearly breaking the springs, and started out again. We arrived at a large house and the guide vanished, reappearing with the most unpleasant-looking Boche officer; a large creature, unshaven and with the most repulsive face. He talked French, and while talking a Frenchman came out and asked if the German doctor could remain to look after French civilians wounded in the village. I liked the look of the Frenchman as little as the German, and as usual in France a crowd had collected, all shrieking at the tops of their voices; some were for keeping the doctor but most for removing him. I gave up and said I would return for him tomorrow; the fellow then had the impertinence to ask for two of the other prisoners as orderlies. This I refused in no uncertain manner and I at least got a good Luger automatic from him. I heard that evening that he was roped in by Commandos less tenderhearted.

*

From Major S. P. Thomas RA (Retd)
... It was impossible to reach the beach at the appointed place because the whole length was occupied by craft of all kinds In addition wrecked and drifting ships made the landing difficult. We eventually went in to a 'dry' landing with the SPs coming off in about 12 inches of water.

It now became apparent that problems were to beset us all day. The beach exit had been blocked by a flail tank shedding a track and there was no forward movement. During this time the troop sergeant, who had landed earlier in the day, made contact, reported the arrival of the other section and awaited the opportunity to lead the guns to the rendezvous in Hermanville. The beach was crowded with armoured and soft-skinned vehicles and came under fire from time to time from the open flank to the west.

The troop eventually cleared the beach at about 1.15 p.m., kept the rendezvous at Hermanville, unbolted and discarded waterproofing, formed up and set off up the brigade axis round about 2 p.m.

As soon as we left the village we came upon five Sherman tanks on fire and a very unhealthy look about the whole area. The only information obtainable was from walking wounded coming back and from them it appeared that the infantry was 'over the hill' and finding progress pretty difficult. As we came up to the top of the rise a tank came roaring up and the officer asked where we thought we were going. It appeared that the Yeomanry too were trying to get up to the infantry, but were held up by 88s over the hill. It was agreed that we should hold fast where we were and move up when the tanks moved.

During this wait the troop came under fire from a small calibre mortar which seemed to be unable to make the range, by about fifty yards at the upper end of its zone. The No 1 of No 4 Gun came up to the head of the column and reported seeing puffs of smoke coming from a wood some distance away. He was told to lay on the point and fire five rounds of HE the next time it opened up. He did so and, although it is unlikely that any great damage was done, the mortaring ceased . . .

*

From Mr Thomas Dalby, 121 Medium Regiment, Royal Artillery
. . . We sailed with an enormous convoy on the morning of the 10th and, in rising seas, off-loaded our guns and vehicles into tank landing craft and headed towards our landing point near La Rivière. The weather caused much disorganisation, but A Troop, 275 Battery, was in action during the afternoon, and all 276 Battery's guns were in action during the night, supporting 50 Division.

That night, I went to my first OP in Normandy. After the North African Desert and the open hills around the Volturno, the Bocage country crowded in on us. I didn't like it. We joined the forward defence line of an infantry unit and snuggled down in a damp ditch whilst red tracer streamed over our heads. Amidst the noise and growing tension, I still remember a quiet sobbing from one of the infantrymen : maybe some of his friends had died earlier, or the layers of fear gathered in Africa and Italy were becoming too heavy for him to bear. I never knew what happened to him. We edged our way to the right and in front of the infantry, expecting a counter-attack which never came and reporting back to the gun position compass bearings of enemy fire.

And so it went on during those early days of June. Much too close to the enemy for comfort, and far more air-burst shelling than previously experienced. And sniping. OPs must always be in rather obvious spots, even if cleverly camouflaged, and to have enemy shells landing close to hastily scraped out slit trenches, or mortar bombs smashing their splinters against the thin armour plate of the OP carrier are terrors difficult to forget – especially when it is not possible to move between first-light and last-light.

I was also an amateur photographer. Quite against rules and regulations I took with me a camera, films, developing and printing gear. This enabled me to photograph our landing on the beaches, scenes around the gun position and, on 21st July, at our OP at Point 103, an historic visit by Winston Churchill. This was Winston's first personal visit to a forward area where he could overlook the enemy, during World War II, and he witnessed an AGRA concentration fall on the enemy along the Tilly–Villers Bocage road. All these films I developed on the gun position – loading the tank in the attic of the farmhouse and trying (but usually failing) to do the job during a quiet lull, when the dust was not swirling from the vibrations caused by the firing. Luckily, my negatives were delivered to me in a dressing station near Mont Pincon, where I was wounded in early August. So – I sailed back to England in a hospital ship, taking with me some permanent memories of the Normandy campaign.

During June, the regiment supported 7 Armoured, 11 Armoured, 15, 43, 49 and 50 Divisions and fired more than twenty thousand 100-pound shells in seventeen days: a weight of metal in the region of a thousand tons.

CHAPTER TWELVE

The Chaplains

Chaplains, doctors and pioneers probably see the worst of battle. For them there is no excitement or elation but they share the general danger and fear. Chaplains help and comfort the wounded and help bury the dead; as with doctors there is no relief for them once the shooting has started. There is always another wounded man, always another crisis.

*

From the Reverend Victor Leach, HCF
I was posted to the 27th Armoured Brigade with the 3rd Division and attached to the 13/18th Royal Hussars in January 1944.

I embarked on LCT 217 which was due to land at H + 45. On the Sunday morning I held a service. I think everyone attended. Previously it was difficult to get anyone to a service. The only thing I remember about the service was that we sang the hymn 'Eternal Father, strong to save'. Never before or since have I heard the refrain sung so feelingly, 'O hear us when we cry to Thee, For those in peril on the sea.' The LCT that was to the lee of ours signalled asking me to conduct a service on that landing craft. The midshipman came across in a dinghy and I duly held a second service.

Sleeping on the deck of an LCT was probably the hardest thing I slept on, or so it seemed, and with waves washing around you all night it was not too comfortable. One of the sailors on board collected 200 cigarettes from other crew members and gave them to me. I was able to supply some of the men who had been able to swim ashore after their tanks had sunk.

I landed in an American half-track along with the MO. We landed on time. I kept a diary for a day or two (against orders, of course). I quote :

Approaching shore a feeling of jitteriness, but passed off quickly when I realised I was a fool for worrying. Drove up beach without meeting mines. Machine gunners potting at us. Crossed to second lateral. Here things got sticky. Mortar bombs dropping either side. Just before turning left one dropped very close throwing earth and concrete on to us. A flail in front of us had one track blown off. We drove round him and carried on. Arrived at rendezvous before RHQ who arrived soon after. Shortly, called over with doctor to 8th Infantry Brigade HQ. A shell had dropped amongst them killing five and wounding four. A terrible mess. Good initiation . . .

Before I could do what was necessary RHQ sent for me, as they were moving. I said I cannot come yet. Give me a map reference. I had no maps. All officers were issued with maps except the padre. But the men who had been killed were officers. So I 'borrowed' a set of maps and after doing what I could I went off on foot in search of RHQ. On arriving at the spot there was no one to be seen. I was sure I was at the right place. The Intelligence Officer arrived shortly after and we agreed we were at the right place. I then sat on the top of his scout car and we roamed around looking for RHQ. Eventually we found them. They had moved to the place indicated but found it too hot and then moved again.

In the evening the doctor and I decided to dig in, much to the amusement of everyone else. We dug only to about a foot, and thought we were safe even though there were snipers all around.

A tank from one of the other regiments in the brigade turned up. A shell had penetrated the tank and killed the co-driver. We left him there till the following morning, when we had to cut him in two (he was almost in that state) in order to get him out of the tank. I buried him there and whilst saying the burial service a photographer from the magazine *Illustrated* photographed us. It appeared in the next issue. That was the first indication to my wife that I was alive and in France.

*

From the Reverend A. L. Beckingham
Shortly before the units of the 6th Airborne Division moved into transit camps in May 1944, there was a switch round of chaplains within the division and I found myself posted to the 224th Parachute Field Ambulance.

On 5th June we took off from Down Ampney before midnight. We seemed to reach and cross the Channel in next to no time and all very comfortably in the Dakota. But from the French coast onwards the pilot took strong evasive action to avoid the heavy flak that met us and it was not easy to stand in the swaying aircraft whilst waiting to jump. At last the red light went on, followed by the green, and then the first man of the stick was on his way down to the earth of Normandy.

I was too nervous to be much aware of the rest of the stick but no doubt it was their courage and example that enabled me to step out when my turn quickly came. Joyfully I heard the crack of the parachute opening and looking down it appeared as if we were descending into a cornfield. But that was an illusion of the dark of night. I had instead the softest of landings in a wet and muddy ditch. At least that is what I supposed it to be until, eagerly removing my parachute harness and clambering up the bank of what I thought was a ditch, I discovered that in fact we were in the middle of a marsh.

Cliff Phillips, my friend and batman, was only a few yards from me and together we watched other men clamber to their feet, like us no doubt recovering from the shock of landing in water and with their movements impeded by thoroughly wet clothes and equipment. As for the enemy, there was no sign of him. Phillips and I offered our prayer of thanksgiving that at least we had arrived, although where our real dropping zone was, we had no way of telling in those first minutes in Normandy.

Fortunately our group soon discovered that in fact we had landed near to the edge of the marshes and within a brief time we left the marsh and found the road to Varaville. On the outskirts of this village we found the Canadians were finishing off their job of taking the village. Whilst sheltering from the firing, I became separated from Phillips and could only assume that he had been taken prisoner.

In Varaville, my group met the Brigade Intelligence Officer who guided us to the main dressing station at Le Mesnil, which we reached at 11 a.m. Within a few minutes, the body of the Reverend G. A. Kay, CF, was brought in. He had dropped with the 8th Battalion whose job was to destroy the bridges at Buves and a single bridge east of Troarn. Immediately after the drop, the chaplain had assisted the doctor by bringing in wounded. He was killed that morning while doing this. Almost my first job on reaching my unit's headquarters was to bury my brother chaplain.

With Kay dead and Chaplain Harris of the Canadian Parachute Battalion unaccounted for (later found to have been killed on descent by enemy fire) it fell to my lot to look after the 8th Battalion and the

Canadians. I saw as many men as time and circumstances permitted in the first few days before the link up with the seaborne troops. Most of my time was occupied with the wounded brought into the 224 Parachute Field Ambulance Unit at Le Mesnil. During those first three days, despite one surgeon taken prisoner and the anaesthetist killed on the descent into Normandy, the Field Ambulance performed no less than 112 operations and during that time were under continuous and heavy pressure from the enemy. It is true to say that the Field Ambulance worked day and night to deal with the casualties, which of course could not be evacuated for some days.

*

From the Reverend C. Raymond Scott
... Then began as part of my work, the grim task of attending the wounded, collecting and identifying the dead, dealing with their effects and recording burials. My first 'cemetery' was an ordinary garden, just off-shore, and one of my earliest services was featured in the *Sunday Pictorial*. The mourners were RAF personnel. I spoke for a few minutes on the text from St John's Gospel, '. . . in the place where He was crucified there was a garden'. Later on we used a field and after wrapping each man in a blanket we buried them in rows of sixty.

There were, later on, lighter moments, much to our relief. My batman, a dour Scot, when asked what BDS stood for should have replied, Beach Dressing Station, which is self-explanatory. Instead he paused a moment, possibly prompted by wishful thinking, and then said, 'Beach Demobilisation Centre.' A commanding officer asked if I could deal with a very swollen dead cow. The weather was hot, the ground hard, and there were no spare men to help dig the large hole required. I knew the CO sufficiently well to be able to reply, 'Not unless you can specify the cow's religious denomination.' Chaplains had been told to bury not only corpses, but also to give Christian burial to bits and pieces of human flesh, however small. Pieces were washed up on the beach. I came to the conclusion that on one occasion the flesh was not human but beef. The MO confirmed this, but hesitated about one tiny bit. I had no option but to bury this consignment, which I believed had drifted ashore from a damaged or sunken ship. What service should I use? There were no mourners. I happened to possess a Canadian Service Book containing the burial services of a number of denominations. I was determined not to read the Methodist Form of Burial, but recalled how often the Anglican Church had claimed to be a comprehensive church. So I now tell my Anglican friends, including my son-in-law who is an Anglican priest, that when they get to the part of heaven reserved for the C of E, and they hear the mooing of a cow, they will be able to say, 'This is a bit of Padre Scott's dirty work.'

But those lighter moments were few. More deeply imbedded are the memories of the many sacrifices made by so many men, to use the words of David (1 *Samuel* 25.v.16) in another context, 'They were a wall unto us both by night and by day.' If these men had failed, said the late King George VI, then the last barrier against world tyranny would have fallen in ruins. These men were not trying to advance the cause of Christianity, as Christianity cannot be advanced by war. The vast majority hated war. They were there to stop a ruthless foe. Some of that ruthlessness I was to see after D Day in Breendonk prison where men were hung three at a time from a crossbeam in the open air. Others were kept in cells the size of a normal lavatory for months on end; sacks were placed over their heads on the rare occasions they were taken outside. I saw where some had scratched in the brickwork of their cells, with their fingernails, last messages or pictures of Christ!

D Day memories. One is proud to have had any association with the men and their successors who made possible so much of the freedom, social, political and economic freedom we enjoy today.

*

From the Reverend Leslie F. Skinner, TD
... The three chaplains of the brigade were attached to the tank regiments with prearranged responsibilities for the other troops of the brigade. Being responsible for Brigade HQ squadron in addition to Sherwood Rangers and other elements of support units, I travelled with Brigade HQ, two platoons of KRRC and half a company of Dorsets, in a small landing craft, being in charge of the second medical half-track vehicle of the Sherwood Rangers with a crew of four including the medical sergeant, the driver and two troopers of SRY as stretcher bearers. The LCT had been loaded on the last on, first off basis, and having been anchored out in the Solent since Friday evening, 2nd June, conditions were grim by daybreak of Tuesday, 6th June, the decks being awash with oil, sea water and vomit. We were all very cold and wet.

Stand to was at first light and by 6 a.m. the enormous convoy stretched out alongside and behind us was a remarkable and stirring sight. Tiredness and dirt were forgotten in the excitement. The rain cleared before 7 a.m. and we were running hard for the beach and under fire by 7.10, touching down by 7.25 a.m.

Lawrence Biddle, the brigade major of 8th Armoured Brigade, called for volunteers to unroll the great drum of coco-matting that was standing just behind the ramp at the forward end of the LCT, and I with three or four others took our places behind the drum ready to push once the doors were opened and the ramp went down

As we beached the ramp dropped on a mine which exploded, jamming the doors. The men standing either side of me were wounded, one losing a leg and dying almost immediately. I was blown backwards on the top of a Bren carrier being badly bruised and momentarily stunned in the process but otherwise unhurt. The damage to the doors took several minutes to release and in the meantime Sergeant Loades, the SRY medical sergeant, and I treated the wounded with dressings and in the case of the dying man with heavy doses of morphine.

Once the ramp was released we shoved the roll of matting out and followed it into about six feet of water, while the carriers and tanks behind us revved their engines preparatory to making their rush for the beach. The theory of the landing matting was no doubt good. In practice however the great length of matting about seven or eight feet wide whipped up and down in water making swimming, let alone pushing impossible. The tanks and carriers behind threatened to crush us in their advance, so that all we could do was to leave the vehicles to take the matting to the bottom as they came, while we swam aside as best we could and made for the beach.

For a few minutes everything on the beach was chaos. The Germans were firing everything they had got. Our own off-shore naval guns bombarding the beach defences a few yards ahead did not make life any more pleasant. There were so many tanks and fighting vehicles trying to get off the beach that all exits soon became blocked. A little track in the dunes ran parallel with the beach through the minefields in the direction of Le Hamel, but the ground either side of the track was heavily mined, and not a few tanks and carriers were blown up to make the confusion worse. Bulldozers pushed them out of the way, and more mines were exploded in the process. Surprisingly enough the actual casualties to men were light.

For an hour or more we gathered the casualties and treated them as best we could. I then joined a detachment of Engineers, wielding a pickaxe to help clear additional exits from the beach. It was heavy work and my bruised back and chest hurt like hell in doing it.

Once the new gap was made we managed to get the half-track into the queue and moved about 100 yards along the track before coming to a halt again. A huge land mine exploded under a bulldozer a few yards ahead of us and the great hole prevented further movement forward. While that was being attended to I dealt with the casualties then walked forward half a mile to the SRY regimental command tank to get 'the form' and learned that the battle for Le Hamel was going well.

Seemingly as yet there was no medical unit established on our part of the beach so we pulled the half-track out of the queue and returned to the beach – somewhat nerve-racking procedure crossing the minefield where it seemed that a tank had made its exit – and set up ourselves as a beach dressing station, and began gathering casualties, mostly infantry with gunshot and shrapnel wounds, informing Brigade and Regimental HQ by radio what we had done. Shortly before noon the Dorests' medical officer came back on foot to see us and give more expert treatment before returning to his own dressing station on the outskirts of Le Hamel, which by this time was more or less cleared and in our hands.

During the afternoon I swam out about twenty yards to rescue two men in a three-ton truck, who were non-swimmers and who for some reason were not wearing lifejackets and in danger of being drowned in the rising tide.

By 16.30 hours there was still no sign of any medical section on the beach near us – we heard a rumour that they had been 'drowned' in landing, but how true this was we had no means of knowing. By this time we had gathered forty-three wounded men, mostly infantry, and I became anxious to get them into more effective care, and to allow us to get off the beach and rejoin the regiment that was already moving well on the way to Bayeux.

The French Viewpoint

In the foregoing accounts there have been many references to the welcome the invasion forces received from the French. It was an unforgettable and dangerous experience for the invading troops but equally unforgettable and, at times, nearly as dangerous for the people whose country it was. For them, after four years of occupation, the experience of the days of liberation must have been traumatic. There follow the experiences of two who were in at the very beginning, one in Ranville where the parachutists landed, the other at Arromanches where 231 Brigade liberated the town.

*

From Monsieur Gabriel Anne of Ranville
I am seventy-five now and at that time I was thirty-nine years old. On the evening that the landings took place I went with my little son – nine years old then – to listen to the English radio. Of course this was forbidden, but the set was hidden in a friend's house outside Ranville, about 800 metres away. We should have been home by 10 o'clock; it was forbidden to be out after that time. We came back very quickly that night. It was a quarter to eleven and there were Germans in the château and a sentry at the gate. We passed the sentry as quickly as possible in case he stopped us, but he said nothing and we came into the house.

Perhaps a quarter of an hour afterwards we heard a noise and went to the door. It was beautiful moonlight – as light as day – and we went outside and saw aeroplanes and parachutists coming down. It was then 11 o'clock or just before. We went back into the house at once, wondering if this was a landing – one didn't know what was happening. There was a trench, a shelter, in the garden of our neighbour and then we all went into it. There were thirteen of us in the trench – little children and women, of course. Then one of the English parachutists came down like a bomb right into the shelter. He said, 'Are there Boches here?' and we said, 'No, babies!' There was one

279

who wasn't even a month old.

We knew he was English – he had a blackened face and speaking of the Germans like that. So, we all went back into the house and left the trench to the parachutists. We were afraid the Germans might come back and start shooting us as well! Then, about five o'clock in the morning, when it was getting light, I went to the door and saw that there were parachutes everywhere.

*

From Madame Bernadette Renouf of Arromanches
I was twenty-two years old at that time. On the evening of Monday, 5th June, I remember that – even physically – there was a very strange atmosphere here. My cousin and I had been to our little church that night. Each evening the priest used to recite the Chapelet, specially for the prisoners, and we had been that evening. We came out and were coming down the road here and I said to my cousin, 'I have the strangest feeling as though I'm surrounded by cotton-wool,' and she said, 'I can feel something under my feet.'

We came in the house, but we didn't say anything because I have a brother who was then eighteen and he would have teased us. We had the usual family evening. I was very close to my father and later I told him.

He said, 'Well, if you're wrapped in cotton-wool, my dear, you won't be damaged.' But then he stayed quiet for a moment and said, 'No, it's not just you, I can feel something too.'

We passed the evening, some went to bed, I stayed up late because I always did. And then I really did feel the earth moving under my feet, faintly but quite definitely. And I thought, there must be something wrong with me, but then I raised my eyes and I saw an extraordinary light and I thought, what on earth is that? I called my mother, who hadn't yet gone to bed, and asked her what she thought it was. We called my father, who was asleep and, at that moment, a terrible uproar started, it was a bombardment of a really rare intensity, very rare indeed. My father, who was an old soldier of Verdun, said, 'My word, something very serious is in preparation, we must be ready for it.' The noise went on, sometimes getting a little less, then starting again. We watched, having turned off the lights, of course, so as not to draw the attention of our illustrious occupants, and we saw that the sky was on fire over the sea, of course over the land it was reflected light.

I had a brother, of whom I have spoken, and a little sister, who was nine, and my father said, 'Get your things ready, children.' We each had already got our things – papers, etc. and basic necessities – in little cases, ready for an emergency. Then he told us to go and lie down but with our cases ready. Of course I didn't sleep and towards half past two I heard the noise of footsteps and I got up and went into the room opposite mine from which I could see the front.

I called out to my brother, 'Come and see – the Boches are going!'

He said, 'What on earth are you saying?' and then we actually saw . . .

I must say here that all that section of the road where we were was houses, and part had been evacuated in October 1943 and some of the houses had been actually taken over by the Germans, and one on the corner of the Rue de la Marine was occupied by officers, I don't know what rank, and also there were troops there. And we saw them running, one losing his boots, losing their caps, trying to get on bicycles, fixing their things on their backs, and – oh, it was lovely! Then I remember I said something which was not very distinguished in a young woman – but I said it.

Then we called Papa and told him and he said we must all get dressed because something was certainly going to happen. Then sometime towards morning, I'm not sure of the exact time but when it had started to get light, my brother was called by a neighbour of ours, a Monsieur Georges Aligot. He slept on the second floor of a house just opposite ours. He said, 'Come and see – it's splendid what I can see from my room. Come and see.' Naturally, without thinking, because we weren't supposed to go outside before 6 o'clock, we rushed across to look. And then, in front of the Hotel de Normandie, we had a view on to the sea, and it was really something.

It was splendid, with the sun just coming up, we could see – a multitude of ships, but a multitude . . . What we felt is almost indescribable, we were suffocated by emotion. Just suffocated. I have a son, and I have tried to tell him what I felt at that moment, but it just isn't possible to convey it. I can only say suffocated by the sight. No one can imagine how tremendous it was, what a splendid spectacle. And then, on the square there, there used to be a little washing place, where washing was done, tables with little walls behind them just by the sea-front. And suddenly from behind one of the little walls came a helmeted head and a machine-gun. And I said, 'Quick, quick, quick' and we all ran for our lives inside. I think I was the first to see him.

I remember half-past-six chiming on the church clock and the bombardment went on. There was the sound of firing – we heard later that the Germans had fired into a garden and some unlucky ones in a shelter had lost their lives. Anyway, we preferred to stay in the house with all the doors open. We passed the day there, in the dining room of that house in the corner opposite the Hôtel de Normandie. Some friends joined us and we talked; we prayed sometimes and we watched to see what was going on. The Germans didn't interfere with us that day at all.

Then in the evening our young neighbour came and said to my father, 'Monsieur André, the English – the English are up on the cliffs.' And my father, with his marvellous calmness, said, 'Then they'd better come down here so that we can have some peace.' Then someone told us that the daughter of some close friends of ours had been killed, her mother gravely wounded. The elder daughter, twenty years old, such a pretty girl. The little sister fought for her life for ten days, but she died too. Three dead in the family – the father too. We were very upset.

Then someone called us and we went to the crossroads, just where it is now, by the hotel and the butcher's – and I looked, I couldn't speak, I didn't know what was happening but my brother and the neighbour's son ran like maniacs to meet the English soldiers. I said to my father, 'Oh goodness, suppose they're Boches disguised.'

I saw the first of them, helmeted, carrying one of those big things, mine-detectors I think they were. There were about four of them. I suddenly felt as if I would fall down. That was when I realised it all at once – liberty, joy, the prisoners coming back, family life sweet as I had known it before – that was when the tears came, I wept and wept with joy. And of course I wasn't the only one. We all kissed and hugged each other, it was sensational. Then my father asked them if they needed anything and got the wine and we took the photograph.*

Then Papa said that if the church was still standing we should go and give thanks – and it was still standing.

Well that's how it happened . . . exactly as I remember it. There's a nice little thing I remember about my grandmother. She was eighty-two at the time, a marvellous old lady, but she had difficulty walking. Some time that day with all the shooting and bombardment she went towards the door and my father said, 'Where are you going, Mother?'

She replied, 'I'm going to get some sorrel to make some soup.'

*See page 221

So he said, 'Are you trying to commit suicide?'

She answered, 'Not at all. But this could go on a long time, the young ones are going to get hungry, and after all at my age what does it matter, it should be me who goes.'

And my good grandmother, in the bombardment, went to our garden which was some way to get sorrel and made soup and a bit later she said, 'Come on children, the soup is served.' Afterwards she used to sit in her chair outside the door and the soldiers used to know her and talk to her. They were so kind and respectful to the old lady. The bars and cafés were closed and when it was hot and the soldiers were thirsty she liked to put a little table outside the door with a big jug of water, covered with a cloth against the dust, and glasses and she had a notice in English : 'We have only this to offer you, but we offer it with all friendship. Please have a drink, the water is fresh.'

* * *

From Lady Mark Fitzalan Howard

We at the Royal School of Needlework have embroidered the entire story of the D Day landings, in a series of thirty-eight panels, each 8 feet long and 3 feet high. It measures 272 feet in length and, being 41 feet longer than the Bayeux Tapestry, is the largest of its kind in the world.

It is on permanent view to the public at the D-Day Museum at Southsea, Portsmouth, Hants. All the panels are correct in every miltary detail, as well as being a moving record of those days of epic heroism.

Further Reading

The Second World War, Winston S. Churchill; Cassell
    History of the Second World War : Victory in the West, Vol 1,
    Major L. F. Ellis and others; HMSO
The Battle of D Day, William McElwee; Faber
The Intelligence and Deception of the D Day Landings, Jock Haswell;
    Batsford
The Struggle for Europe, Chester Wilmots; Collins
Storm from the Sea, Brigadier Peter Young; William Kimber

The Allied Armies

UNITS INVOLVED IN THE FIGHTING BETWEEN 6 JUNE 1944 AND 31 AUGUST 1944

TWENTY-FIRST ARMY GROUP

General Sir Bernard L. Montgomery
Commander-in-Chief
Major-General Sir Francis W. de Guingand
Chief of Staff

G.H.Q. AND ARMY TROOPS

79th Armoured Division

Major-General Sir Percy C. S. Hobart

30th Armoured Brigade
22nd Dragoons
1st Lothians and Border Horse
2nd County of London Yeomanry
(Westminster Dragoons)
141st Regiment R.A.C.

1st Tank Brigade
11th, 42nd and 49th Battalions R.T.R.

1st Assault Brigade R.E.
5th, 6th and 42nd Assault Regiments R.E.

79th Armoured Divisional Signals
1st Canadian Armoured Personnel Carrier Regiment

Independent Brigades

4th Armoured Brigade
The Royal Scots Greys
3rd County of London Yeomanry (Sharpshooters) (to 28.7.44)
3rd/4th County of London Yeomanry (Sharpshooters) (from 29.7.44)
44th Battalion R.T.R.
2nd Battalion The King's Royal Rifle Corps (Motor)

6th Guards Tank Brigade
4th Tank Battalion Grenadier Guards
4th Tank Battalion Coldstream Guards
3rd Tank Battalion Scots Guards

8th Armoured Brigade
4th/7th Royal Dragoon Guards
24th Lancers (to 29.7.44)
The Nottinghamshire Yeomanry
13th/18th Royal Hussars (from 29.7.44)
12th Battalion The King's Royal Rifle Corps (Motor)

27th Armoured Brigade (to 29.7.44)
13th/18th Royal Hussars
1st East Riding Yeomanry
The Staffordshire Yeomanry

286

31st Tank Brigade
7th Battalion R.T.R. (to 17.8.44)
9th Battalion R.T.R. (to 31.8.44)
144th Regiment R.A.C.
   (23–31.8.44)

34th Tank Brigade
107th and 147th Regiment R.A.C.
153rd Regiment R.A.C. (to 24.8.44)

33rd Armoured Brigade
1st Northamptonshire Yeomanry
144th Regiment R.A.C. (to 22.8.44)
148th Regiment R.A.C. (to 16.8.44)
1st East Riding Yeomanry
   (from 16.8.44)

2nd Canadian Armoured Brigade
6th Armoured Regiment
   (1st Hussars)
(10th Armoured Regiment (The
   Fort Garry Horse)
27th Armoured Regiment (The
   Sherbrooke Fusiliers Regiment)

H.Q. Anti-Aircraft Brigades
74th, 76th, 80th, 100th, 101st, 105th, 106th and 107th

Heavy Anti-Aircraft Regiments
60th, 86th, 90th, 99th, 103rd, 105th, 107th, 108th, 109th, 112th, 113th,
   115th, 116th, 121st, 146th, 165th and 147th; 2nd Canadian

Light Anti-Aircraft Regiments
20th, 27th, 32nd, 54th, 71st, 73rd, 93rd, 109th, 112th, 113th, 114th,
   120th, 121st, 123rd, 124th, 125th, 126th, 127th, 133rd, 139th and
   149th

Searchlight Regiments
41st 356 (ind) Search Battery

56th Infantry Brigade
(Became integral part of the
   49th Division from 20.8.44)
2nd Battalion The South Wales
Borderers
2nd Battalion The Gloucestershire
Regiment
2nd Battalion The Essex Regiment

1st Special Service Brigade
Nos. 3, 4 and 6 Commandos
No. 45 (Royal Marine) Commando

4th Special Service Brigade
Nos. 41, 46, 47 and 48 (Royal
   Marine) Commandos.

Other Formations and Units
Armoured
G.H.Q. Liaison Regiment R.A.C. ('Phantom')
2nd Armoured Replacement Group
2nd Armoured Delivery Regiment
25th Canadian Armoured Delivery Regiment (The Elgin Regiment)

Artillery

H.Q. Army Groups Royal Artillery: 3rd, 4th, 5th, 8th and 9th; 2nd Canadian

> *Heavy Regiments:* 1st, 51st, 52nd, 53rd and 59th
>
> *Medium Regiments:* 7th, 9th, 10th, 11th, 13th, 15th, 53rd, 59th, 61st, 63rd, 64th, 65th, 67th, 68th, 72nd, 77th, 79th, 84th, 107th, 121st and 146th; 3rd, 4th and 7th Canadian
>
> *Field Regiments:* 4th R.H.A., 6th, 25th, 86th, 147th, 150th and 191st; 19th Canadian

Engineer

H.Q. Army Groups Royal Engineers: 10th, 11th, 12th, 13th and 14th; 1st Canadian

> *G.H.Q. Troops Engineers:* 4th, 7th, 8th, 13th, 15th, 18th, 48th and 59th
>
> *Airfield Construction Groups:* 13th, 16th, 23rd, 24th and 25th
>
> *Army Troops Engineers:* 2nd, 6th and 7th; 1st and 2nd Canadian

2nd and 3rd Battalions Royal Canadian Engineers

Signal

Twenty-First Army Group Headquarters Signals
Second Army Headquarters Signals
First Canadian Army Headquarters Signals
Air Formation Signals, Nos. 11, 12, 13, 16, 17 and 18
1st Special Wireless Group

Infantry

4th Battalion The Royal Northumberland Fusiliers (Machine Gun)
First Canadian Army Headquarters Defence Battalion (Royal Montreal Regiment)

Army Air Corps

Glider Pilot Regiment: 1st and 2nd Glider Pilot Wings

Royal Marine

Armoured Support Group: 1st and 2nd Royal Marine Armoured Support Regiments

Special Air Service

1st and 2nd Special Air Service Regiments
3rd and 4th French Parachute Battalions

European Allies

1st Belgian Infantry Brigade
Royal Netherlands Brigade (Princess Irene's)

ARMIES, CORPS AND DIVISIONS

Second Army

Lieutenant-General Sir Miles C. Dempsey
General Officer Commanding-in-Chief
Brigadier M. S. Chilton
Chief of Staff

First Canadian Army
Lieutenant-General H. D. G. Crerar
General Officer Commanding-in-Chief
Brigadier C. C. Mann
Chief of Staff

I Corps
Lieutenant-General J. T. Crocker
The Inns of Court Regiment R.A.C. (Armoured Car)
62nd Anti-Tank, 102nd Light Anti-Aircraft, 9th Survey Regiments R.A.
I Corps Troops Engineers   I Corps Signals

VII Corps
Lieutenant-General Sir Richard N. O'Connor
2nd Household Cavalry Regiment (Armoured Car)
91st Anti-Tank, 121st Light Anti-Aircraft, 10th Survey Regiments R.A.
VIII Corps Troops Engineers   VIII Corps Signals

XII Corps
Lieutenant-General N. M. Ritchie
1st The Royal Dragoons (Armoured Car)
86th Anti-Tank, 112th Light Anti-Aircraft, 7th Survey Regiments R.A.
XII Corps Troops Engineers   XII Corps Signals

XXX Corps
Lieutenant-General G. C. Bucknall (to 3.8.44)
Lieutenant-General B. G. Horrocks (from 4.8.44)
11th Hussars (Armoured Car)
73rd Anti-Tank, 27th Light Anti-Aircraft, 4th Survey Regiments R.A.
XXX Corps Troops Engineers.   XXX Corps Signals

II Canadian Corps
Lieutenant-General G. G. Simonds
18th Armoured Car Regiment (12th Manitoba Dragoons)
6th Anti-Tank, 6th Light Anti-Aircraft, 2nd Survey Regiments R.C.A.
11th Canadian Corps Troops Engineers   11 Canadian Corps Signals

Guards Armoured Division
Major-General A. H. S. Adair

5th Guards Armoured Brigade	*32nd Guards Brigade*
2nd (Armoured) Battalion Grenadier Guards	5th Battalion Coldstream Guards
1st (Armoured) Battalion Coldstream Guards	3rd Battalion Irish Guards
2nd (Armoured) Battalion Irish Guards	1st Battalion Welsh Guards
1st (Motor) Battalion Grenadier Guards	

Divisional Troops

2nd Armoured Reconnaissance Battalion Welsh Guards

Guards Armoured Divisional Engineers

55th and 153rd Field, 21st Anti-Tank and 94th Light Anti-Aircraft Regiments R.A.

Guards Armoured Divisional Signals

7th Armoured Division
Major-General G. W. E. J. Erskine (to 3.8.44)
Major-General G. L. Verney (from 4.8.44)

22nd Armoured Brigade

4th County of London Yeomanry (Sharpshooters) (to 29.7.44)

1st and 5th Battalions R.T.R.

5th Royal Inniskilling Dragoon Guards (from 29.7.44)

1st Battalion The Rifle Brigade (Motor)

131st Infantry Brigade

1/5th, 1/6th and 1/7th Battalions The Queen's Royal Regiment

Divisional Troops

8th King's Royal Irish Hussars

7th Armoured Divisional Engineers

7th Armoured Divisional Signals

3rd and 5th Regiments R.H.A.; 65th Anti-Tank and 15th Light Anti-Aircraft Regiments R.A.

11th Armoured Division
Major-General G. P. B. Roberts

29th Armoured Brigade

23rd Hussars

2nd Fife and Forfar Yeomanry

3rd Battalion R.T.R.

8th Battalion The Rifle Brigade (Motor)

159th Infantry Brigade

3rd Battalion The Monmouthshire Regiment

4th Battalion The King's Shropshire Light Infantry

1st Battalion The Herefordshire Regiment

Divisional Troops

2nd Northamptonshire Yeomanry (to 17.8.44)

15th/19th The King's Royal Hussars (from 17.8.44)

11th Armoured Divisional Engineers

13th Regiment R.H.A.; 151st Field, 75th Anti-Tank and 58th Light Anti-Aircraft Regiments R.A.

11th Armoured Divisional Signals

3rd Division
Major-General T. G. Rennie (to 13.6.44)
Brigadier E. E. E. Cass (acting)
Major-General L. G. Whistler (from 23.6.44)

8th Brigade
1st Battalion The Suffolk Regiment
2nd Battalion The East Yorkshire Regiment
1st Battalion The South Lancashire Regiment

9th Brigade
2nd Battalion The Lincolnshire Regiment
1st Battalion The King's Own Scottish Borderers
2nd Battalion The Royal Ulster Rifles

185th Brigade
2nd Battalion The Royal Warwickshire Regiment
1st Battalion The Royal Norfolk Regiment
2nd Battalion The King's Shropshire Light Infantry

Divisional Troops
3rd Reconnaissance Regiment R.A.C.
3rd Divisional Engineers
3rd Divisional Signals

7th, 33rd and 76th Field, 20th Anti-Tank and 92nd Light Anti-Aircraft Regiments R.A.
2nd Battalion The Middlesex Regiment (Machine Gun)

6th Airborne Division
Major-General R. N. Gale

3rd Parachute Brigade
8th and 9th Battalions The Parachute Regiment
1st Canadian Parachute Battalion

5th Parachute Brigade
7th, 12th and 13th Battalions The Parachute Regiment

6th Airlanding Brigade
12th Battalion The Devonshire Regiment
2nd Battalion The Oxfordshire and Buckinghamshire Light Infantry
1st Battalion The Royal Ulster Rifles

Divisional Troops
6th Airborne Armoured Reconnaissance Regiment R.A.C.
6th Airborne Divisional Engineers

53rd Airlanding Light Regiment R.A.
6th Airborne Divisional Signals

15th (Scottish) Division
Major-General G. H. A. MacMillan (to 2.8.44)
Major-General C. M. Barber (from 3.8.44)

44th (Lowland) Brigade
8th Battalion The Royal Scots
6th Battalion The Royal Scots Fusiliers
7th Battalion The King's Own Scottish Borderers

46th (Highland) Brigade
9th Battalion The Cameronians
2nd Battalion The Glasgow Highlanders
7th Battalion The Seaforth Highlanders

227th (Highland) Brigade
10th Battalion The Highland Light Infantry
2nd Battalion The Argyll and Sutherland Highlanders
2nd Battalion The Gordon Highlanders

Divisional Troops

15th Reconnaissance Regiment
R.A.C.
15th Divisional Engineers
15th Divisional Signals

131st, 181st and 190th Field, 97th
Anti-Tank and 119th Light
Anti-Aircraft Regiments R.A.
1st Battalion The Middlesex
Regiment (Machine Gun)

43rd (Wessex) Division
Major-General G. I. Thomas

129th Brigade
4th Battalion The Somerset Light
Infantry
4th and 5th Battalions The Wiltshire Regiment

130th Brigade
7th Battalion The Hampshire
Regiment
4th and 5th Battalions The Dorsetshire Regiment

214th Brigade
7th Battalion The Somerset Light Infantry
1st Battalion The Worcestershire Regiment
5th Battalion The Duke of Cornwall's Light Infantry

Divisional Troops

43rd Reconnaissance Regiment
R.A.C.
43rd Divisional Engineers
43rd Divisional Signals

94th, 112th and 179th Field, 59th
Anti-Tank and 110th Light
Anti-Aircraft Regiments R.A.
8th Battalion The Middlesex
Regiment (Machine Gun)

49th (West Riding) Division
Major-General E. H. Barker

70th Brigade (to 20.8.44)
10th and 11th Battalions The
Durham Light Infantry
1st Battalion The Tyneside
Scottish

146th Brigade
4th Battalion The Lincolnshire
Regiment
1/4th Battalion The King's Own
Yorkshire Light Infantry
Hallamshire Battalion The York
and Lancaster Regiment

147th Brigade
11th Battalion The Royal Scots Fusiliers
6th Battalion The Duke of Wellington's Regiment (to 6.7.44)
7th Battalion The Duke of Wellington's Regiment
1st Battalion The Leicestershire Regiment (from 6.7.44)

56th Brigade (from 20.8.44)
See under GHQ Troops
(page 523)

Divisional Troops
49th Reconnaissance Regiment R.A.C.
49th Divisional Engineers
49th Divisional Signals

69th, 143rd and 185th Field, 55th Anti-Tank and 89th Light Anti-Aircraft Regiments R.A.
2nd Princess Louise's Kensington Regiment (Machine Gun)

50th (Northumbrian) Division
Major-General D. A. H. Graham

69th Brigade
5th Battalion The East Yorkshire Regiment
6th and 7th Battalions The Green Howards

151st Brigade
6th , 8th and 9th Battalions The Durham Light Infantry

231st Brigade
2nd Battalion The Devonshire Regiment
1st Battalion The Hampshire Regiment
1st Battalion The Dorsetshire Regiment

Divisional Troops
61st Reconnaisance Regiment R.A.C.
50th Divisional Engineers
50th Divisional Signals

74th, 90th and 124th Field, 102nd Anti-Tank and 25th Light Anti-Aircraft Regiments R.A.
2nd Battalion The Cheshire Regiment (Machine Gun)

51st (Highland) Division
Major-General D. C. Bullen-Smith (to 26.7.44)
Major-General T. G. Rennie (from 27.7.44)

152nd Brigade
2nd and 5th Battalions The Seaforth Highlanders
5th Battalion The Queen's Own Cameron Highlanders

153rd Brigade
5th Battalion The Black Watch
1st and 5th/7th Battalions The Gordon Highlanders

154th Brigade
1st and 7th Battalions The Black Watch
7th Battalion The Argyll and Sutherland Highlanders

Divisional Troops

2nd Derbyshire Yeomanry R.A.C.
51st Divisional Engineers
51st Divisional Signals

126th, 127th and 128th Field,
61st Anti-Tank and 40th Light
Anti-Aircraft Regiments R.A.
1/7th Battalion The Middlesex
Regiment

53rd (Welsh) Division
Major-General R. K. Ross

71st Brigade
1st Battalion The East Lancashire
Regiment (to 3.8.44)
1st Battalion The Oxfordshire and
Buckinghamshire Light Infantry
1st Battalion The Highland Light
Infantry
4th Battalion The Royal Welch
Fusiliers (from 5.8.44)

158th Brigade
4th and 6th Battalions The Royal
Welch Fusiliers (to 3.8.44)
7th Battalion The Royal Welch
Fusiliers
1st Battalion The East Lancashire
Regiment (from 4.8.44)
1/5th Battalion The Welch Regiment (from 4.8.44)

160th Brigade
2nd Battalion The Monmouthshire Regiment
4th Battalion The Welch Regiment
1/5th Battalion The Welch Regiment (to 3.8.44)
6th Battalion The Royal Welch Fusiliers (from 4.8.44)

Divisional Troops

53rd Reconnaissance Regiment
R.A.C.
53rd Divisional Engineers
53rd Divisional Signals

81st, 83rd and 133rd Field, 71st
Anti-Tank and 116th Light
Anti-Aircraft Regiments R.A.
1st Battalion The Manchester
Regiment (Machine Gun)

59th (Staffordshire) Division
Major-General L. O. Lyne

176th Brigade (to 26.8.44)
7th Battalion The Royal Norfolk
Regiment
7th Battalion The South Staffordshire Regiment
6th Battalion The North Staffordshire Regiment

177th Brigade (to 26.8.44)
5th, 1/6th and 2/6th Battalions
The South Staffordshire Regiment

197th Brigade (to 26.8.44)
1/7th Battalion The Royal Warwickshire Regiment
2/5th Battalion The Lancashire Fusiliers
5th Battalion The East Lancashire Regiment

Divisional Troops

59th Reconnaissance Regiment R.A.C. (to 31.8.44)
59th Divisional Engineers
59th Divisional Signals

61st, 110th and 116th Field (to 31.8.44), 68th Anti-Tank (to 26.8.44) and 68th Light Anti-Aircraft (to 22.8.44) Regiments R.A.
7th Battalion The Royal Northumberland Fusiliers (Machine Gun) (to 24.8.44)

4th Canadian Armoured Division
Major-General G. Kitching (to 21.8.44)
Major-General H. W. Foster (from 22.8.44)

4th Armoured Brigade
21st Armoured Regiment (The Governor General's Foot Guards)
22nd Armoured Regiment (The Canadian Grenadier Guards)
28th Armoured Regiment (The British Columbia Regiment)
The Lake Superior Regiment (Motor)

10th Infantry Brigade
The Lincoln and Welland Regiment
The Algonquin Regiment
The Argyll and Sutherland Highlanders of Canada (Princess Louise's)

Divisional Troops

29th Reconnaisance Regiment (The South Alberta Regiment)
4th Canadian Armoured Divisional Engineers

15th and 23rd Field, 5th Anti-Tank and 8th Light Anti-Aircraft Regiments R.C.A.
4th Canadian Armoured Divisional Signals

2nd Canadian Division
Major-General C. Foulkes

4th Brigade
The Royal Regiment of Canada
The Royal Hamilton Light Infantry
The Essex Scottish Regiment

5th Brigade
The Black Watch (Royal Highland Regiment) of Canada
Le Régiment de Maisonneuve
The Calgary Highlanders

6th Brigade

Les Fusiliers Mont-Royal
The Queen's Own Cameron Highlands of Canada
The South Saskatchewan Regiment

Divisional Troops

8th Reconnaissance Regiment (14th Canadian Hussars)
2nd Canadian Divisional Engineers
2nd Canadian Divisional Signals

4th, 5th and 6th Field, 2nd Anti-Tank and 3rd Light Anti-Aircraft Regiments R.C.A.
The Toronto Scottish Regiment (Machine Gun)

3rd Canadian Division

Major-General R. F. L. Keller (to 8.8.44)
Major-General D. C. Spry (from 18.8.44)

7th Brigade

The Royal Winnipeg Rifles
The Regina Rifle Regiment
1st Battalion The Canadian Scottish Regiment

8th Brigade

The Queen's Own Rifles of Canada
Le Régiment de la Chaudière
The North Shore (New Brunswick) Regiment

9th Brigade

The Highland Light Infantry of Canada
The Stormont, Dundas and Glengarry Highlanders
The North Nova Scotia Highlanders

Divisional Troops

7th Reconnaissance Regiment (17th Duke of York's Royal Canadian Hussars)
3rd Canadian Divisional Engineers
3rd Canadian Divisional Signals

12th, 13th, and 14th Field, 3rd Anti-Tank and 4th Light Anti-Aircraft Regiments R.C.A.
The Cameron Highlands of Ottawa (Machine Gun)

1st Polish Armoured Division
Major-General S. Maczek

10th Polish Armoured Brigade
1st Polish Armoured Regiment
2nd Polish Armoured Regiment
24th Polish Armoured (Lancer) Regiment
10th Polish Motor Battalion

3rd Polish Infantry Brigade
1st Polish (Highland) Battalion
8th Polish Batalion
9th Polish Battalion

Divisional Troops

10th Polish Mounted Rifle Regiment

1st Polish Armoured Divisional Engineers

1st and 2nd Polish Field, 1st Polish Anti-Tank and 1st Polish Light Anti-Aircraft Regiments

1st Polish Armoured Divisional Signals

LINES OF COMMUNICATION AND REAR MAINTENANCE AREA

Headquarters Lines of Communication

Major-General R. F. B. Naylor

Nos. 11 and 12 Lines of Communication Areas

Nos. 4, 5 and 6 Lines of Communication Sub-Areas

Nos. 7 and 8 Base Sub-Areas

Nos. 101, 102 and 104 Beach Sub-Areas

Nos. 10 and 11 Garrisons

Engineers

Nos. 2, 3, 5 and 6 Railway Construction and Maintenance Groups

No. 3 Railway Operating Group

No. 1 Canadian Railway Operating Group

No. 1 Railway Workshop Group

Nos. 2, 6, 8, 9, 10 and 11 Port Operating Groups

Nos. 1, 2, 4 and 5 Port Construction and Repair Groups

Nos. 3 and 4 Inland Water Transport Groups

No. 2 Mechanical Equipment (Transportation) Unit

Signals

Nos. 2 and 12 Lines of Communication Headquarters Signals

No. 1 Canadian Lines of Communication Headquarters Signals

Infantry

5th and 8th Battalions The King's Regiment

7th Battalion The East Yorkshire Regiment

2nd Battalion The Hertfordshire Regiment

6th Battalion The Border Regiment

1st Buckinghamshire Battalion The Oxfordshire and Buckinghamshire Light Infantry

5th Battalion The Royal Berkshire Regiment

18th Battalion The Durham Light Infantry

UNITED STATES TWELFTH ARMY GROUP

Lieutenant-General Omar N. Bradley

Commanding General

Major-General Leven C. Allen

Chief of Staff

First Army
Lieutenant-General Courtney H. Hodges
Commanding General
(Succeeded General Bradley from 1.8.44)
Major-General William B. Keen
Chief of Staff

, *Third Army*
Lieutenant-General George S. Patton, Jr.
Comanding General
Major-General Hugh J. Gaffey
Chief of Staff

Corps
V. Major-General Leonard T. Gerow
VII. Major-General J. Lawton Collins
VIII. Major-General Troy H. Middleton
XII. Major-General Gilbert R. Cook (to 18.8.44)
    Major-General Manton S. Eddy (from 19.8.44)
XV. Major-General Wade H. Haislip
XIX. Major-General Charles H. Corlett
XX. Major-General Walton H. Walker

Divisions
Armoured : 2nd, 3rd, 4th, 5th, 6th and 7th; 2nd French
Infantry : 1st, 2nd, 4th, 5th, 8th, 9th, 28th, 29th, 30th, 35th, 79th, 80th,
    83rd and 90th
Nos. 10 and 11 Garrisons

Index

Index